S0-BCO-162

Take A Deep Breath

Take A Deep Breath

A Life Examined

David E. Burns, M.D.

Board Certified, Internal Medicine

iUniverse, Inc.
New York Bloomington

Copyright © 2010 by David E. Burns, MD

All rights reserved. No part of this book may be used or reproduced by
any means, graphic, electronic, or mechanical, including photocopying,
recording, taping or by any information storage retrieval system
without the written permission of the publisher except in the case
of brief quotations embodied in critical articles and reviews.

iUniverse books may be ordered through booksellers or by contacting:

iUniverse
1663 Liberty Drive
Bloomington, IN 47403
www.iuniverse.com
1-800-Authors (1-800-288-4677)

Because of the dynamic nature of the Internet, any Web addresses or links
contained in this book may have changed since publication and may no longer be
valid. The views expressed in this work are solely those of the author and do not
necessarily reflect the views of the publisher, and the publisher hereby disclaims
any responsibility for them.

ISBN: 978-1-4401-9055-1 (sc)
ISBN: 978-1-4401-9056-8 (ebook)

Printed in the United States of America

iUniverse rev. date: 01/19/10

Copyright 2009: David E. Burns, M.D.
<takeadeep@gmail.com>

*"**The Old Milk House**,"*
a watercolor by David E. Burns, MD

For My Family:

Marcia, Marie, Michael, and David

… for subsequent generations

Contents

Getting Serious

Spiritus Fermenti

Lighter Moments

In Their Vale of Tears

The Nature of Life

Preface

At seven a.m. a mother was driving her two children to school, running a bit late but that's not out of the ordinary. That morning, however, the day began with freezing rain. The weather change came in quickly, especially where they lived, in the high plateau countryside of upstate New York. No one knows why, but the mom failed to make that sharp turn in the road, the same road she drove everyday. As their compact car skidded, it broadsided a maple tree on the driver's side. Everyone was found pinned in the wreckage. All were critically hurt. Apparently, no one wore the seatbelts. After all, it was only a short couple of miles to the school.

The mother was the first to be brought into our ER: unresponsive, multiple fractures of her pelvis and chest, and no recordable blood pressure. An urgent diagnostic tap—a needle inserted into her abdominal space, yielded fresh bright red blood, indicative of a likely ruptured spleen. She was whisked off to immediate surgery, but every effort that the surgeons attempted was for naught. In the meantime, her two little ones required a difficult and protracted amount of time to become freed from the twisted wreckage. Both of her children had evidence of head trauma: we knew this from the first responders. A call was placed early for a "chopper" and pediatric trauma specialist to fly in to assist in their transport. Despite the weather, the team arrived at our hospital before the two additional patients were brought in. Dr. Kantor, the Pediatric Specialist, a man whom I had previously spoken with—numerous times about this and other past difficult cases—was now on-site in our ER when the two young victims were carried in. Both had multiple fractures and both were unresponsive; at least one required Dr. Kantor to perform an immediate craniotomy—a opening drilled into the skull to relieve and monitor the internal pressures within the skull— (an attempt to save the child's developing brain and his life).

This entire early morning was reminiscent of the first story in this book, *Lessons for a Lifetime*.

In the popular children's rhyme of "Humpty-Dumpty," the Egg that fell off the wall—then cracked. Most remember the exasperation of that told story—putting all the pieces back together is not an easy task in life, even though we try, try to put lives back together.

My presence at these sad accidents—events that involve young children, the outcome of such stories have prompted me to write about these circumstances—accounts with human emotions too powerful to leave solely as a memory, to leave untold.

*David E.
Burns, M.D.,*

(Past) Chief of Medicine of Little Falls Hospital

Director of Critical Care

Past President, Herkimer County Medical Society

Internal Medicine Residency

Albany and Winston-Salem

Albany Medical College, MD '72

Seton Hall University attended '67–'68

Utica College, BS '67

Acknowledgements

I'm grateful to so many people—individuals who have assisted and shown encouragement to this doctor's manuscript: words that describe the life that I have led. Clearly, the medical situations that I had been a part of surely heightened my perspective. The wonderful people whom I have met and cared for, the extraordinary events that have come my way, these are in part what has shaped this manuscript.

Many nights I came home from events that were emotionally far too intense to relate to anyone, even to my wife. However, Marcie knew that every day in my practice of medicine there were real-life stories filled with sadness, sometimes tragedy or human situations bursting with elation—bold stories that needed to be told.

Marcie was the first to encourage me to write, to engage those past accounts, those exceptional moments: beginning with my simple childhood memories through the bedside witness of untimely deaths. Unbeknownst to me, my wife had assigned me to Peter Saunder's Writers Group at our Eldredge Public Library in Chatham, and through Peter's diligence and inspiration, I began to put into words ... a lifetime of past emotions. Thank you, Peter.

My first writing assignment was "I Couldn't Believe He/ She Said That." We needed to write about an event where someone had been confrontational. I immediately recalled an ER episode from so long ago, and I wrote about a grieving mother who accused me of killing her son. The memory of her pain, her direct physical threats came to life through my prose. Those in Peter's class could feel that mother's anguish and the tension of that moment. Others were held spellbound by the emotions that my words evoked. It was through these vignettes of my past medical experiences that I found a voice—it seemed that each week, this class of beginning writers all yearned for more, more of my perspective on the human events from so many patients past.

Fleur Jones was the first to urge me to combine all these vignettes into a book—thank you Fleur.

John Nostrand had previously published a book *The Art of James H. Cromartie*. John took charge of my initial process: demanded organization, subtitles, and a serious analysis of the content. John's organizational skills were 'engineered' perfectly, and through his direction, this manuscript began to take shape and demonstrate clarity. Thank you, John.

Nancy Patterson's encouragement after her first reading was enlightening. Her commentaries advanced my efforts as well. Thank you.

Alayne Tsigas labored for weeks on weeks to improve the readership and sentence structure; repeatedly, she dissected the individual stories line by line, with unerring perseverance. I am indeed indebted to Alayne—thank you, thank you.

Finally, I am indebted to the many patients that I had helped and to those whom I have failed, those with disease processes that could not be altered, I believe I had given my all. We all learn through our human weaknesses—in spite of my occasional failure, the care of the sick has indeed been my special privilege.

Introduction

How many times have I seen visitors in a hospital setting, cautiously or even reluctantly enter an ICU or a Special Care Unit, visiting a loved one or a friend—and not recognize that patient? Because many people critically ill will have drastic physical changes: lying in a hospital bed, attached to multiple lifelines, perhaps after an accident or from a serious illness—patients maybe unrecognizable. Maybe edematous, swollen beyond recognition, whether from the impact of his injury or from overwhelming infection or from massive blood loss—Swelling of the tissues of the body is predictable. Perhaps the person was on a mechanical ventilator, a machine that assures the continued breath of air. A visitor might gasp at the sight ... take in that deep breath ... perhaps, place a hand to their mouth with a silent exclamation: "Oh, my gosh!" and then quickly retreat to a waiting room. Life is like that—so is disease.

Take a Deep Breath—a repeated command to patients while I examined their lungs, but also, this book is about the physical and psychological deep gasps one may take when faced with a diagnosis that will shorten ones life, while their facial expressions silently shout: "Oh, my God ... what has happened?" Many of these stories are up close and in your face.

I practiced medicine in a "remote" community hospital, perhaps a "St. Elsewhere," an institution, some thought, was out in the "Boonies" where a patient, an accident victim from the Interstate highway, could end-up ... at this small hospital. Maybe that person was from a metropolitan area and thought they were now in some Godforsaken corner of the world ... surprised that medicine was even practiced in such a remote setting, but it was. Doctors, nurses, and technicians worked long and hard for the welfare of a few.

My writings take the reader into a country setting of growing up on a farm, surviving shameful family situations and tragedies like many other families. However, while working a generational farm, I began to dream—to consider other possibilities far beyond the farm.

Against all odds, I made that leap of faith and became a Board Certified Internist, in fact, the very first one to practice medicine in the entire Herkimer County. Further, I made sure we had the best equipment, and honed our skills to care for those critically ill. Some patients could find themselves miles from "anywhere," certainly anywhere but a university hospital setting.

These patient details reflect my love for the profession. I've attempted to 'paint' that emotion which was part of my daily activity. One friend stated that the book should be titled: "A Love Story." I believe you will re-live some of that emotion through my text.
D.B.

The Beginning— the Evolution of a Student

Lessons for a Lifetime

She kept screaming over and over, claiming she was going to die. Shouting hysterically: "God! Oh, God, I'm dying!" It had been suggested that students observe at the Trauma Center and I had just walked into the Department. Standing at a distance, I tried to figure-out what was happening. As a second-year medical student, I was filled with all sorts of knowledge from years of studying science: textbooks read, then read again. Clinically, there was little a medical student at my level of training could have done, short of observing. However, I had never seen anything quite like the situation that was unfolding that evening.

The patient continued shouting and carrying-on, and I wondered in awe if she was truly pleading for her life or perhaps simply a neurotic soul wanting attention. Perhaps she was excessively emotional following her auto accident. "Goddamn it," she went on, "won't someone listen to me? I'm dying, can't anyone realize it?" As she stared at me, she exclaimed with disgust, "Christ Almighty!"

I was at the Emergency Department (ER) in the University Medical Center at Albany, New York, trying not to be in anyone's way when this young woman had been admitted. She had been involved in a serious car accident: one of her passengers was DOA (dead-on-arrival); the other two women with her were critically injured. This patient seemed to be without a scratch when the doctors examined her, finding no physical or any abnormal neurological signs that would indicate a problem.

This accident had happened years ago at a time before effective brain scans, before computerized technology. Patients like this woman would have been closely observed. When a neurologist reexamined her, he again looked carefully at her neurological systems, and all were clinically normal.

This emotional accident victim was moved closer to the nursing station for more immediate observation and perhaps for some reassurance to her. Propped-up on a stretcher, she remained restless, agitated, upsetting everyone by her screams and repeated outbursts that she was going to die. I remember reluctantly approaching the gurney on which she was placed. Naively, I tried to calm her but to no avail. I will always remember the profound fright in her eyes. When she stared at me, it felt like she looked straight through me. Again she angrily shouted, "Can't you understand that I'm dying?" As she conveyed her sad plight to me, I was embarrassed and even frightened by her pointed emotions. In my dismay, I moved a little further away.

On and on she lamented her pending doom. The staff, busy with others, seemed to ignore her further pleas. Occasionally, a nurse would attend to her side, but the staff was engrossed with those who were critically injured. As I stood by, I was made uneasy by her unrest as well as with my own ineptness. Clinically, the staff was not allowed to give her any sedatives, knowing these drugs could mask any subtle change that would point to an internal brain injury. Patients like her needed continued close observation.

Suddenly, the woman had a seizure and stopped breathing right before my eyes! Before I could shout, "There's a problem here," the professionals had reached her side. The attending neurosurgeon, working on the other injured passengers, approached this patient with clear anticipation. The doctor grabbed the electric clippers, shaved off a swath of her hair on the right scalp area, and after a quick wipe of disinfectant, sliced a cruciate incision into her scalp. Without hesitation, he picked up a gleaming surgical bit-brace, similar to a workshop tool my dad had frequently used; however, this instrument was shinny and sterile. With it, the doctor drilled a one-inch hole into the woman's skull. Just like that, he drilled into her head.

Within seconds, his drill had cut through her calvarium; visible were the thin, curtain-like membranes that line our brain: the meningeal tissues, the Dura Mater. With the doctor's procedure, through this opening, the patient's blood and spinal fluid oozed from the excessive pressure against her brain. His action quickly lessened the patient's intracranial pressure; however, her injury remained. The patient was resuscitated, intubated, and whisked off for urgent surgery. Unfortunately, she would later die from a severely ischemic brain.

The next day, at her autopsy, I viewed the terrible injuries. From the impact of the accident, too many small blood vessels had been ripped apart inside her skull. The finely fractured elements of bone at the base of her skull all contributed to her fatal internal bleed.

This one individual with such a profound immediate death marked a change for me. This change, perhaps better termed a quantum leap, propelled me from being a student to the stark beginnings of becoming a clinician.

At that moment, that witnessed episode as a student, my life changed. It was a distinct transition. I knew my life would never again be the same. The impact of that young woman's plea has lasted a lifetime. *"Listen, listen always to the patient,"* was the voice of my mentors.

The bewilderment I felt following her sudden demise brought forth a mixture of yearnings. I realized the need to hone the skills necessary to find the subtle aspects of serious disease before Death walked in.

Much later, a month after graduation from Medical School, I was an Intern working in the Albany Medical Center, ER. A sixty-year-old patient entered complaining of very vague symptoms. The man had recently been discharged from the neurosurgical service at the Medical Center. He was very anxious and told of an onset mild headache and intermittent blurred vision. I completed a careful neurological exam with no major findings except, that is, the lack of a pupillary reflex to a bright light and only absent from the lateral aspects of his left eye. This finding was so very subtle; everything else appeared normal. All his other reflexes, his sensory and motor skills were good, including his fundoscopic* exam. I had the

---

* **fundoscopic:** *viewing the retina (internal eye) with a hand-held instrument*

senior medical resident check the man, but he thought the findings I had described were not significant. I begged to differ with him, and held my ground. Since there were no CT exams available in those early years, careful physical exams were crucial.

I called Dr. Skilp, the neurosurgeon. He was a very diligent doctor, plus a physically impressive individual. Tall, fit, a no-nonsense sort a man, he was a person of few words. Further, there was a great deal of 'mystique' that surrounded him as an individual. Rumors about his obscure past were most intriguing. As a teenager in Holland, it was purported that he was the Head of Dutch Underground Resistance to the Occupying Nazis and was on Hitler's most wanted list. No one had the courage to ask him whether this rumor was true, although many, including myself, would have loved to hear his reply.

I had reached him on an evening when he was not on call; however, this was his patient. As I described my findings, he told me to hold the patient there in the ER and he would be right in to check my findings for himself. In a way he also was challenging my abilities.

"That's an amazing find," he told me. "Without papilledema♣ it's very unusual to find an absence to a light reflex—isolated to one-half of an eye.

The patient was admitted that night—required further surgery, and the placement of a temporary shunt in his brain to relieve his elevated intracranial pressure.

"Listen. Listen to what is happening. Listen always to the patient. LISTEN," echoed the voice of my mentors. Through my years in practice, this command was not always an easy task to carryout.

♣ **Papilledema:** *a change in the optic nerve from increased pressure on the brain*

A New Decade–Growing Up

Questions do exist, and I ponder—reflect on them—perhaps as the reader does also: how did I manage to become privileged to be a witness at the previous critical situation? Why was I present at such an extraordinary event?

With all probability, I should have spent my life working on the family farm, but I didn't. For each of us, life can be a strange and wonderful journey. I remember, as a small boy, asking my mom's uncle, my great-uncle, just how he managed to "land" in Little Falls, New York? His words became indelible: *"I left Ireland as a young man, left behind all my friends and family, and sailed to America with only a small knapsack and the clothes on my back. After I was processed through Ellis Island, I kept my eyes and ears open for available work. I hopped on a rumor—then onto a barge that was to travel north to Albany, volunteered my labors for "grub," then on another barge into the Erie Canal system with promises of work. As the barge headed west, through numerous locks, it eventually halted at a boat basin in Little Falls. When I disembarked that night, someone offered a job, an offer that I didn't refuse."* My great-uncle had found his new home, and soon two Irish immigrants would become one family of my mother's ancestors.

We never truly know where our path through life will take us. So it was with me. I was raised on a farm in upstate New York with two older brothers and two younger sisters. No one in our family had a medical background. It was assumed that I would continue the work of my Dad, which was farming the lands of his father and his father's father.

So I write about my own transition through life, a life probably not as harsh as had my great-uncle, but a transition just the same. My first three years of education were at a one-room country school; all eight-grades were managed by one teacher, Miss Agnes Kelhi. I completed primary, then secondary schooling at St. Mary's Academy in Little Falls. After graduating from Utica College, I went to Seton Hall University for a year and then onto fulfillment with graduation from Albany Medical College. One photo I've included is a snapshot taken in front of the one room school; pictured are seventeen students, and three of these kids would go on to achieve their doctorate, quite an impressive leap from that ragtag group of country kids. Miss Kelhi must have instilled something beyond average into her students: The few pictured in that old photo, in old cow-feed burlap bags—ready for the race.

I've care for so many patients, and tried my best to do what was right. Even with that, at times I failed. Like that famous baseball player speaking years ago at Yankee Stadium, I feel I am the luckiest guy alive: having a loving wife, a wonderful family, and having achieved a profession that allowed me to be firsthand at the worst and the best of the human condition. Caring for those less fortunate in so many ways has indeed been a privilege.

My own journey from farming to that of becoming a physician has been a similar extreme shift in purpose. After high school, I essentially operated the family farm from the age of 17 to 23 years of age. My transition through the first thoughts of becoming something other than a farmer was a slow and deliberate process.

During the transition of growing from a boy into manhood, besides my parents, there were just a few individuals that made an impact on me. The two individuals who did were a coach and a doctor. These two did so with their actions as well as words. Their demands, maybe a word or two or an offhand comment, would cause me to stop and ponder what was told. A heroes' influence becomes like a pruning exercise, someone that snips at our branches (of thought) or cuts off our actions—a snip that starts one on a new course—a new thought, a direction not previously considered, an awakening, a new process. Coach Hubie Brown was one of two men who would become my hero. Dr. Bernard Burke became a hero later in life. They were somewhat diverse personalities but shared a similar intent in life and had certain characteristics

8

that caught my attention early on. Both were easy to like, and for me these were two people to emulate. Only God knew why or how both of these men landed at different times in Little Falls. However, each man, in his own separate endeavor, became larger than life.

Coach Brown arrived at our small parochial school when I was sixteen. Hubie was very charismatic, a disciple of sports. He entered our small, forgotten valley town like a new wave, and the entire school became energized. As the Athletic Director he coached the baseball and basketball teams at St. Mary's Academy. Coach Brown had a personality greater than life, but he wasn't perfect: he openly cussed and swore and had a temper. He always carried a green towel during the game ... a "worry" towel of sorts that would be twisted, rolled-up, chewed, or thrown as tensions soared. It was tossed at the game floor, at a player or rarely near a referee. These antics were very novel for the Mohawk Valley schools and especially for St. Mary's Academy. The crowds admired him, and rarely was he ever reprimanded in a game.

At every practice session and during the games he would yell and curse much like my dad. Hubie would shout: "Goddamn it!" or "Jesus Christ, Burnsey, block that goddamn shot." The parochial crowd loved it, even the Monsignor began showing up for the exciting sporting events and "cutting" the Coach some slack as Hubie carved-out and shaped-up winning teams. We learned by his intensity, his coaching method, and his demanding practice. He taught that there's no such thing as a moral victory, not in sports, despite what the nuns taught us. He expected our whole demeanor to improve, attitudes toward life itself, not simply at basketball: our grades, our habits, our dress, and players' attitudes all had to improve and be honed. And I, well, I had to be a part of it.

Hubie put up with me. Since he knew the situation of every kid on the team, of course he knew about my need to work on the farm. He also knew very well that I could do better: "Goddamn it, Burnsey, if you'd work harder, make every practice, you could become a decent player." It seemed that I was one who could be excused from missing an occasional practice. There were times when after farm work, I'd hop in our pickup truck, and show-up ten or more minutes into practice, fresh from barn chores. This was when others began to call me "Barney."

Arriving late for practice was usually accompanied by his tirade of expletives and public denouncements; however, he kept me on the team. All said and done, he apparently had hope for this youngster, and in turn I would occasionally score a winning basket or make that rare final defensive block that would redeem my shortcomings. He allowed me a certain favor, time and time again.

My basketball coach was kind, stern, instructive, and demanding; yet, he was a man that either felt sorry for my limited talents or saw beneath my unpolished exterior. Perhaps he saw a youngster with some possibility. When we traveled, it was with jacket and tie. There were so many little things he pointed out to the team. For instance, how to fold ones sport jacket; he would never allow one to be worn in a car (it would ruin the lining). These small incidental directions I continue to honor to this day.

He went out of his way to keep players under his wing. He had been one person who had opened my eyes to many different aspects of life. He stressed, to the entire team, how to become a better person, encouraging the players to become unique, rise above, set a different style and be responsible individuals. He prodded this kid to look beyond the obvious in life. Not that he explicitly pointed out any particular path, yet he clearly coached me to look beyond, to tap talents yet hidden. Coach took this parochial team to winning tournaments all across our region.

Hubie would on occasion drive me home, out through the hinterlands, delivering me back to my awaiting farm responsibilities. I believe he knew and respected the labors that were required of me. I remembered being embarrassed by the late winter thaws that laid bare the mud and manure, the crudeness of the hill farms, the smells from cattle that were evident as we turned into our drive. However, Hubie never said anything negative about me, never chided me about being a farm kid. His whole demeanor was towards stressing the positive.

* * *

After high school I was essentially running the family farm full time. Dad worked for the Post Office delivering rural mail to the old RFD #2, a mail route that covered thirty plus miles. Each day he traveled through the rugged countryside, through the Townships of Fairfield, Salisbury, and the North side of Little Falls. Dad loved the work and he faithfully delivered farmers' mail regardless of weather. Jack, my oldest brother was attending Cornell University. My brother Tom, a year older than I, was the one whom I always believed would assume stewardship of the home farm. Tom had started out on his own, however and rented the Kelhi farm a mile down the road. By this time we were renting two additional farms to gain extra forage that was required to feed our expanding herd. Tom was also negotiating to buy the hundred and seventy acre O'Hara farm, also a mile away.

I loved the setting of our generational lands, enjoyed the rugged fieldwork and had all the necessary talents that one required for farming. There were all sorts of needed trades for farming: plumbing, animal husbandry, agronomy, mechanical skill, and construction. Farmers must know how to cut and thread a pipe, to repair a broken water line, to know a street el from an elbow. There was a need to know all the ins and outs of electricity, know the basics of the large electric motors used, necessary to have mechanical know-how as well. Because money was so short, most farmers worked alone—most could not afford to hire this extra labor, nor waste the time waiting for the repairman. To compensate, I learned the methods for both electric and acetylene welding that enabled the repair of broken steel or cast iron gears, parts of the equipment that inadvertently broke or fractured. These machine parts took a beating during the harsh fieldwork, required welding or brazing for quick repair. Perhaps working alone, sometimes against exceeding odds became a philosophy of labors for me personally; no doubt, this temperament would reflect on my style of medical practice in later life.

It was my brother Tom who was the true farmer in our family. It was Tom that knew animal husbandry; he alone understood the bloodlines of the Holstein cow. However, he wanted his own farm, and that made me more responsible for the work at hand at the home farm, work that anchored me to the generations past.

Farming was and is such a labor-intensive endeavor: twenty-four hour days seven days a week. Dairy cows needed to be milked every twelve-hours or even, in some cases, every eight-hours. Money was short; farmers are always the ones to receive the last nickel for their product. Government agencies, utilizing antiquated pricing formulas from the nineteen-thirties, always paid the dairy farmers weeks and weeks after the milk had been processed and sold to the consumers. Federal and State agencies still make a point to visit most farms, and their agents have preached for years that farmers need to become more efficient, house more cows, work harder. Never was it mentioned that this class of American workers needed a more equitable price for their milk products, never was there a mention for greater economic relief, never was the fact brought up that milk was priced too low to be called a business, and never will farmers be free to earn a decent living from their land or afford to be mortgage free.

These are some of the reasons that I abandoned thoughts of farming as a career, walked-away from the lands where three prior generations had toiled for so long. I could not live and work under those conditions, knowing that as a farmer, I would never get ahead, never be treated equitably, never be given a fair voice in the pricing of my product.

Farmers make up less than one percent of our population, yet they work harder and longer hours than most and earn so little in terms of respect, in terms of wealth. Too many farm families now could receive State and family social aid but don't apply. Their plight is a national disgrace, and yet the average person on the street has no idea that the price of milk can vary by thirty percent, or even fifty percent, lower than a prior month for no good reason. Our society believes that this endeavor, farming or ranching, is something near idyllic. But it isn't.

Since becoming a physician I have cared for many farm families, have seen first hand the physical wear and tear, plus the psychological trauma that they exist with. Many families cannot financially walk away; they're shackled by their debt, faced with losing both the farm and their home. They instead wait until foreclosures forces that issue and they walk away empty-handed and depressed.

Looking back to those farming days the family situation was more serious than I knew. Our Dad was physically failing although we were not aware of the reasons. He was slowly backing away from the work of the farm. After lunch he would frequently go to the living room windows, light up a Lucky Strike, pull back the lace curtains and just seem to stare out for too long a time. These patterns caught my eye. I always wondered if he was daydreaming; certainly he was pondering something. I wondered just what were his thoughts and much later, far too much later, we would know the reason.

Dad never did enjoy having his photo taken. On one occasion I saw him filling-up our Chevy with gas (we had our own fuel storage), and I grabbed our aunt's camera and took several shots through the bushes as dad filled the car. He was traveling to Buffalo to see my oldest brother. Something urged me to snap that picture, told me that a photo was important. I hid in the shrubbery and snapped away. A month later our dad would be dead.

One Sunday shortly after my picture taking, dad appeared ashen and sweaty. I was unable to equate this episode with anything that would become suddenly life threatening. I drove him to Dr. Burke's office. For some reason Mom stayed back at the farm. Although she was crying and very anxious, she chose to stay home which was an unusual decision since Dad had appeared very, very ill. As I drove, I never asked him about his symptoms; I assumed it was some type of virus. How naive we are in our youth, so young, assuming life always stretches far in front of us.

When we arrived Dad told me to wait in the car. I don't know why I just sat there, and didn't go in with him. If I had, perhaps I would have learned from the doctor that our dad had a bad heart. Times were much different then in 1960, and I was only a kid. Dad returned about twenty minutes later, looking much better and wanting to go home. I have revisited that day countless times: Why did I not go into the office with dad? Why was I so unassuming? However, as we went home, he did look much better. I never realized that life as we knew it was nearly over.

About a week later, Dad had increasing symptoms of unstable angina. (I learned of this only much later.) He had been delivering mail, stopping numerous times, along his route, battling severe chest symptoms and taking several nitroglycerin tablets under his tongue but to no avail. His chest tightness lingered with aches into his arms. Even though he had bouts of vomiting and diarrhea, he continued to deliver the mail. He stopped at our neighbor Don Millington's farm and told Don just what was happening. He told Don things about his heart symptoms, symptoms that he wouldn't tell our mom. Dad told Don that he was really scared that day, that his bouts of pain extended far too long in time and into his arms … told how that the pressure in his chest seemed unrelenting. Coming home he went directly into the "pool room," a room where he frequently rested after his mail route, a room that was used for storage, a cluttered space, a sort of hideaway that was cool in the warmer months. This room had housed a full size pool table left from our great uncle, Father Thomas Burns, here Dad rested as usual. I'm sure he likely had had similar bouts of angina and hoped his nap would help; however, he would never wake up this day … there in the old poolroom, Dad died.

Mom, who arrived home after Dad began his nap, also had a routine to sit in a recliner and take a 15 or 20-minute nap. Something abruptly caused her to awaken from a sound sleep. She later claimed that she had a peculiar sensation come over her … an unsettled feeling that someone had gently brushed her face, her cheek. When she felt this light and loving touch, she awoke, knowing instantly that something was terribly wrong with Dad. What had awakened her? Mom always insisted that this was her love departing, caressing her for the last time. Perhaps, it was an Angel. In any event, as she awoke she rushed into the room where her love usually rested, in that poolroom.

I had just come in from completing some fieldwork and was alerted by my mom's screams. As I rushed into the hallway, Mom was besides herself sobbing, her screams ceased as I walked towards that end of the hallway. Mom had an unusual air about her, almost a resolve that this was that dreaded day that she somehow knew "was to be." With one hand clutching her mouth, I recall that she simply pointed to the old unfinished poolroom where dad had taken his final nap. She was crying so hard … yet so pitiful as her words poured forth: "Your father's dead." Words so foreign, and unbelievable, a statement that stopped any response—then her voice now suddenly subdued, and in a quiet, yet painfully calm voice, Mom re-stated, "Your father is dead!"

On that day, at that hour, the farm became my whole responsibility.

Bob

On most occasions when a patient of mine died suddenly, I would think back to that day when my dad died. Those feelings would be intensified by the similarities to that personal loss. Although with my dad's death, I had not shared any responsibilities, sort of an innocent bystander in that family's tragedy. With a patient, however, I would have been deeply involved in their care, committed to their health, and their death would become very personal. Every time I would see a patient die, particularly a farmer, it took me back to my dad's death and even more so if that person dropped dead. My Dad's death was a tremendous loss, with my patients' deaths, especially if it was sudden, their passing became a personal defeat. One of my teachers said it best: "Remember, David, as hard as you try, Death will always beat you in the end."

The last time I saw Bob was only hours before he died. Although he was in real tough shape, "*in extremis,*" but he was very mentally alert. His wife had called and asked if I could come this day and see him. "Please," she added, "he really wishes to see you. He needs you." That particular day had been extremely busy for me. Fridays can be like that: a week's summation of all kinds of ills. Disease seems to ripen on Fridays; symptoms from Monday that didn't expect to cause anyone a problem usually reach their pinnacle at week's end.

That morning, I had admitted several critically ill people through the Emergency Room to our ICU. Consequently, carving an hour or more out of this day to drive out to Bob's farm hardly seemed feasible. His wife's voice, however, held a distinct element of despair. It was already passed noon, I had not eaten my lunch, had not finished my "rounds" at the hospital, and had a list of patients at my office for follow-up. Yet the plea in this woman's voice, especially when "please" was added, would cause me to drive far that day. These

patients and the others would have to await my return as I
headed out to Bob's farm.

The drive out was a long 12 miles, through the winding
county roads, along the hardscrabble uplands, down and up
the glacial hills past Fairfield. These secondary roads were
not the type where one could cut corners, but I had to hurry.
Heaven knew that neither Bob nor I had much time that day.
As I drove past these dairy farms, my old haunts, I thought just
how far the past twenty years had carried me: from tending a
farm to tending to the farmers.

I turned my thoughts to Bob, a gentleman always, a man
of amazing grit. Never once did I hear him bemoan his plight.
When he presented with an "angry," out-of-place lymph node,
he knew as I, what the node represented. An excisional biopsy
demonstrated a tissue-type with severe dysplasia, an
anaplastic* aggressive malignancy, a cell-type that is never
kind. No primary site of origin would ever be located; even in
Boston, experts were baffled over its pathology. The metastatic
node was so malignant that no one could identify its tissue
type nor from where it had arisen. After his biopsy, his
chemotherapy, his radiation, he just went about his heavy work
schedule.

When his cancer returned 18 months later, it was
aggressive, cutting him down quickly, attacking almost all of
his vital organs. Weekly or sometimes more often I would
place a large bore needle into his chest, into the pleural space,
the area between his lungs and ribs, and relieve the pressure
from the buildup of malignant fluid that squeezed against his
lungs, fluids that compromised his ability to breathe. With an
attached large syringe, I drew off quarts of "straw" colored
fluid. He appreciated his newfound depth of breath. However,
over the ensuing weeks his large strapping muscles would
quickly fade. In only a few weeks his malignancy caused Bob
to evolve from a hulk of a workman into a wasted shell.

** Anaplastic: *malignant undifferentiated cells–poorly defined
cellular characteristics.*

I had seen him just a few days earlier, and I knew why he and his wife needed me this day. We had spoken openly about his approaching death, and he had his "affairs" in order.

Early in my practice while visiting patients at their homes (this was usually when their disease had become terminal), I found myself distracted. It was difficult to adequately examine people lying in a soft bed or on a sofa, although just being allowed into their world was always a real eye-opener. Sometimes these visits were my first glimpse into just how meager some of their lives had been. Most patients when they came to my office were presenting their best side, but seeing someone in their home showed me the reality of their existence. It's an unsettled time for the patient, for his family, and for a physician viewing individuals so ill that they're housebound and in their final days. However, attending to the dying patients in their homes always taught me lessons in life, lessons about vulnerability and empathy.

Disease was particularly difficult for me to yield to, and many times I thought that a dying patient only pointed to my own failure as a physician, highlighting my own inadequacies. I wondered if others could notice this subtle element of insecurity.

That day turning into Bob's drive, I was taken aback, amazed by the number of cars present. I felt more anxious—unsure of the scene inside, evidence of Bob's extended family, his friends likely present, and then simply wondering if I had arrived too late. I have thought on many past occasions, in such situations, that I could never represent the doctors of old, with their three-piece suits, perhaps smoking a pipe, having a grace and presence that would put all at ease. This day for some reason I could not be at ease. I felt rushed, disappointed that I could do no more for this man, that this disease had beaten me again.

I entered through the side door, into the large country kitchen. It was crowded with young and old, babies fussing, women in quiet prayer, working men standing idle, uneasy, and wishing they were elsewhere, mentally searching for obscure reasons to leave this death watch. I saw the strain and fatigue on their faces, the toil from caring for their dying. Bob's wife introduced all three generations of the family. There were so many that I could not remember who was who, except for his sons; they all had a strong resemblance to their dad. The sheer numbers present in the oversized kitchen demonstrated how important this man was to them, whether their father, brother, uncle, or spouse; they were all there to see him, to honor this man in his last hours.

Their anguish was palpable. Soon after my entrance into that home I noted a distinct air of relief; it was like everyone exhaled, a momentary break from their deathwatch. One could almost hear a communal sigh while they put their watch on hold, at least for a while. Something else: I found that my presence in that home as the doctor was indeed a stand-in for the old fashioned-type physician. There was a genuine relief by my presence, it spelled out a definite comfort, however temporary, to the entire group.

Bob was in the living room, sitting before a large picture window through which he looked out over the vast acreage where he had worked for so many years. He was pale, drenched in a cool sweat, propped up in a leather recliner, appearing very terminal. Yet here in his home, I noted a level of comfort, the strong family bond that had been forged through the years, yet Bob was dying.

The old leather chair in which he sat creaked as this farmer moved, a sound reminiscent of him being still in the saddle. He was moderately short of breath, and I found difficulty comprehending his faint words, his efforts lost through the oxygen mask he wore. So I sat and moved close, leaning nearer to his weak voice.

He first thanked me for coming. His speech was slow, deliberate; he looked a lot older, more compromised, further wasted since the last office visit of a couple of days before. He tried to speak with more energy, but this only made his breathing more labored, his color pasty but without any cyanosis. He labored to speak in a very faint voice, and then asked his wife to leave us alone. The request surprised me, furthered my uneasiness, as his wife stepped back.

Bob struggled to raise himself in his chair, to bring himself even closer to where I sat. Naturally, I leaned even closer, my ear nearer to his quiet words. I felt a tinge of fraudulence, as if I were a priest about to hear someone's last confession. I was made further uneasy when he motioned to his wife, now a few feet removed and ordered her completely from the room. With his limited strength, he strained, and struggled while I moved my chair ever closer.

Hush, I signaled with my finger to my lips as I placed the stethoscope to his chest, quietly listening to the wet rales, sounds of fluid in his chest and throughout both lungs, fluid that now filled his chest cavity. I knew he would save his strength as I listened intently. With his cool hand drenched in sweat, Bob pulled the oxygen mask to the side, and spoke in a hushed tone, "I can't go on like this," a pause. "I don't know how to die," again a pause. I wasn't sure if I heard him correctly or what exactly he asked or if he was kidding in some obtuse manner. Yet on he forged: "How is it going to happen? Am I doing anything wrong?" he asked. I did not answer but let him continue. I was perplexed, hoping he was not asking for this doctor to help his exit from this life. Again I did not respond but let him go on: "Everyone's exhausted," another pause. "I worry about my wife," Bob stated clearly. I was humbled by his frank honesty. Here he was dying and yet his concern was for his caring spouse. His words seemed too light for such a serious moment, but then I realized this meant everything to him. Death surely was imminent, but he really didn't know how it all would happen--and why should he?

All he really needed was knowledge, to know how death would take him, the simple mechanics of it. He wanted me there for that single reason. He was in no pain. He needed only information, and he didn't wish to put his wife through any more of this misery. At first, I feared that he was asking me to do something to end his life, but no, that would not be in keeping with this man's precepts. There was no request for narcotics. He simply was inquisitive. I was astounded. No one had ever asked me so pointedly.

Bob gazed into my eyes, and then he raised the corners of his mouth with a weak but gentle smile. I smiled back with a reassuring glance. I told him that he was my kind of man; again he gave a faint smile. I explained why it's called "expiring" and how he would breathe his last. It's as simple as that; he would not be bothered laboring for another breath.

"That simple?" he asked.

"You will no doubt be unconscious when it happens," I told him. "You'll be asleep."

I could see contentment steal over him. "Thank you, thank you," he responded as he leaned back in the recliner. He placed his thin, wasted, bony fingers on my forearm in an attempt to grab hold, but he was so weak. He was an exceptional man, too young, too needed, to die. We were both indeed relieved this day. He then knew that for him, death would not be a painful struggle but simply eternal rest, a kind exit from his disease. He thanked me for coming. "It meant a lot!" he said. I squeezed his hand and held on with a prayer.

Before I left, I spoke with his wife privately. I told her the pointed questions Bob had along with his concerns. Earlier, she was frightened; Bob had appeared very uneasy, and she was concerned whether he was in pain. Now she was relieved, relieved that I had come to see her husband in his final hours, relieved to know his need had not resulted from something she had done or not done for him.

I took away something from that afternoon: a maturing, a further understanding of life and death, a personal growth. I had a greater understanding about my professional duties and the knowledge which people appreciate—a doctor nearby, someone to professionally and just simply hold someone's hand.

As I left that farmhouse, I was pleased that I had driven the distance, left the hospital this hectic day. Now as I left Bob, this sad day became joyous in an odd sort of way. I felt that I did my very best, that I had 'performed' as well as any old-time doctor could have, that I had acted as the professional, reassuring even without that three piece suit, without the pipe, without the horse and carriage.

Contemplative as I drove back towards the office, this day was special for me as well as for this wonderful man. I thought about so many patients I had been with when they died. Only a few made their exit as gracefully as Bob, surrounded by a loving family and in his own home. Later that evening Bob died. After several hours of being unresponsive, he quietly expired. He was an exceptional man.

Returning to the hospital that afternoon, when I passed-by our family farm, the homestead about five miles from Bob's farm, I reflected on that day, years ago, the day on which my own dad had died. In too many ways, that was a long time ago.

Mom's Second Chance

I had just arrived at the hospital, attempting to obtain an early start on a busy schedule. I also wanted to check how my mother had fared. Mom had been admitted the previous night for evaluation of a possible cardiac arrhythmia, a heart rate that might have been either too rapid or too slow.

Our mother was found confused, sitting out-of-doors on the lawn—physically and psychologically shaken. When my brother Tom found her, she claimed that she did not know what had happened or how it occurred, she thought perhaps she had fallen on the wet grass; however, that did not explain why she had left her home on a cool day in March and out-of-doors but lightly attired. Her regular physician was away on vacation, and so after I had examined her at home, I had her admitted for monitoring in ICU. She had previously been known to have periods of an irregular heart rate, bouts of atrial fibrillation, but no other arrhythmia had ever been recorded on the several Holter* recordings she had worn over the past several months.

As soon as I awoke that morning, I called the ICU; the nurse related that her heart rhythm had been very stable throughout the night. However, when I entered the hospital early that morning, a nurse came running down the hall to show me Mom's startling rhythm strip. They had recorded more than a ten-second pause in which not a single heartbeat was recorded—a pause far too long to sustain life. Mom's heart was now failing, now beating far too slowly, and there had been no response to the standard medications. The IV atropine° should have "kicked" her heart into high gear, but it hadn't.

---

* Holter, *a portable heart monitor that recorded every heart beat for 24 or 48 hours.*

° Atropine, *a drug when given intravenously should increase ones heart rate*

Without question, mom needed a heart pacemaker to save her life, an electrical "wire" placed inside her heart to maintain her heart rate. The morning's urgent situation demanded the insertion of this temporary device, until a permanent one would be later placed. Her heart had ceased beating for far too many seconds, and the result was that Mom lay somewhat confused, her heart failing, her speech slow—slurred from a diminished supply of blood to her brain.

After a hurried surgical scrub and wrapped with a sterile gown, a sterile mask, and gloves, I approached her ICU bedside. I had already asked myself, "Should I be doing this?" Even though there was no one else that could intervene—no one to step in—I still wondered. Our hospital had only a small number of doctors on staff, and that day I was the only physician who could deliver. It was as it was; my mom was now my patient, like it or not. I had no qualms about meeting that need.

Mom's head and face were now covered under the sterile drapes, a nurse held her hands (for comfort and as a precaution to prevent Mom from reaching out and inadvertently contaminating the sterile operative field). Mom surprised everyone by asking, "Is that you, David?"

The nurse replied, "Yes, it is, Mrs. Burns, It's your son."

"Glory be," she acknowledged.

I focused on the obvious, to get on with the procedure. The large bore needle sliced easily through her thin skin and then slid beneath her collarbone, seemingly without effort. I knew how easy it would be to puncture the lung or the subclavian artery lying very nearby (Both could be a major complication.) This procedure is always urgent, always tense, as the needle was inserted blindly but with anatomical confidence. However, inserting a pacemaker into ones own mother drew that much more meaning.

As the needle entered her subclavian vein, her dark venous blood filled my syringe. I then removed the syringe and threaded a spring-like guide wire through the needle into the large vein. Then I pulled out and off the original needle, leaving the guide wire in; over that guide wire I advanced the introducer, a device with a significantly larger bore opening that would stretch a larger opening into the subclavian vein. All of this manipulation would afford an opening for the pacing catheter to be inserted. Things progressed very well with no complications; all this while her heart continued to fail, beating too slowly.

The pacing catheter was then advanced about twelve inches into Mom's vein, when the balloon, at the pacing catheter's tip was filled with a small amount of air, the tiny balloon (about the width of a pencil's eraser) now positioned in the Superior Vena Cava, the large central vein deep in ones chest. The catheter then floated within mom's sluggish venous blood flow towards her heart.

Beads of sweat formed on my forehead, I felt the sweat trickled down over my ribs, while the emotion swelled from within. Questions continued to linger as the pacing catheter slid through this woman's vein and into the chamber of her heart. I watched the monitor as the catheter wire advanced into her ventricle. With voltage set on high and the air at its balloon tip removed with a syringe, the wire blindly lodged onto the wall of her right ventricle. Then "Bingo!" Mom's heart jumped to life, about as easy as it gets, all in less than a couple of minutes. That wonderful resilient heart beating because of a simple, small wire placed inside, a wire that supplied the timed electrical charge, that jolted my mother's heart into action. "A piece of cake," I thought.

Yes, "A piece of cake," but this was, by far, my most emotionally draining medical procedure. Not during, not while mom's chips were down, but after, after stripping off my sweat-soaked surgical wrap, snapping off the wet-from-sweat gloves, it was then that I realized the full consequences of that early morning. Urgent events that unfolded all too quickly, medical necessities that did not allow me time to fret. My eyes filled when I realized, with pride, my accomplishment. Immediately after, however, both hands shook and everything inside this man trembled. Certainly I had an adrenaline rush and one filled with that rising sense of fear, fear of all that could have gone wrong during a procedure like this. Although I had never punctured a lung searching for that elusive subclavian vein, I have, on others, spent far too much time finding this access. Occasionally, I would choose the internal jugular vein in a patient's neck, but that approach poses its own difficulties. Other access sites are available but all at a cost of time.

Time, this day, had been critical. I knew how some previous procedures had consumed ten, fifteen, twenty minutes or more. Time … time that Mom didn't have that morning.

Young at Heart and Restless

District #7 Country School

It was always chocolate milk in an old mayonnaise jar, its top turned tightly with wax paper in-between. The sandwich was peanut butter and home made jam or jelly, always this same sandwich of homemade bread placed in a paper bag. My two older brothers carried a similar lunch. This was my first year of school, the first of three in that one-room schoolhouse, first of what would become twenty-four years of studies. However, I began here at District School #7, a country school with classes for all eight grades in one room, a short mile from the farm. Miss Kelhi was everyone's teacher, always in print dresses and white beads about her neck, matching large button-like earrings, leather shoes with sturdy heels. I noticed how she rocked back and forth as she taught, standing on a platform by her desk, rising on her toes then back to her heels; all day she taught, all eight grades.

We walked to school, walked in all sorts of weather. There was little time to lolly-gag. Returning home was generally a leisurely walk that gave us kids' time to check the small stream for fish and minnows or the bluish craw-daddies hiding beneath the rock-ledges. Other days offered only a quick glance though the railings on the bridge for those "Trolls" that might be down under that concrete. We would inspect the fresh water spring that flowed all year beside the road, spilling water out from the slate under Comstock's pasture; we usually would check there for snakes and salamanders.

On mornings we walked along with other kids from other farms, except for one of our neighbors. They were a family of a dozen or so kids; of course, half were at home in diapers, but it seemed that each grade held one of their boys or girls. They always squabbled among themselves and, generally, were late arriving for school.

Two other families a mile further away on Hard Scrabble Road had kids that walked with us. However, when Billy

Gornshek, a seventh grader, drove his father's green John Deere tractor to school, we would all ride on the attached hay wagon, sitting on the edge of its flat rack watching the road slide by. Billy would stop and pickup other students along the way. That two-cylinder tractor sure made the trek fun. Billy parked it right in the schoolyard between the building and the swing-set. Those were rare treats that occurred in warmer weather and only on days when his dad went fishing.

In winter months we rode our sleds down the road and over the bridge, riding about halfway to our school, pulling them across those patches swept bare by the wind. This became a daily race to see whose sled was the fastest. The road never had any salt spread and the snow-packed surface made sledding perfect. By December the drifted snow piled high along the roadway that had made our run carved like a canyon. As the wind-swept snow settled into this channel, it could make for whiteout conditions. There was no need to worry about traffic, only the snowplow of course, but that great machine could easily be heard approaching.

One day, with my small, slower sled, I could not keep up with the older kids as they disappeared into that snowy mist. My attitude grew from disappointment into a tantrum. Angered at my siblings and their scheming fast sleds, I buried that jar of chocolate milk in a snow-bank, turned and walked back towards home with eyes filled, believing my mom would give me shelter and the day off. I told her how in the blinding snow I lost the jar of chocolate milk. With all the Wisdom of Solomon she said, "Go straight back there and find that milk, and then go to school." Walking alone into that one room schoolhouse an hour late, I was scared and ashamed. Miss Kelhi could see my discomfort and that alone was her punishment for this pouting lad

Miss Johnson was the District's music teacher. She would arrive in a black Hudson coupe, parking it always on the roadside, on a slight grade. She probably came a couple times a month. I can't recall ever singing as she played the upright piano or learning any music. After the music lessons Miss Johnson would leave about noontime. If we were in recess or playing outside, the older kids would gather around the fence by the road to watch her zoom the engine. Then taking her time releasing the clutch, her car would roll backwards several feet before the clutch engaged and her car lurched forward, spinning the fine stones from the roadside. Everyone would send her off with a loud cheer. On one occasion, Billy Gornshek brought along several large spikes from home and wedged some behind the Hudson's rear tires, angling these large nails so that when she rolled back both rear tires would have likely been blown-out. However, that day Miss Johnson zoomed off without a hint of that clutch slipping as her car charged forward. We all roared with laughter and dismissed any of our disappointment

Every May, Miss Kelhi would deem a certain day Arbor Day. On an exceptional sunny spring day, the entire school went into the Atutis' woods to select a sugar maple sapling among the hundreds that sprouted there. With shovels the older boys dug the sapling from the soft, rich soil and carried it, in water, back to the schoolyard, and after a low-key ceremony the students gathered around as the sapling was rooted. A used ink- bottle with every student's name in it was placed into the dug hole. This became a time capsule, buried along with the tree roots. There were many stately maples of all sizes growing around the circumference of that small schoolyard.

Then in 1947 the State closed all country schools. It was sad seeing the old one-room schoolhouse vacant on Harry Comstock's field, surrounded by the many various maples that kids had planted through the years. We were carted by bus to the "city," where the Burns kids attended St. Mary's Academy. A year later, Al Carney bought the old school structure to become living quarters for his hired help. There was a slight problem: Al's farm was a couple of miles away. He and his helpers raised that building with large screw-type house jacks, and then lowered that wooden building onto several long, old wooden poles placed under it for skids. Then they hitched the building to an array of farm tractors of all sizes, all makes and various colors: neighbors helping neighbors. With attached chains and wire cables, they pulled and pushed, huffed and puffed over ditches, across fields and meadows, under power lines, and over three roads. It was a show much like an ill-rehearsed three-ring circus without a director. Even Mickey Steele got into the act with his massive tow-truck. When pulled, that old school building twisted and creaked, bending as it coursed over the uneven ground, but eventually Al had his new tenant house.

The schoolyard was cleared of trees, outhouses, foundation stones, and returned to a productive meadow for Mr. Comstock. Good soil on that site continues to grow wonderful corn and alfalfa. Sadly, no one ever found a single ink well; no one ever discovered the hidden history of the many past students, their names buried therein like so many memories.

Of Life and Limb

Jack was late for lunch and decided to take a short cut home. All of fourteen years old, he had worked alone all morning. He chose to follow a cow path up and over the older but steeper embankment from the past wanderings of a creek bed. That decision would cost him dearly.

Like others his age, Jack was an impulsive youth. He thought not at all about the possible consequences of choosing that shortcut instead of following the established pathway through the pasture. Indeed he chose a course that would forever become the long way home. As the tractor he was driving began to climb the steep grade, its center of gravity shifted drastically; mechanically speaking the rear wheels no longer turned forward. Instead, the wheels remained still, while the motor's torque lifted the tractor's frame up and backwards, throwing Jack off. He attempted to run away from the danger, but even Jack couldn't be that nimble. In a millisecond, the tractor turned topside down and caught Jack at his flexed right knee as he ran, attempting to flee the danger. There he lay under the tractor's mighty weight, unconscious and face down. He would lie there for untold minutes, maybe even for hours.

Mom's intuition told her that something was terribly wrong. Jack was never late for lunch and hours had passed. It was fortuitous that Tom and I had been farmed out for that day to Gram's house downtown, for we could have been victims as well. Mom walked the half-mile, a mother on a mission, through the day pasture. Those abundant June flowers, the bright yellow buttercups, would not be noticed this day. No, mom's focus was elsewhere.

As she hurried towards the creek bed, no one will know her heartache, her panic and despair when the tractor came into view. The machine's position so strange, so foreign with its wheels high in the air, must have caused her heart to sink.

Mom's first born—where was he? Calling out his name, she rushed towards this strange, God-awful scene. Would her son be crushed or still alive?

She called, "Jack where are you?" However, there was no response. Over and over her shouts went unanswered as she closed onto the accident scene. Jack, just a kid, was pinned beneath the tractor's weight. The heavy cast steering column at the tractor's front end caught him from behind, narrowly missing his shoulder but catching his right leg, smashing his right knee, driving the shattered bones into the pasture's turf.

As Mom knelt at his side, the bloody scene seemed hopeless. There was no way to free her son. Alone with him in this cow pasture, I'm sure she wiped his brow as her mind raced. Mom left him beneath that machine … there was no other choice. She then hurried to climb the pasture's hills, back to the house to call for help.

First, she rang for an ambulance, and then she called her many neighbors, farmers who dropped everything to race to the scene. Harry Comstock raced his small orange Case tractor directly across his pasturelands, crashing through the barbed fences to reach this remote scene.

When Jack came to, he recalled only the smell of wild spearmint that he had crushed nearby where he lay. A flurry of neighbors arrived and worked to free him, lifting that enormous weight off of him. He was then placed in the waiting ambulance that had been driven into this strange pasture scene.

Unfortunately, after Jack was carried into the hospital, a surgeon opted to immediately remove the injured leg, despite the objections of other doctors. Sure, there were major concerns for tetanus (a Clostridial infection), especially a crushing injury to that knee joint occurring in a pasture where cattle and horses had grazed, animals known to carry this bacterium. There were other conditions: the surgeon was someone with years of experience, but someone whose decisions may have been tainted by alcohol. This doctor had acted with impunity, despite starting each day with a nip or two. On this day, he failed to realize another important fact of Jack's trauma—his right hip was dislocated. No one discovered this additional factor until it was too late. Treatment was delayed for weeks. Jack now had a double injury: his hip would become atrophic and nonfunctioning as a result of the loss of blood supply to a youthful, growing bone in his hip-socket. This tragedy along with the loss of the knee and lower leg would cripple our older brother. Furthermore, it would take months and months for his recovery. Jack would spend much of the following year in a rehabilitation hospital.

The rehab facility in Utica was more like a prison with limited parental visits and no visits allowed for his siblings. We could only wave from the lawn. Jack was now an above-knee amputee and had great difficulty being fitted with an artificial limb, primarily because of his non-existing hip joint. Today, as then, it's well known that such trauma is frequently associated with dislocation of a hip. Further, when a dislocation of a joint is recognized, and then "reduced" (joint articulation reset into its socket), the joint will heal. Later in my own practice, this fact was foremost in my assessment of any traumatized patient.

Jack spent many weeks in a wheel chair. After he returned home, I remember pushing him through the hay field below the farmhouse. I was eight years old, trying to help Jack's return into the farm scene. The entire setting was so foreign: a wheelchair in the hayfield, Jack's impairments, the cuff of his missing pant leg blowing in the breeze, his frustrations spilling out, his shame palpable, and his anger near a rage. Tears and frustrations flowed from both of us—so many things had gone wrong, his leg sheared short like the hay stubble in that field.

I thought back to that day when Jack ran across our lawn, through the sun and into the shadows from the large maples, to phone the police when our dad was drunk and trying to drive our old truck. Time had changed so many things. Extreme situations had come into our family: Jack became crippled, while dad became sober.

Looking back, Jack's accident was a pivotal point in time for our family: it marked the beginning of a major transition in Jack's life, but more importantly, it would become the critical point in our Dad's life as well. For there was no question in my mind that this catastrophic event, though nearly taking

Jack's life, clearly saved his father's life from alcohol abuse. In the scheme of things, no other force within our family could have turned the course of events that Jack's tragedy had. In a manner of destiny, Jack became--sort of a "sacrificial lamb," for the continued life of our father. Although difficult to understand—miracles do occur.

***

Jack's story did not end here. Our brother's adult life in some aspects began there. After he graduated from high school, Jack attempted to resume a normal life. However compromised, he would never let his handicap get in the way. Furthermore, Jack tried very hard not to let his disability slow him down as he limped his way through life. He helped with the farm work; Jack would try to do anything and everything, and following his accident he set a wonderful example of perseverance.

In mid-August he was mowing pastures, driving the same old tractor that four years earlier he over-turned and crushed his leg. Out of the blue, a black sedan drove into the field where Jack was mowing weeds. Oddly, this stranger never stopped at our house to find our brother but drove directly into the field. The gentleman in a dark suit and tie got out of his car and walked up the slope to where my brother had been working. In the cow pasture he introduced himself, and immediately asked Jack to come to the farmhouse and sit with his parents to "discuss some future plans."

At the house Mom, Dad, and Jack, all of us, heard the man describe a possible future for our brother. The gentleman thought Jack should seriously consider college, namely Cornell, in the fall. "That's only two or three weeks away," someone stated.

"Correct. I'd like to see Jack start this fall." Because higher education had never been discussed … Jack was caught off guard. "Well," the gentleman went on, "I've gone ahead and arranged for you to simply visit the college. Perhaps your mom and dad could drive you there next week, to look over the school."

I'm sure everyone was dumbfounded at that point, but Dad agreed to take Jack to Cornell University for a look. "Oh, that's great," said the man, "I believe that College is right for him, and we'll see what can be worked out." Then he added, "Perhaps Jack would consider becoming a veterinarian at some point in the future." That again was the farthest consideration from Jack's mind, definitely not something that he had ever considered.

The following week, our parents and Jack drove to Cornell University. They started at the admissions office as the man suggested. "Oh, yes," they said, "We had expected you. Your appointment time was left open, but we're glad you could make it. We'll start with a tour of the Campus."

Later back at the office, Cornell personnel stated that they had a reserved a "spot" for Jack that fall in the Class of '55. I was not present, but I'll bet Jack had to have been shocked, astounded that only a week earlier, the thought of college was not on his horizon, not even in his most remote dream.

The most wonderful, most intriguing part of this story is that no one ever heard of that man in the dark suit, the man who drove the dark sedan into the cow pasture and into Jack's life. While at Cornell, Jack attempted to find out who was that person who appeared out of nowhere? Who was the one who made all those arrangements without consulting the family? Try as Jack did, he was never able to find anyone who could remember such a person or who fit the stranger's description. The Admissions Office and their Director knew of no one. They showed Jack all his preliminary application, papers that contained only his Mom and Dad's signatures. The office staff insisted that the personnel in that office only spoke with Jack's parents; they were the only ones who set everything up through phone calls. No one ever heard of that anonymous gentleman, the mysterious Angel that started Jack down this path to become a professional. There was no possibility that our parents or aunts or any relatives or friends could have set these unbelievable sequences in motion.

37

Blue

I couldn't believe just how blue he was … and still, very, very still. The only sound I heard was from the hallway, Mom's anguished, "Oh my God, Oh my God. Your father's dead." Grief came rushing in that day, and for all of us his death became repeated over and over for hours, for days, for the weeks. Dad's sudden exit from our lives is still my foremost memory.

Up to that day it had been an exceptional autumn, with fine reds from the maples, bright yellows from the poplars, and majestic greens from the meadow filling the lands. Blue, I thought, was a primary reserved for the skies, not for my dad. His last breath was long gone! Blue suddenly became a prominent feature in our family. Blue was no longer reserved for our skies--blue became us.

Alerted by my mom's screaming, I rushed into the hallway of our home. Mom had one hand over her mouth, distressed as she pointed to the old unfinished poolroom where Dad lay. I couldn't believe a person, our dad could die just like that: alive one minute and dead the next. I was so stunned. I wonder why I did not push on his ribs or shake him or try to squeeze the life's blood from his heart? So many subsequent times at others' bedside, I would ponder my Dad's lonely death. Modern medicine was still around future's corner. Truth-be-known aggressive resuscitations would begin in earnest in Vietnam. Strange that it takes a war to save lives.

I simply turned and walked to the kitchen. I called the doctor's office. I'll always remember Bernard Burke's response as I told him, "Dad is dead." I recoiled as I heard my own words.

"Damn it," Bernard exclaimed, acknowledging the loss of another in his charge. There was so little a physician could do in those years, so little medicine, no CCU, no angiography, certainly no resuscitation. "I'll be right up!" said the good doctor, and then he added, "Make sure you call the priest."

Seemingly in a flash the doctor was entering our home. It was sad seeing the doctor helpless, for we had surmised what little could be done, and comfort was all he could give. He spoke with Mom about Thomas's virtues, repeatedly told her that Thomas was a good man. I remember the comfort in the doctor's words. I could not return to the "pool" room—fearful that Dad was still that awful shade of blue. I knew he was dead, but I could not enter that room again, at least for a while. (In later years, I would see all too many patients with that similar shade of blue.)

Doctor Burke waited until the priest arrived before he would leave. Bernard was very Irish and being Irish he was raised to appreciate how sacred a household is when someone dies. His Faith had taught him that in these precious minutes an Angel comes and carries the soul to Heaven. Years later he would remind me of those sacred moments in the hospital and stress that it was my responsibility to be there when patients die. He would never let one of his elderly patients die alone. Giving comfort to a person or their family in their final moments was an obligation for any physician. Now older, all this makes sense; it's such a vulnerable emotional time, likely the most important moments in anyone's life, the moments before death.

Mom had always insisted that when Dad died, something or someone brushed her face, gently, as perhaps her husband had many times before, and this tender touch woke her in a start. Her first thought when awakened was that something terrible had happened to her love. For she also was 'fast' asleep, taking a nap after working all day in the school cafeteria. It was a daily routine for both Mom and Dad. Mom had taken comfort by this last tender touch, by an angel or from Dad's final goodbye.

The last time I remember kissing my Dad was just before his casket was closed. The family alone in the parlor at the farm after everyone left for the funeral procession, we waited. Together we quietly paused, not wanting to go on, not wishing to stay. I was uneasy. Flights of ideas clouded my thoughts at the last moment with our dad's body. Our mom was so distraught she could have gone with him. I can't speak for anyone else but I was scare--afraid of the present as well as the future. I stood there looking at him, feeling sorry that he died so young, so quickly. I was becoming a man but knew him only as a kid. I could see the lines in his face, aging over the past few days, lying there in 'State,' in the parlor of his wonderful home.

So many people came to his wake. For three days neighbors, friends, and relatives from afar gave tribute to him as a person. I hadn't realized how many people his life had touched. I felt bad that I had only known him as my dad. This day in our parlor, I wondered why, years before, he had lowered himself to become a drunk. Now his past was only between my dad and his God. I wondered, at that profound moment, how God would judge him. It would be years and years until I let go of my grudge over his drinking, a grudge held no doubt much longer by me than by God.

Yet for those few days at his wake, we laughed and cried, reflected on so many humorous times. Though with every laugh, every joke relatives raised, the fun times revisited— these only pointed to our loss.

Mom gave him a hug—I remember that—it messed up his tie and lapel. Her grief would almost pull her in. There was such reluctance on my part. Should I run? Should I hide my tears or should I simply shout, "*No, no, no! You can't go; you can't leave me with this farm, with these responsibilities. I'm not ready for this.*" Yet, I bent and kissed his forehead. He felt strange, lifeless, inert—I was taken back by the coolness of his skin. It was the most trying few seconds of my life.

In our sorrow, we watched the black cars coursed the country roads. On the way to the Church, we saw neighbors honor our Dad by stopping whatever they were doing at the roadside or in the fields—they tipped their caps, lowered their heads—I was struck with farmers showing this degree of respect—farmers, hard working, some unpolished, others having been distant, yet giving public notice to our dad. Perhaps they even murmured a prayer. Their gestures still remain strong in my heart.

The Catholic Faith gives strong comfort in Death as well as in Life. Dad's distant cousin said the Mass. The Monsignor acknowledged our dad with personal accolades, spoke at the Mass of how much he enjoyed his many visits to our farm. This priest was himself a unique man. Frequently he drove to the farm for Mom's wonderful creamed potatoes with her homemade bread, her homemade chili sauce, and a special cake or pie. He was a learned man but appeared ordinary; he put everyone at ease. When he visited, the Monsignor would engage all, even bring us kids into the conversation. I was especially pleased the day when I was fourteen; he gave my older brothers and me a great cigar after that wonderful home cooked meal. I knew the picture didn't fit; however I lit the cigar, pretending at least for a while to be a big deal.

In those dark hours of the funeral, the colors of autumn continued to stand out. The cobalt blue skies, the bright sun-filled days were the norm. The brilliance of the foliage remained, as if each tree held its every leaf as a highlight to a life given; and the meadows were still lush with the deep greens of alfalfa, yet to be harvested.

After the Mass the entourage of autos headed to the cemetery. Again the vivid foliage clung to the varied branches, unusual this far into October. The forecast did tell of a change, but this funeral morning was summer-like. As Dad's casket was lowered and prayers said, handfuls of dirt were cast upon the finished wooden casket. It was done.

Later that day back at the farmhouse as everyone gathered before going back into their own lives, before Mom and I faced the farm without Dad, before the sorrow and grief really set in, the skies quickly darkened and the air turned cool. Then gusting winds scattered the leaves, raised the dust, and shook not only the maples but our lives. The ill winds indeed blew in that day ushering in a whole new era, new responsibilities, and a new emptiness. I sat on the front porch, alone in thought as the winds picked up nature's past. The day turned dark, forbidding. The sun was blotted by the clouds and stirred my dad's son to think: think of life, think of death—a death so quick.

Goals in Mind

Make Straight My Path

As I think back, before professional school, before college when I worked our farm, after the sudden death of our dad, many things had changed. Particularly, all the responsibilities of the farm were on my shoulders, and there were plenty. A mortgage remained on the farm, left over from those years when our father lived as a reckless drunk. Furthermore, money is and always was scarce on any farm. Yet as I tried to get a handle on my future, at times becoming a doctor all seemed so nebulous, too remote.

Indeed, I loved so many aspects of farming. Besides the economics, there were so many wonderful rewards about the work at hand: simply helping a cow give birth to an eighty pound calf in the middle of the night. The calf, covered with a proteinaceous slim from birth, lay on fresh clean wood shavings, bedding for the animal, the wood clips adhering to its hide. Then in one or maybe two attempts, the calf lifts itself to its feet and staggers towards its first taste of colostrum. Wow, anyone should marvel at such an event.

I remember every spring preparing the soil for a new crop, turning the earthen sod onto its side—about a week later, the field of dark brown soil, maybe twenty acres, is made green by rain and Mother Earth. Certainly very corny, yet a truth emerges from every seed ... life restored.

As my days on the farm unfolded, a recurrent thought continued to surface, a daily mental nudge, directing a basic tenet: "*David, you can do more.*"

One summer after the majority of crops were safely stored, tons and tons, the entire winter's feed for the livestock was in the barn: two friends and I decided to drive across this great country. In spite of my Mom having a conniption, I hired a neighbor to milk the cows, care for the farm, and to look-in on my mom. As we drove through the wondrous dimensions of this country, Mom came to realize that in her future, she might become the sole person, along with old Frank, to live on the farm. I believe this was her fear that she might lose this son to some other endeavor in life. In this situation Mom sensed her own uncertain future, an uneasy future for the farm, particularly if my wandering went further than this two-week tour of this Country.

We headed west driving the northern route to Seattle and then on to California and the arid southwest. We returned by way of Route 66, all driven in a new Impala convertible, robins-egg blue with a white top, owned by my friend Sam Sterusky. The two of us along with another friend, Jim Collins, drove this dream of mine, a fantasy to explore the West.

The trip was a wonderful experience, a vision come true; many areas were simply seen from afar, but other Western areas were noted in depth. In Wyoming, perhaps traveling at ninety plus miles per hour, we 'flew' past a young kid standing beside this very straight, flat road. I decided to stop and quiz him about the workings of a ranch. It required a half-mile to slow and turn. He couldn't believe that three men from New York State would stop and speak with him.

None of us had ever been on a ranch while this fifteen year old had never seen such a beautiful car. I prodded the lad take us to see his father's ranch. We followed him as he drove his old tractor, not knowing how far off the road to the ranch. The dust was thick enough to choke us all. We had to stop to shut the convertible's top. The drive seemed miles to the ranch house. Their setting was so disappointing: no horses, no cattle, a couple of broken-down buildings with an artesian well pouring out a vivid stream of cool, fresh, sulfur water, water that no one would drink except myself—cool pure water that quenched my thirst.

Although this hard-luck ranch was a far cry from our idealized image, stopping was a needed break in our travels. The young lad took us into the stark farmhouse. Without paint, its clapboards blended with the surroundings, matching the weatherworn barn-boards. There were two older women watching TV in a spacious room with a small TV that had "rabbit-ears." The women were watching intently an afternoon show. They never looked up at the three strangers who walked through to their kitchen—there the lad gave us cold Cokes. An hour later, we were back on the road and heading west: we had yet to see a true ranch.

Ahead lay were the Grand Tetons and Yellowstone, then the mining and lumbering sections of Idaho. One of the more poignant moments for me was a roadside stop outside of Spokane, Washington. It was so hot and dry; the elevation had to be several thousand feet. There were these huge combine harvesters, the type that worked the steep, rolling hills, harvesting wheat fields, fields with soil so dry that the earth could actually burn. A huge cloud of dust followed every machine. In the distance, perhaps a mile away, a fire raged, consuming the wheat, while multiple fire departments raced to the inferno.

Then a middle-aged woman ran onto the scene, commanded the huge harvesters to hurry: "Get moving," she yelled, "faster," as she motioned with her arms, fearing her own economic disaster. While the fires consumed her distant crops, those machines rumbled along the slopes of the steep hillsides. This left an indelible image of the hazards of farming in that arid northwest.

Driving the West Coast from Seattle to LA, the sites were all a great awakening. I felt free, released from the farm, free to think of other possibilities. The trip was, perhaps, an effort to show myself that the generational farm would still be there, even without me. When I returned, I was glad to be back, back with a fresh look into my future.

I knew I needed challenges beyond, and I realized I was less grounded because of the trip. I found myself less 'anchored' by the prior generations that had toiled there: yet that feeling, that lineage, continued to be strong. Then one day, it was as if I had an Epiphany, an understanding, of a clear idea that had been so foreign. Truly, I believe to this day that this was Divine Intervention because out of the blue, I had this one thought, one endeavor, and only one. The seemingly impossible 'task' of becoming a physician lay before me. I thought long and hard of this one goal, but I kept my thoughts quiet. Because of fear, I kept silent, because of the possible ridicule from friends and family. I felt alienated, isolated from people through this one endeavor to keep my dream silent. I was six or seven years after high school and had never taken a single college course; yet I was planning and plotting to become a doctor.

Although both a great aunt and a great uncle had chosen to dedicate their lives to religious orders, there was no direct connection to any family member that was a medical professional; so what made me consider becoming a physician? I do not know, but again, I believe there are Divine plans, however exaggerated that sounds. Perhaps a directed series of thoughts are induced into everyone's conscious, and a person can grab hold and think the process through or have the choice to discard such ideation. I believe strongly that my path was spiritually guided, for the manner of success, for this single entity was far too remote without heavenly guidance. I do believe that God helps us choose, but how many of us meditate or listen long enough?

There were several reasons that may have influenced my thoughts towards medicine. First, I had considerable problems with allergies and bronchitis from molds that concurred with harvesting grains in the fall, plus seasonal asthma symptoms with cattle dander throughout the winter months. These were problematic and required frequent visits to Dr. Burke's office.

Waiting in his crowded office, along with so many others, I was fascinated by the diverse group of people entering and leaving: people sad, some crying, people so ill as they left his exam, sick babies screaming, all sorts of medical dilemmas. As I sat there, coughing and wheezing, I wondered about every waiting patient. What possible conditions existed? What secret concerns had been exchanged or explained by the doctor?

The second fact was my dad's sudden death and its strange aftermath: the wonderment about life and death, disease and health. The third factor, an event that had occurred much earlier, was my brother Jack's farm accident and the resulting amputation of his right leg, another improbable happening at the farm. All these conditions became cumulative and heightened my curiosity with the medical profession.

I can't say with any certainty what one thought had been more compelling or if any added weight to my future plans. It seemed like "out-of-the-blue" my mind had become convinced that this one profession was a doable idea and one that I needed to pursue. It became important to "catch the bus" that would lead to my future. As I thought, I became increasingly convinced that I would make every attempt to become a doctor. It wasn't that I might become one, no—it was more clear than that—I would become a doctor.

I had to start with a single college course, to test my diligence while I had full-time responsibilities operating a relatively large farm. My 'dream' was daunting, a tedious pursuit one step at a time towards that goal. I was twenty-three and I could feel the anxiety over the fact that my 'true' future could simply melt away as an unattainable figment of my imagination.

As others my age spent weekends sipping beers and having a carefree time, I became more serious. I no longer continued my weekend nights of going out. Instead on Friday evenings around ten p.m., after the doctor's office hours ceased, I would call upon Dr. Burke and ask if I could stop and speak with him. We spoke of so many things other than medicine, and it would take numerous visits before I had the courage to ask his opinion of my desire to become a physician.

Bernard could be intimidating and boisterous; however, he responded in kind. In analytical conversations he asked about the farm, asked what would my mother do without her son working the land. While I concerned myself more with questions on the requirements and the intelligence needed to make a good physician, Dr. Burke forced me to look at the whole picture, not that I had skirted these points in my own deliberations, but the entire picture was so complicated. I simply needed his nudge to take that first step. I thought my age might preclude this endeavor. I was not a bookworm. My academics had never been seriously tested. Although I never strived in high school, I had achieved some honors in mathematics and Latin. I always remember Bernard's reply to that one question: "Hell, anyone can be a physician. Look at me. If a doctor doesn't know what the Hell's wrong with a patient, just get on the phone and call someone."

His statement, although elemental, leveled all my academic fears. Although I was not that naive, his statement seemed so logical. From his early responses, I knew I would eventually return to this small Upstate community and practice medicine. It was a goal so remote, yet so tangible. Without a moment of college instruction, I knew I would return home as a doctor.

My most daunting thought: 'What if I failed at this extreme goal? What if I stepped out from the farm, pursued a college degree, and never achieved Medical School? How would I feel with that fact? The thought was unnerving. I never enjoyed failure and thinking of the possibility of failure was very debilitating, discouraging, and most frightening. These thoughts halted my Progress—thoughts of failure caused me to take pause, made hesitant that first important step; through this fear I wasted months of forward motion.

Three years after my Dad's death, I was seven years from high school, and I had no idea of the demands that college would place upon me or if I had the academic fortitude. Furthermore, there were other problems: both Mom and the farm were huge considerations. I grappled with the decision. There were days when I surmised it might be easier just to stay put. Leaving Mom alone was an enormous psychological barrier. Leaving her essentially alone with our old hired hand, poor Frank did not help.

I was stepping into deep waters and was unsure of so many facts. For sure, I prayed a lot, mediated with professional school on my mind. On occasions, I would sit in our church at two or three a.m., during exposé of Blessed Sacrament, particularly on First Fridays. I would sit, kneel, and meditate, asking for guidance, praying for direction, for fortitude to carry out my desires.

Other times, I'd walk through our wonderful woodland, walk the Hogs Back, taking in its beauty, its severe geological contours. Eventually, while coursing down life's road, my needs became more clarified. I dreaded the moment when I had to tell Mom that I would be leaving the farm where prior generations toiled, working these hardscrabble acres.

Mom would not take my news lightly. I was, after all, abandoning her in her senior years. When I finally told her of my quest, she was predictably angered. Tears flowed as she felt the pain, the hurt in my decision. She could readily feel the future emptiness that would exist in our wonderful farm home, the absence of her five children now gone from her nest. I knew the decision would further crush her with the disappointment, the fears of living in a fourteen-room house, with only herself and the aging hired man. Mom was not encouraging. I didn't expect anything more from her initial reaction. I guess I couldn't blame her. Some might believe Mom was selfish, but like all of us, she didn't wish to be alone. It was an Irish way to have ones offspring care for a parent when they become older and Mom, of course, did not wish to see the farm lost.

Poor Frank

Truly, my first patient became our old feeble hired man, Frank Manion. Before I went to college and shortly after Dad's death, Frank fell and fractured a hip. "Poor Frank," as he was sometimes referred to (however never addressed by) lived at the farm for as long as I can remember, perhaps thirty years or more. Without family, Frank became assimilated into ours. Even though Mom had her hands full with her three young boys and two daughters along with our great aunt, Frank was accepted into our household and was given his own bedroom. Dad had taken him in, perhaps because he had nowhere else to go. From that point on, Frank seemed to be always present: caring for the animals, cutting grass or weeds or simply puttering about. The farm was never a place without something that needed to be done, whether out-of-doors or inside. When we sat at our large kitchen table at family gatherings or playing cards in the evenings, Frank was present, yet somehow apart. A simple man with simple needs, he worked everyday on the farm whether in the barn or in the fields or in summer time tending to our large garden.

In our eyes Frank was always physically and mentally slower, especially when we were younger. He appeared frail, deformed with a slight humped back, shoulders slumped, unsteady on his feet. However, considering the number of frequent stumbles and falls, these left him generally without injury. In the barn he usually wore knee-high, stiff rubber boots, which made it more likely for him to confound his gait. I remember his apparel, his demeanor, his clumsiness, and yet he would accomplish many tasks, always moving in low gear, whether hoeing weeds in the garden or trimming overgrowth about the barnyard with his large awkward scythe.

I don't believe Dad ever gave him directions; rather Frank saw what needed to be done and worked at it. Wherever he toiled he had a nervous habit of spitting "O Be Joyful" tobacco juice everywhere as he worked, and if the work became more intense, the hired man increased the frequency of spitting the fine spray of tobacco juice. Something else: he always came along with us, whatever the task, for he would have been insulted if someone told him otherwise. For example, in the spring as the frost left the ground, most fence posts needed to be reset and the barbed wire re-stretched and fastened. Frank would be there, repairing fences up and down the steep embankments in our woods or pastures or wherever the property lines divided the fields. Otherwise, he would be in our barn tending to those rambunctious calves. Often he would climb the ladder into the haymow and toss down the bales of hay for the cows even though he was told not to. On one occasion, my brother Tom and I found Frank stuck in the muddy barnyard, those high rubber boots nearly topped by the soft spring mud. I remember both of us lifting him without his boots and carrying him to safety, retrieving the boots later.

On Sundays he would shave, put in his dentures, and get into his only JC Penny suit, his fedora, and together with the family ride to Sunday Mass. After church Frank would stay a few hours in town; someone would usually drive him home later or he hired a taxi. After Mass, he would often walk, more likely saunter, dressed to the nines in his collared shirt and tie. He would walk a couple of blocks to the downtown area, talking with himself or whomever he noticed along the way, and then he strode into Bride's Pool Hall. Frank would sit on one of those high-chaired gallery seats to watch the teenagers sharpen their "sticks." He'd sit and light up a White Owl cigar, looking around as if he were King of something yet unnamed.

Our family would always stop at Grandma's house after Mass for coffee or to chat. Mom would catch-up on the news from her old neighborhood and ongoing problems within the family. Perhaps a half hour would pass and then back into our Chevy to stop for the Sunday paper, a copy of the Syracuse Herald American, which Bill Bride would always set aside for our dad. There, at the pool hall, we'd see Frank sitting in all his glory, sitting in the back gallery watching the sharks chalk their sticks.

Looking back, it was shameful just how embarrassed I would act. As a youngster, perhaps ten years old, I would rush into Bill Bride's Cigar Store and Pool Hall to plunk down the exact number of coins for the paper to avoid waiting for my change. Frank always sat in the back billiard room, but he could easily be seen through the open archway to the left of Bill's cash register. God forbid, if Frank caught my eye or shouted a "Hello, David." What if my peers would be watching? Heaven forbid.

Bill Bride, what a character! Probably eighty years old for too many years, he ran a seedy establishment, seedy because he never cleaned or painted his store or changed a thing. He waited on customers, always with a used cigar in one corner of his mouth, always wearing that old fedora to cover his baldhead, a cardigan sweater (the same old ratty one), and a fingerless glove that jingled the customer's money.

For thirty years Frank shared our meals, our joys and the necessary work. Quietly, he took-in everything but asked for little. He was family, although as I grew into my teens, there were times when I was embarrassed, if not outright ashamed, by his ever-presence or with his simple comments about the news or a show seen on our newly acquired TV or about a new style of automobiles he had noticed traveling on our back country road. He always could spot his favorite cars, a Buick, with their three or four air-vents aside the front fenders. I thought like most teens: "Who really cares about what type of car traverses our roads?" But to Frank, his notice spoke volumes.

Frank never could drive a tractor or any vehicle, never could coordinate himself. I was told that dad gave him one chance, and that one time Frank needed to steer the old REO Truck as the tractor pulled it out from a deep snow drift, that episode almost killed our dad. Although Frank was instructed as to where the truck's brakes were, as the truck became freed and started, the old vehicle charged into the rear of the tractor and damn near climbed over those large rear wheels before Frank could figure out which pedal was the brake.

As friends or relatives gathered about our large kitchen table to talk, to eat, or to play cards, Frank was always there.

He loved the various relatives and friends that frequented our home. He also loved the TV programs, especially Peggy Lee, even loved her rendition of "Fever." I found it difficult to connect Frank to the song "Fever," but then I was just a kid. However, when he hummed that song, I would be embarrassed just the same.

After our Dad died, poor Frank fell and fractured his hip. He spent weeks in the hospital and even though not fully recovered, he was brought home. I drove to pick him up at the rear of the hospital where most patients were met and one's car would be close at hand. A problem arose: I had failed to bring any winter clothes with me! I had not brought a damn stitch of clothes for him to wear home, nothing. Here he was still in his hospital "Johnny" sitting in a wheel chair, while Dr. Burke gave me instructions on his care. Yet I was still a kid at heart and never thought much about what Frank should wear. I never thought about the cold winds that winter day; I simply never considered whether Frank had clothes to wear or not. No doubt I figured that he had gone into the hospital with clothes on and those were likely still in his possession. Dr. Burke could not believe just how ignorant I was that day, upon not bringing an appropriate pair of pants or socks or shoes—not even a warm jacket. Bernard Burke simply howled with laughter as he learned of this absurdity, and so I warmed the car, and then wheeled poor Frank near the rear door of the hospital. The nurses helped; they kindly bundled him in several warmed blankets, extra socks, and I simply picked him up and carried him to the car's back seat, butt bare and very happy to be out of the hospital. I was embarrassed and yet Frank was so happy to be going home, full of joy—all smiles, in spite of the brief exposure to the bitter cold and the flurries of snow in the air.

Frank was heading home, not in good shape physically, not even able to lift himself from the chair; but no matter, he was happy. Mom, on the other hand, was annoyed as hell that Frank was coming back and back as an invalid to boot.

Mom, of course, was not glad to have him back in her house; Frank required complete care, care that Mom could not bring herself to readily accept. Even though I could well understand Mom's position, I felt Frank was family and needed a home. Frank's status and Mom's attitude both spiraled downward. To make matters worse, Frank was all but helpless. He urinated in the bed, soiled his pants, and over time things did deteriorate. Frank grew steadily more infirmed and I became increasingly his private duty nurse. The reality was that Frank needed more than both of us could give, and soon he was placed in an extended-care nursing home. There he improved slowly but was so unhappy that anyone could see he wanted to be back on the farm.

The first plea I ever heard from Frank occurred months later. His frail status became static: Frank's infirmity continued with bedsores and more weakness. During this time conditions at our home were sad. With my dad dead, it appeared that Mom's happiness had left her. Her widow's burden precluded any possibility for Mom to care for poor old Frank. Mom was adamant; she would not or could not care for an old man, even old Frank. Her Cross of Sorrows, her husband's death, was all she could bear. Her love died so suddenly, with no chance given for her to be a caregiver for her husband. She became bitter about Frank, probably vindictive of sorts. Mom, I'm sure, was angered because "God took her husband" and not old Frank. Not necessarily logical but Mom was firm: her husband was gone, her sorrow deep, and Frank would spend his days in a nursing home—period.

Frank pleaded every time I visited: "Please, David, can I go home?" My mother, at times, found it impossible to visit the old hired man. Mom could not relate to his plight. Week after week, however, Frank would continue to plead his case. With my siblings off in their world and my dad long buried, the large fourteen-room farmhouse felt empty. Mom continued to work at the school cafeteria, a job she loved. Her friends there were an important factor for Mom's mental health; her socializing with the other women at work had relieved some of her sorrows by day, but at night she cried alone.

Yet anyone could see the loneliness of this old hired-man. Frank could have been the old man in a Robert Frost poem, awaiting his place back on the farm, his place to die. Every Sunday after Mass I would visit Frank in an old Victorian house, turned Nursing Home. Frequently his physician, Dr. Burke was there to examine patients. He would shout loudly from across the rooms, "David, for God's sake when are you going to take Frank home?"

The doctor's honesty would continue as he admonished me, "So he may not do well, but he'll at least die with his boots on; take him home and carry him to the barn if you have to."

Everyone heard his inferences. I felt Frank's pain, and these visits, plus the doctor's urging both drew me to notice the reality that I had silently ignored. Clearly, I felt sorry for the old man. I, too, imagined him being at the farm, and steadily I saw my responsibility. Further, I did not wish to hear Dr. Burke's weekly remarks. Perhaps it was solely the doctor who intimidated me to act, or possibly it was a first nudge from Divinity towards my future of care giving, a profession yet defined.

I decided to bring Frank home. I'd be his caregiver. More than enough work existed, but by God, I knew Frank deserved more than those four sterile walls of a nursing home, even if Mom disagreed. This one event became an awakening in my life, or maybe this was simply my maturing. Like his doctor said, "If he goes home and dies, at least he dies happily."

Frank was smiling and I was apprehensive as we headed out into the rural landscape. For both of us months had passed. It was indeed a different season as we coursed the country road home. Frank did not have the strength to walk. He was so frail, just skin and bones with a ruddy bedsore on his butt.

My plan was simple: feed him, get him up and out to a new day. If I had to, I'd carry him into the stable each day—well I guess I could. He would require weeks of care before anything that extreme could take place; that is if Frank improved. All this turned out to be anything but simple. Since I had no foresight of the consequences of incontinence, attempts to become a nurse took on a whole new meaning for me. This twenty-year old farmer was redirected towards a softer side of humanity. Usually each day, I had to give Frank a bath. He returned to wearing long johns, the ones with a large button-up flap over the backside. One thing for sure, I don't believe he ever had a problem with constipation, for each day Frank needed fresh clean clothes. Most mornings, I needed to carry him directly to the tub, wash his clothes, dress him, and carry him down the stairs over my back. He was never heavy.

There were ungainly moments for Frank and me while I cared for his aged, wasted body. The shame of incontinence and his general inability must have bothered him, but I can't recall either of us complaining. Slowly one could see the huge bedsore begin to improve. There were embarrassing moments and many difficult presentations, but the baths helped both his self-esteem and his ability to move.

Physically putting him into the tub and soaking his skinny, frail body in the hot sudsy water helped his contracted knees to say nothing of his soiled, ruddy bottom. In time, he could stand (assisted) and raise his stork-like limbs in and out of the tub. Weeks went by before he could wash himself. Then eventually his pride and strength returned. While snows swirled outside, I would lift Frank—dripping wet out of the tub and wrap the soft terry cloth towel about his skeleton sized body. Soon all his sores healed. Further, I found a comfort level with nursing and realized anew the power of 'caring' for the infirm. I learned to appreciate the care and understanding I've seen with the many nurses I have had the privilege to work with. It's infectious: the response people receive when caring for a less fortunate patient. There is clearly a love present in that work; and sometimes that feeling is only transmitted one way.

Over time, Frank was able to return to his favorite barn chores: sweeping the silage and hay up to the housed animals, spending all those winter months in the warm barn, puttering about, talking to himself, and chewing tobacco, spitting its juice indiscriminately. Although still very frail he puttered about the calves, helped keep the animals clean, and found contentment in his old age.

As I began college, Mom continued to work at our high school, and Frank would spend the day in the barn. This one particular winter day, there had been freezing rain all through the night. I told Frank to stay in because it was just too dangerous for him to attempt to climb the hill to the barn or get safely over the slippery terraces that were between the barn and our house. After sanding the driveway and driving off for class, in my rear view mirror I saw Frank crawling on all fours inching his way to the barn. I thought to turn about and admonish him; instead I admired that old man's grit and determination.

This hired man who came into our family with nothing, had nothing, and was nearing the completion of his life should likely offer little. Yet he was very much a part of the family and in his own quiet way opened something very lasting in my life. Frank, truly, had been my first patient. After I started college, Poor Frank lived and worked for another ten years at the farm.

I can still recall that awful autumn day when Dad died. Frank, of course, was out in our cow barn. Because the weather had been exceptional, the window sashes were out of their openings, and so there wasn't much that Frank wouldn't take notice of, especially the cars coming and going, the ambulance's brief stop. It was likely he knew from the commotion that there had to be a serious problem.

After the priest and the doctor left, I walked to the barn and told Frank that our Dad died. I was taken back by his response, not that I had any idea how Frank would react, but it was unexpected. This was the only time I saw Frank cry openly. He said not a word but buried his face in his calloused hands. His whole little body shook as he cried out loud. I'll never forget that moment out in the cow barn, next to the pile of burlap bags full of freshly ground cow feed giving off the aroma of sweet molasses and mixed grains, standing next to Frank as we both cried out loud.

That was the first time I fully appreciated how much love and respect Frank had for Dad, for our entire family. Suddenly, on this, my first day as an adult, I understood Frank's feelings for our family, his love for Dad, his gratefulness to him for giving Frank a home. Perhaps Dad was the first to treat Frank with kindness when others, throughout his life, had not.

When I was in my sophomore year at Albany Medical College, Mom called and told me that Frank had died. She found him on the floor in his room, the room he had for almost forty years. Every day, he had walked to the barn to help in any way he could. As Dr. Burke had suggested, Frank did die with his boots on, at least one anyway; he dropped dead before the second one was in place. All those years he kept our Mom from living alone, and even though we were miles apart and on the phone, Mom and I cried over our loss, knowing that Frank would no longer be in our lives.

Poor Frank

Getting Serious

Starting College

When I started college, I tried to please everyone, do everything.

I drove one hour to and from classes and then back to the necessary farm work. My first college experience was a course taken in the evenings. I was twenty-three and I felt old; however, I enjoyed the class work, and silently held onto my secret goal. I sat with mostly eighteen year olds, most of whom had no clue what their future held. Mr. Murphy was the instructor, a person that worked at the GE plant during the day, then taught philosophy and social studies at these evening classes. I found him inspiring; he put forth a great spirit for learning.

The college required that I sit for the SATs and I did a few months later. After six years away from scholastics, however, I found many of the questions foreign. One multiple-choice question that has stayed with me was: "In what sport would one find a divot?" After farming seven days a week all my life, turning the sod every fall, one would believe I'd know that answer. However, it would be years before I could ever play golf and learn where divots are generally found.

At midyear I began classes full time at Utica College. Running the farm and attending college full time was an extreme situation. There definitely was no time for collegiate socializing; it was work, then more work. I studied from ten p.m. to whatever time I fell asleep. I learned to pace, to walk while studying, in order not to fall asleep. Other nights I never got that far and was found head-down on the kitchen table, the cup of strong coffee now stone cold, with old Frank shaking me at five a.m. to awaken and start the pattern all over.

There were so many things on a farm that could go wrong and did. Cows would "freshen," that is, labor for hours before birthing a calf. Someone needs to be present, to assist, or to call a veterinarian for additional help if that was necessary. After a cow freshens, a calcium imbalance may affect the animal. Frequently a cow could become paralyzed from a condition called 'milk-fever,' a low blood calcium level secondary to the sudden flow of milk, a parathyroid disorder, which could kill an animal unless intravenous treatment was soon initiated.

There were all sorts of aliments: cows could accidentally ingest nails, pieces of old barbed wire, parts of machines that were picked up in the hay bales. These sharp metal foreign objects caused intestinal obstruction or perforation in the animal's gut. The problem can be prevented by the placement of a large magnet, nearly the size of one's fist into the cows' stomach where the magnet's weight causes it to remain in the first portion of its stomach where it would attract ferrous metal objects, and the stomach's tough lining would not be affected by the magnet, nails, fragments of wire, staples, etc..

Occasionally a cow would up and die without a diagnosis. It would require great effort to drag the carcass, the remains out from its stall. One would need ropes, block and tackle, and then a tractor to pull the dead 1200-pound weight from the stable.

Then there were mechanical problems: water lines could break, freeze, or even flood the entire stable. There were days when winter's lake-effect snows would bury most roads and driveways. All that required extra work, extra time, time that was a commodity that I had so little of. However, I did persevere, but there were those other days, especially before or on the day of an exam, that I could count on a major problem to develop at the farm. At times, it seemed that the Fates were working hard against me, days when I felt like the Biblical Job.

On one occasion, rushing to college (every drive was a race of sorts, trying to make up time), a woman driver pulled out in front of my car in East Herkimer, on a slippery snow-packed road. In another instant, there would have been a collusion of two cars at a high speed. Making a snap decision, I choose to leave the road and hit a snow-covered, six-foot tall lilac bush. In a second I flattened that shrub and continued driving straight through someone's front yard, with several inches of snow cover on the lawn. I simply "hit" the gas and plowed over a few other small bushes, never pausing. I returned to the road, and made Utica for my Chemistry class on time. I can still recall that New York license plate number on the car. These events mirrored my entire college experience in pursuit of my goal, sometimes on the road to my future and too many times off the road (to success).

In the second year of college, morning chores had to begin even earlier, and some nights of studies ran into the morning chores. There developed too many variables that needed to be resolved before I headed to Utica College. It seemed I was chronically late for classes, particularly in the second year in organic chemistry class, coming into class, some mornings, five, ten, or more minutes later than the professor would like. He always gave me a wary eye as I entered—I'm not sure I had ever met with him, to explain my work commitments before his class. Perhaps I felt he might not care or understand my situation.

Then, at the first quiz that semester, I was not well prepared and two students, one that sat to my left and the other to the right, decided to cheat on that particular quiz. They both copied my answers verbatim, the correct ones and those incorrect. The professor hauled the three of us into his office that next day and read us the "riot act." He was very indignant but so was I. The two cheaters thought I was the more diligent student—were they wrong. The Professor never accepted my explanation or my innocence; I felt that he never trusted me after that first quiz, for which I remained always aware.

However, I settled down and studied. The organic chemistry laboratory requirements were a very important part of my grade and in one experiment, a lab quiz, the Professor gave out "unknown" crystals, crystals from a variety of organic compounds that each student had to identify. Each student had his own different unknown; one needed to accomplish all sorts of testing, everything from smell, color, shape (appearance under a microscope), to the precise melting temperatures. Each substance had its own definite characteristics.

I uncovered the identity of my compound rather quickly. It was a white, odorless, crystalline substance that melted at a very high temperature. The Professor inferred that I had somehow been less than honest with my quick identity of that unknown. I was very much putout by his inference, and I asked him why this continued distrust, when indeed I had succeeded. I challenged him: he stated that I could not have heated the oil-bath to that temperature without producing smoke. (The crystals were placed in a separate tube with a calibrated thermometer in the oil bath, with glass beads on the base of the oil bath that lessened the surface tensions for the oil to boil.) The Professor stated that the oil would definitely smoke at that highly elevated heat, and further, that he would have noticed (the smoke).

I was very disheartened by his attitude. The test on my part was a complicated trap of sorts; the teacher knew, or at least thought the oil should become a problem. I asked him for another similar crystal and proved to him that this oil had to be especially pure (because it had not burned or smoked as he predicted). I had the professor standby as the crystal melted and there was absolutely no smoke. I remember the satisfaction I had felt at that moment while the teacher looked on as the crystal melted, while not a whiff of smoke was noted. However, the Professor would continue to cast a wary eye my way (my opinion).

My final grade was a C+ which caused great difficulty when Medical Colleges began to scrutinize my admission process. Certainly, some degree of my mediocre grade was caused by the distractions from the many, many hours required for farm work and the major setbacks that continued at the farm.

In my second year at college, I hired a young farmhand for certain jobs during the daytime when I was not on site. However, this caused more problems: some machines broke from his carelessness, and then he quit. Another man was equally careless and rolled a tractor on to its side, fortunately without injury. However he soon left the job. Then the winter weather became extreme and caused further delays in my arrival time at class. And always Frank was a concern. These were more "reasons" for my mediocre grades. Certainly a part of my final grade, for that most important chemistry course, was from the bias of the Professor; however, most was from my absurd attempts to serve two masters: the farm and my college studies. My grade for organic chemistry, the most important course on which professional schools would judge me ... was not stellar.

As my senior year rolled around, even though I had several medical college interviews, I was left with no promise of admission. I was frustrated, and soon surmised that I would definitely need some personal influence from someone who would "go to bat" for me, someone connected who could push for serious consideration of my application in spite of my academic record. Dr. Burke suggested that I see a retired surgeon who lived in Little Falls, a man that was Past-President of New York State Medical Society. Perhaps he could help.

I lost no time in contacting him. Even though I had never met the man, when I called upon him, he invited me into his home dressed in a three-piece suit and pocket watch with a gold chain; he was most gracious. I realized in these meetings with various distinguished professionals, that these accomplished people represented far more than their own success. They also carried a weight of the spectrum of the entire profession. Dr. Burgin took me into his study, where he introduced me to his lovely spouse. Even I would notice her deteriorating health, notice her pallor, notice the pall over the entire household. I could feel the sadness of the surgeon, a man that had helped so many others—now no longer needed by his profession, now helpless with his wife's battle with cancer. Dr. Burgin went on to state that he currently had only one patient, his wife, and further, that he wasn't effective with her needs. The doctor went on about their loneliness, no children, no longer any professional responsibility.

I felt compassion for the man, and he in turn appreciated my coming to him for help. I spoke of my desires and frustrations; he was most helpful and his assistance would turn out to become so important for my future. In essence we both leaned on each other that day. We spoke about many things. I was aware that he enjoyed the fact that I had involved him in my pursuit of professional school. Perhaps this renewed his importance, by assisting in someone else's life. Dr. Burgin had also attended Albany Medical College, an institution where I had based all my hopes for admission. The doctor directed me to contact Dr. John Carter, a surgeon at Albany. Dr. Burgin added, "I know if anyone can help, he will." Further, the doctor went on, "I haven't spoken with him in a long time, but I will call him before you meet with him."

Dr. John Carter's office was at a very classy brownstone facing Washington Park in Albany, and walking into his office, I was immediately transposed into a different world. His office reflected academia, a sense of class, of the "old guard" in the Profession of Medicine. John Carter gave me a striking amount of attention. Dressed in his summer suit and striped tie; he was the exact opposite of the casual, small town Dr. Burke. Yet Dr. Carter rocked back in his oversized office chair, placed his polished 'wing-tips' upon the pullout of his large oak desk, and continued to quiz me about my wants and desires. In spite of the many patients awaiting his surgical advice, he spent considerable time assessing this want-to-be-physician. He called the Admitting Office at the College, and while on the phone, he gathered my academic profile for what it was worth.

As he hung up the phone, Dr. Carter bluntly asked, "What-the-hell have you been doing in the last four years?" He continued to scold me for not concentrating on my studies: "You look bright enough; why aren't you earning higher grades?" He drew attention to my future, insisting that this process of admission was not some sort of game. "We have literally thousands of applicants who have excellent grades, and yet here you are, asking for favors, for me to scrutinize your admission with a B average. Sure, you've done well in some. Why? Why should we consider you when we have so many others from which to choose?"

After telling him my story of college and farming, he again scolded, "What are you doing? Decide now whether you'll be a farmer or become a physician. You can't do both." Again he reiterated, "Very serious attention must be given to studies." He insisted that I enroll in graduate school for a Master of Science degree. He promised me a serious look at next year's process if, and only if, I earned all A's, further accompanied by strong academic recommendations. Of course I heeded his advice and succeeded. I was admitted to Albany the next year. I will always be indebted to Dr. John Carter for his kindness, his scrutiny. Finally my dream began to take form. I would become a physician.

A Doctor in the House

In the year I was to finish my undergraduate college, a wonderful woman came into my life. I had been introduced to her a few years earlier, when a friend brought her to our farm for a visit. She would visit often, and I was quick to realize that this woman possessed all the wonderful attributes I had been searching for. As if with perfect timing Marcia became the one I would marry. Together we realized what a tough and strange road I had chosen, along with all of Life's other uncertain times that lay ahead. With absolutely no money and the cost of four years of Medical School weighing heavily, plus many postgraduate years ahead; the only security we had was our love. We were married only few weeks before we moved to Albany for the start of my professional training. Life was good, in spite of a host of bumps on the road we had chosen. Fortunately there have been no detours.

On our first trip to Albany we found a small three-room apartment in a private home. This clearly was serendipity. After walking through too many dumpy, dirty rentals and 'walking' through the advertised portion of the newspaper, nothing was clean enough or affordable. Then when a secretary in the Office of Student Affairs at Albany Medical College (AMC) over-heard Marcia's inquiries, the clerk's simple suggestion led us to our first apartment on Berncliff Avenue. Our small living quarter was in a beautiful setting on a quiet residential street—it was perfect.

From the start we both desired a large family. Our first son was born at the beginning of my sophomore year. A year later we moved into a larger space and befriended the landlord, Walter and Anita, who lived on the first floor of a new duplex. They treated us like family. They helped us in so many ways: lowered our cost for rent and supplied a new refrigerator, while we helped with small tasks about his property such as clearing snow from their drive, watching their ten year old or tutoring their son in math.

I rode a bike to and from the Medical College, a used bike that had been given as a present upon acceptance into AMC. I rode that old bike, one that probably had thousands of miles chalked up by a neighbor, Roger Tibbitts, who lived near our farm but was now working the home farm in my absence. I rode his bike in all kinds of weather, in good and not so good. Of course, in the winter months, I either walked to Medical School or Marcia drove me.

***

Roger Tibbitts was legally blind, and when he started working our farm he had just completed high school. I would be going off to Graduate school for a Master's Degree. Roger was someone in whom I had much confidence: he knew the work and knew how to "get it done." Even though he had been raised in a 'suburban' home, since his early teen years Roger wanted to become a farmer. In many ways he already was one; well, sort of. He worked for years helping various farmers in the neighborhood, worked after school, weekends, and during any school vacations. Roger was the most hardworking individual I had ever known, the most diligent teenager that God ever made. His brother Gary was of a similar *ilk*. Both were clever, both were legally blind, and from their mouths, never was heard a regretful word about their plight in life.

Before becoming teenagers, they had managed to travel by bicycles, up and down the hills that surround their rural hamlet of Eatonville. There were several hill farms where they worked at various chores. In the winter, they walked or someone would drive them to the farm of choice. Their parents had built a new home close to my brother Tom's farm, so as they grew through their teenage years, the Tibbitts' kids kept busy. They became capable of completing most tasks that were required for farming. By this time, they owned the first production models of the Bombardier snowmobile to reach their winter chores.

As an interesting note, when I went off to medical school, Roger gave me his old one-speed bike, a bike that had been peddled up so many hills by this energetic kid, that its sprocket shaft had a six inch 'play' when one started off on a ride. I took that bike to Albany for my first semester there and as long as I remembered about the sprocket and its 'play," the bike was my transportation to and from the College. Later in my third year, however, while in a student rotation at the VA hospital, even though I chained and locked it, the urban "munchkins" used bolt-cutters and stole the bike. Even the FBI investigated the crime, a requirement for any theft on federal property. Since it was never a high priority, the bike was never again located.

Roger and his older brother Gary could work at anything and get it right. Roger's eyesight was so poor that he needed to bring a nut or a cotter pin or written directions up close to his eyes to fully examine them, and yet the boys paid attention to details better than most with twenty-twenty vision. Through their diligence, they would have the correct wrench or cut a board square or weld or drive tractors as well as anyone. As a teenager Roger acquired an older John Deere that had but two-cylinders; that was his transportation to and from work sites. After that year he no longer required his bike.

The year Roger graduated from high school was the year he agreed to run our farm. It could not have been a better deal for both parties. With this arrangement Roger began to hone further his skills of farming and kept our farm operating. Mom continued to live on the farm, so that there was always someone around. Roger kept the driveways cleared of snow and Mom supplied with fresh milk. The arrangement I made with him was that he could buy the cows over time, rent the land from Mom, and in due time, over the next four or five years, he could find his own place to buy if he choose. As one would expect, Roger was perfect: a good herdsman, a reliable worker, and he knew enough already to build upon. He was an answer to my prayers, an absolutely amazing man. He eventually did buy his own farm.

At the end of my first semester at the Medical College, we returned to the farm for a couple of weeks at Christmas. After milking, Roger came to the house and invited me to join him for a 'run' on his new Bombardier snowmobile. We buzzed up and over the drifted snow towards the Millington farm about a half-mile away. Don had us come in for a test of his newly aged 'hard-cider' that was in a wooden staved, fifty-gallon barrel stored in the cow barn. It was a memorable night as we pulled up a couple of bales of mixed alfalfa and timothy for the bar stools and sipped the great brew of delicious 'cider' that had aged nearly to a fine "champagne." After a couple of hours of camaraderie, Don, and another neighbor, Harry, could not stand up, nor could they get up. Roger and I managed to get them both, as silly as we all were, home and in bed. Then Roger drove me back home across the moon glow on the snow, both of us on his new Bombardier. There I was, silly with cider, cruising across the moonlit meadows, being driven by a man legally blind. It was all so great getting back to my roots and away from the intensity of those books.

Yet I longed to fulfill my dream, to become a clinician. Our class was composed of sixty mostly eager, bright, younger-than-I, students. One of my anatomy partners was only eighteen; he was one of about ten students at AMC who were achieving a six-year MD/PhD degree.

As for money, I had none. I never took a salary for the work on the farm because the goal there was to payoff the mortgage so that the farm would belong to no one else. For medical school, I borrowed everything. After being accepted into AMC, I met with an Assistant Dean of Admissions. He found it difficult working to fulfill my financial needs. He told me, "You're the most financially destitute student we've ever had here." I doubted that he had ever conceived of helping someone who hailed from a farm.

Before classes started, our family doctor, Dr. Burke, gave me a Nikon binocular microscope, a very generous gift that I used, as did other medical students (in later years) including our own son. The amount of reading was enormous; however, I managed to keep abreast until the middle of my second year. That's when I 'hit a wall,' a learning wall; it was as if my mind could hold no more information. Fortunately that occurred just before a one-week break in studies.

Certain subjects were easy. For instance, anatomy, pathology, hematology, and microbiology, for these I could visually memorize everything by sight. The quizzes were also fun; the class would walk around the cadavers or the microscopes one by one, and had a prescribed time to see a tagged structure on a body or under the 'scope.' As a course, pathology was also a favorite, lots to learn and to visualize. Peering into a microscope to identify a tissue or an organism was fascinating. On the other hand, biostatistics had always been a dry subject; I had difficulty with that in undergrad courses as well, and fortunately that course in medical school was brief.

The later half of the second year, we started to hone our clinical skills, the slow and studious start to becoming a physician. Some things were fun, as in psychiatry, where we had to interview a series of patients. Our professor was a character, a great teacher, but still the patients were all "nuts," locked in their shut ward. To attempt a straight answer was almost comical. I recall that this one schizophrenic, a person with auditory hallucinations, told a fellow student to shut up. Then added, I'd rather speak with my other friends."

The student looked around and asked, "Who?"

"My friends, I talk to them every day, all day long! They never ask anything of me. They just tell me what to do."

Life is truly a journey, and we know not where each person's destination lies; however, Marcia and I have been given so much along the way, met so many wonderful people, individuals that have come into our lives, and some have exited but always leave a mark of distinction or lasting imprint on us. We had wished for a large family; however, Marcia had had too many miscarriages, and to end these disappointments, we adopted our next son, Michael, who has been a true gift. Four years later, our wonderful daughter Marie was born.

Living with an acute care physician, my family had many, many interruptions in their normal day-to-day activities, whether during my Residency Program or in private practice. On far too many occasions, my time spent with family had been suddenly but predictably disrupted. It seemed that on any one occasion, an evening meal or a Holiday Feast or especially

76

when extended families would come together, I could be called out for medical emergencies. Our oldest son once stated as a teenager: "One thing for sure, Dad, I will never become a Doctor." However, as Divine intervention may guide us all, that young man is now a General Surgeon. I know for both of us, there is no greater satisfaction than being a part of this professional tradition.

Fulfillment

That first morning walking into the Medical College from the parking lot, the early September sun on my face, was truly an exhilarating sense of accomplishment: my first day at Albany Medical College (AMC). I thought back to my other first days of school when I began at the one room country schoolhouse, and then another 'first' school when we were carted by bus to St Mary's Academy in town. On both of those occasions, I felt skittish, bashful, perhaps intimidated. Back then I recall the fright as I left our farm for the day, but this day walking into the Medical College at Albany there was none of that. I knew I was on the correct path, the one I so very much desired. I knew these four years would be intense, and I knew that I would succeed. I was so excited, sensing the reality of becoming a physician. I believe on that first day walking into the College lobby, there was a greater sense of accomplishment than on the final day, the day of my graduation from the Albany Medical College.

Our classes began with a brief tour, but then it was books and classes nonstop for next two years. Gross Anatomy began the following day, four students to a cadaver. Most were skittish as we began our concerted dissection; our first lesson was on the leg, isolating the femoral artery and vein, with all their branches. For the most, this was everyone's first exposure to a body, and most had never seen anything that was remotely dead. Surprisingly, I did not mind working in the Anatomy Lab, even working after hours when a few of us would finish up the day's assignment; there were no concerns. I believe my experiences from the farm added greatly in preparing me for the anatomy class. The students gave their utmost respect to those men and women that donated their remains to the school.

Months later we finished dissection on the cadaver's hands and face. (The anatomical structures that were to be the most personal, the most intimidating anatomy, were left for our last efforts.)

There was much introspection while working on our cadaver; in my case, here was a man, someone who had dreams like us: someone who laughed, who cried, who loved, and then was taken apart piece meal. His name was Joe. We learned a lot about him: his arteries, joints, lung, everything except his thoughts and his likes and dislikes. In the end, he commanded respect for his formaldehyde soaked remains.

Besides the Anatomy class, the first two years at the College were mostly packed with various disciplines of science, everything from Physiology, Pharmacology through Biostatistics, and then Pathology to Microbiology, Embryology through Senility. Our Medical School class work was intense; our courses compacted into an energetic wealth of knowledge. In a more compelling period, students began rotating through the various clinical duties; it was there that residents and Staff physicians began teaching their expertise, where we learned the art as well as the science of medicine and surgery. The interactions with doctors and patients, during my third and fourth years at the College and as I worked through my Clinical Residency, presented an amazing array of human interest, trauma, and disease.

As I previously mentioned, the first drastic medical situation I was involved in became forever foremost in my mind and cemented further my quest to care for very ill people. I loved the challenge that critically ill patients presented—with a possible success for turning a critically ill person from sure death to a path of restored health; it is a wonderful emotional ride. I knew that some medical students when they confronted similar critical situations vowed, perhaps through outright fear, to only care for people who were well but needed professional help. Many doctors are not comfortable assessing critical patients. I know with the death of that young woman (the accident victim discussed in Chapter One), my reaction was an eagerness to learn more, to hone my talents. At that point in our training, many of my classmates in Medical School vowed never to allow themselves to become involved in such acute stressful situations. These students would gravitate towards caring for a 'well' practice, perhaps Radiology, Psychiatry, or Dermatology, to name a few. I can't say I'd blame them for that choice. Ones personal life is definitely more predictable, his life more orderly, caring for 'well' individuals.

Students' clinical work included medical and surgical rotations at the Veterans Administration Hospital (VAH). Situations there were different from those at the Albany Medical Center (AMC), certainly more relaxed, more informal. Most of the VAH doctors were from the attending staff at the Medical Center. Others were full time clinicians for the VA. All and all, the doctors and nurses were always great, and they appreciated the attention that the students gave to their patients because many inpatients were chronically ill and their stay was long and arduous. Many were suffering from alcoholism; many had severe lung disease, having smoked all too many cigarettes.

One group of students, upper class-men, plotted to play a prank on an attending physician. This doctor had graduated from Princeton, was a distinguished professional who had practiced for years and years in Albany. He was very accomplished, perhaps a bit of a medical elitist. He taught physical examination stressing the old-fashion methods on how to use one's hands to use percussion of a patient's chest. A physician should be able to "sound out," through changes in those tapped sounds, the size and shape of ones heart. So the stage was set. In the past these modalities were very important; however, to this clinician this method was the sine-qua-non of physical exams. There was a time when this was the only method to check lungs and hearts. Times had changed with newer ways: ECHO cardiograms, heart and lung scan and x-rays all gave more exact dimensions and pathologies. For some, old habits would die slowly.

One patient became a setup, a man recently admitted who had a condition called Situs Inverses (internal organs were mirror images of the normal: i.e., appendix would be on the left side (instead of the right), the heart would be opposite (apical pulse felt between the ribs on the right side of one's chest instead of the normal left), one's stomach would be oriented towards the left (instead of towards the right). The patient was also a chronic alcoholic and likely lived on the street. These senior student pranksters selected this man for the doctor to teach the art of physical examination, and before wheeling the patient to the examination room, they had the man wear an old, dirty, white Princeton sweater with a faded orange "P" on its front.

As the doctor (a Princeton graduate) entered, he never missed a beat, introduced himself to this ill-kept patient, and said, "Let's remove that good-looking Princeton sweater."

As he began to help the patient, the man grabbed at his sweater, "Oh, no. no way."

The physician responded, "You will have it back after the exam."

With the man now with a bare chest and in great need of a bath, the doctor began to percuss the man's chest, then outlining the heart where it is normally found, just to the left of his sternum, explaining to all the students present the patient's supposed heart size. When in fact, with this medical condition of Situs Inversus, the heart lay in the opposite position of the sternum (dextrocardia). Every student chuckled as the spoof unfolded. Neither the doctor nor the patient could understand the students' chuckles. The professor never questioned anyone further about that day's exercise, mainly because that particular patient signed-out, against medical advice (AMA). He disappeared into the night with his Princeton sweater and no one became the wiser about the joke the students' had played.

Later in my own training, when completing a physical examination on a new patient, a man who was a physician told me that he had a very unusual medical condition. He challenged me to find it. Then he added an even further challenge: "Other doctors could not differentiate the determination." I missed the condition as well: found nothing unusual in his exam. He had dextrocardia (Situs Inversus).

Politics being what they are, many chronic alcoholics attempted to admit themselves, particularly as the weather became colder. Patients would call their politicians or Congressional staff would call an Intern with some obscure demand: "You should have admitted that person!" I received a few of these political demands myself, although I would rebuke whoever called, exerting what little authority I could muster.

Occasionally a patient would walk into the VA Emergency Room, a Department that did not welcome many acute patients. The VAH at that time was not setup for this service; although by law it was a hospital and that alone forced some requirements. However, the space they allowed for this specialty room, especially for a huge hospital complex of 12 floors, appeared as a closet, perhaps an after thought in design. I'm sure all of these shortcomings have since been changed. The ER in 1960 was low tech and rarely had anyone admitted. More than one creative patient acquired an old suit of clothes three sizes too large, so obvious since ones sleeve length is not affected by weight loss, yet they walked into the admitting department complaining about weight loss. Like at any other hospital, however, most patients at the VAH were legitimate—people with serious ailments. I have worked at seven emergency departments, and all had patients who were devious in their intent. For example, there are individuals who fake their symptoms, make-up symptoms, i.e., Munchausen's Syndrome, men or women, who desire narcotics or are lonely people and seeking nothing more than attention or a place to stay.

As an Intern, one would be commissioned to be MOD, Medical (doctor) of the Day, and be responsible for all that happened between 4:30 p.m. and 8 a.m. the following day. On this one assignment, a patient walked into the ER (at the VA Hospital), not sure how he made it through the "closed" door of the ER. However, the poor soul had profound vomiting of bright red blood. As already noted, the room was small, and before this one patient, it was super clean. The man in charge wanted to keep it that way. It was ridiculous to label it an ER because there was very little equipment available; everything was looked upon as a major distraction to this one man in charge, the ER male Nurse.

When I was paged STAT to the ER, at first I thought it was a prank. There was a patient lying on a polished stainless steel gurney and blood spattered all about as if someone had been shot. Entering, I saw no nurse in attendance, simply the patient prone on the exam table actively bleeding with no IV, no fluid setup, and in extreme distress. Then I noticed the nurse on his hands and knees, distressed while mopping up the blood with a white towel. The vomiting and coughing of bright red blood continued, while the nurse focused solely on cleaning to floor.

I quickly started two IV's but had difficulty finding in which cabinet the nurse kept the IV fluids. The patient and the nurse were both distraught, however for different reasons. Eventually, the nasal gastric tube was placed into the man's stomach, and somehow I found a suction machine to attach which relieved the vomiting. I then carted him off to the ICU, six floors up in the world's slowest elevator. The patient lived and improved without an operation; his problem was a peptic ulcer that had eroded into a small artery at the outlet of his stomach.

A Friend Named Joe

"David!" It was Sal on the phone, "Joe's dead!"

Before I could tell him, "That's not funny," he repeated the absurd comment, but with conviction: "Joe is dead!"

I knew then by his desperate tone that this was not some sort of pun. No, there would be no laughing this day, only sad tales, repeated over and over.

Stunned, I simply hung up the phone, grabbed my coat and ran. I couldn't comprehend what I had just heard. So when my wife, Marcia, half heard that early morning commotion … I refused to use Sal's words—so I told her: "I got to run."

It was 4:30 a.m. this was supposed to be a day away from professional studies. Sal, Joe, and myself, we were headed north to ski. I had only known Joe for about a month, only since his discharged from the Army. He had been a childhood friend of Sal's, and they both shared an apartment.

After this shocking news, I left a note for my wife on the table, "No skiing today, I'll call you." As I started the car, I noticed that much of my face still wore the shaving cream. The early morning was very dark and cold, the evening rain had ceased, the streets were clear and vacant as I drove like a maniac–only slowing for the red lights. At that hour, there was no traffic, streets all but barren. Gone that morning was more than the light, fluffy snow that we had hoped to ski on, instead the cold hard facts of life and death were thrust upon us.

I made the two miles to Sal's place in haste, while trying to figure out in my mind why a twenty-five year old should suddenly drop dead. I kept thinking of all the possibilities as I drove: Was it suicide? Was it drugs or a cerebral hemorrhage? No, I knew Joe and he had recently left the Army with honors, and further was a life long friend to Sal (a Medical College classmate of mine). I was far from being a full-fledged physician, but in my mind–there was nothing in my reasoning for the death of this young adult.

Driving up to Sal's apartment, there were two police cars, with lights flashing. *"Oh my God,"* I thought, *"could he have been shot? Was he murdered?"*

I ran up the stairs where two police officers stood, indifferent to this dreadful unfolding situation. I hurried into the apartment; Sal was frantic, attempting CPR by himself, as Joe's body, bounced from the compressions and from the bedsprings, Joe's one arm slightly raised and outstretched, frozen by the rigor mortis, his pupils fixed. Sal was crying, shouting, hoping for Joe to come around; the entire scene was macabre. Sal was hysterical, as I pulled him away. I could see from Joe's color, the noted livideo color changes of his skin— changes of death, a discolored pattern on his skin told of his passing. It was an awful. I had to force Sal to stop, stop his vain attempts to resuscitate his childhood friend. I found it so strange, as the two of us, two friends stood there, gazing down at Joe's body, now long dead. "How the hell could this have happen?" I asked. Sal stated that he tried to awaken his friend, lying facedown, and then rolled him over. There were no answers, no reasons for this death, and we both sobbed.

Finally the ambulance arrived, but it was all too late for Joe. We both simply sat, mentally exhausted. We were soon to be doctors, but our knowledge—our efforts could not put life back into Joe. I thought back to that day when I rushed in to see my own dead father, that day as well, I could do nothing but stand there. With the death of our friend, Sal's long time friend, reality came rushing in like a real cold winter's day. Bone chilling grief was the first order of the day.

The cops asked a few perfunctory questions, then handed us a paper form to sign; then they took the body to the morgue at our College. Sal was now in real bad shape. "What are we going to do Dave?" He kept repeating, "What are we going to do?" While I asked, "What the Hell has happened?" As it all started to sink in, we simply stood there hoping that this was all some sort of nightmare.

Soon, Sal realized we would have to call his parents. "No, no, no," he said, "we'll drive over there." Then after a long pause, Sal became so anxious as he uttered: "No, No, No, you'll have to go."

"Why me?" I asked, as I pulled back, "I don't even know them." Silently, I pondered what that early morning visit would be like, a stranger knocking on their door, telling this couple of their son's death; it didn't seem plausible. In the background, I heard Sal throwing-up in the bathroom. I was worried about him as well. When Sal returned, he stated that he couldn't muster the strength to go, nor have the courage to tell the Colonel, Joe's dad, the awful truth. "No, no, Dave you'll have to go." As strange as it may seem, at that point, I understood Sal's request. I knew that Sal's family, the Colonel, and Joe had all been the best of friends. Joe was their only son and their one child that the sun arose and set with him. "Dave you'll have to go, you'll have to go now," Sal demanded, as he wrote down the directions to their suburban home.

Sal continued to be beside himself, upset, returning to the bathroom with the dry heaves. I was so torn, whether to stay with Sal or to go to the parents home, about 10-15 miles away. Frankly I did not want this task, to be the bearer of horrendous news to complete strangers. Yet, this is what, someday, I would have to do, breaking terrible news to loved ones, a responsibility that would become a part of my profession. Sal then added, "They sleep late, perhaps you'll need to go across the street." He wrote down their names as well—then added, "These folks, I know, will be awake–the entire neighborhood are all close friends. My parents have known both families for years." Then Sal confessed with these words: "Dave, I don't have the strength to face them," his last words as I left for my mission.

It was now around 6:30 AM, the sun rising, a light frosty snow sparkled in the air from the sunshine. I drove straight to Joe's old neighborhood, along the way I thought long and hard about his parents sleeping and I waking them. They were about to have their world turned upside-down. I thought about such future duties for myself, the doctor, meeting with families after such tragedy. Already, I had seen how some doctors and clergy had failed to adequately connect and adequately address their sad duty. So many fail miserably at this task, but how does one deliver sad, devastating news, anyway? I would soon find out, and discover if I'm any better than others I've witnessed. I resolved to try.

This bright beautiful winter day would soon be darkened for the Colonel and Joe's mom, this would be a day they would like to forget. I spent twenty or thirty minutes to find their home. I wasn't rushing. Slowly the suburbs were coming awake. The well-kept snow covered homes looked all too perfect to even think of the news I carried. Everything looked so perfect, I missed a few turns but eventually found their home just as Sal described.

The entire neighborhood seemed so still: some smoke, rising slowly from a few chimneys, was the only visible motion. Slowly I walked up to the front door. Indeed I was hesitant to say the least, the cold snow crunched under foot. With no answer after repeated rings, I began to knock firmly at the front door. Finally, I could hear someone walking inside the home. A woman, in a bathrobe peeked from a corner, reluctant to approach this stranger at her door. I kept wondering just what she could be thinking? The door opened cautiously, and only a crack. I introduced myself, through the storm door—my words seemed so irrelevant, as I asked if I could come in. That triggered absolute fear in this woman. "No," she replied and slammed the door. "I need to speak with you," but she stood silent behind the shut door. I heard her call the Colonel as she walked away. However, no one came as I stood there.

I decided to go across the street. As I approached that house I could see the other couple peaking out, partly from behind a curtain. The man opened the door before I could knock—then asked me into their home. They both started to scream as I spoke of the terrible news. I stood dumbfounded—wondered if this scene was actually real. Was I living this strange scenario … verses some God-awful nightmare? I questioned myself in these strange surroundings, delivering this strange message of death. These two people whom I had never meet before, in their home, relating this awful news. It was all un-settling. It was quite awhile before we all could settle down. I wondered just how the Colonel and his wife could possibly manage with this morning's dreaded news.

Thankfully, the friends stated they would accompany me across the street, they knew their support would be needed by the Colonel and his wife. The man called first, telling Joe's parents that we would be coming over; "What is it, what's wrong?" I heard Joe's mother asking as I stood near. I heard the mother's anxious voice through the phone: "What's wrong?" Her voice commanding, yet hesitant, not wanting to hear the truth we held.

They put on their jackets and we proceeded to cross the street, and as we walked, again I remember the sound of the crystalline snow crunch under foot, and looking up I noticed Joe's parents standing at the picture window; we must have appeared as an assault team as the three of us bore their awful news. As the Colonel opened the door, I could hear Joe's mother, gasping, crying ... "No, no, no, what is this about?" She stood in the background, covering her ears, as grief came pouring into their lives, all consuming, terrible waves of grief came—for a death, so final.

I could not attend Joe's autopsy, it would have been all too painful, all too emotional. However, I was eager to know what pathology had existed in our mutual friend. What disease within had killed him? The final pathology report noted a moderate degree of cardiomyopathy.*

** *An inflammation of the muscles of the heart—from one of life's many viruses that will infect and irritate the rhythm of a heart.*

Doctor Ralph Alley

He was an imposing man: tall, broad-shouldered, wearing his half glasses in a professorial manner. The rumor had it that he had been born in India to an English couple, missionaries living among the impoverished Sudras. More important for students was the fact that he was the Chief of Thoracic Surgery. As a surgeon he walked the hallowed halls of the Medical Center with distinction, perhaps giving a perception that he was above the others, which I do not believe was the case. From my prospective, however, rarely would he acknowledge anyone while traversing those hallways whether fellow professors, faculty, surgical residents, friends or compatriots. He walked those corridors not trying to ignore anyone but simply in a preoccupied state. He was a man of few words; many feared him, all were driven to respect him.

As students, we had slim margins to function within the Operating Room. There, students were even more vulnerable; they were unfamiliar and, of course, not needed. In truth, those first few times as observers in surgery, most students were excited but uncomfortable to say the least. In our second year of studies at the College, students were split into small groups of two or three and rotated for short periods of time through various disciplines of medicine and surgery. One morning three of us dressed in surgical greens with our jaunty caps and old-fashioned cloth masks, wearing temporary covers over our shoes and entered a surgical suite as if it were some foreign land. It was the scrub nurse that really gave us directions as a group: "Don't touch anything or anybody, keep your hands at your sides or arms folded or better yet keep hands clasped behind you and simply observe. For God's sake don't get in anyone's way." She warned us about contaminating instruments or personnel wrapped in sterile garb. "Fold your arms and stay your distance. If you wish to approach the operating table, you can only reach the backs of the doctors. Look over their shoulders but never, ever point. There are wooden step-stools for those shorter students."

We arrived early and observed as the room had begun to fill, fill with personnel that knew what they were there for. Compared to the larger surgical rooms at the Little Falls Hospital, this space seemed small and definitely more cramped. Of course, for me with my past surgical exposure during those summers, it seemed like old home day. Granted the technical aspects were by far more advanced, more dramatic, plus this was my first look at open-heart surgery. The patient arrived and the anesthetist began administering to his needs. For most students, this was their first surgical experience. The scrub nurse unwrapped the huge display of gleaming, sterilized surgical instruments. Residents scrubbed in an anteroom and then as they entered dried their hands and arms with sterile towels before being clothed in sterile gowns. Soon any extra space became a commodity for the observers. Carefully, we sidestepped everyone.

Suddenly, Dr. Alley entered in haste, dried his arms, then sort of walked into his sterile gown, and then he spun, with his arms outstretched; we feared he might reach us with his tall, large frame. I sidestepped but another student, quickly backed up against the table with the elaborate display of sterile instruments. Not only did he back into this setting, the student brought his hands down and to his back, as if feeling for what he had just backed into. In the process he inadvertently contaminated the instrument table. Not just a few instruments but the entire table was deemed "ruined" for any surgery. The vast spread of surgical tools for heart surgery had to be reset with new sterilized tools.

Doctor Alley roared like no other roar I've ever heard from a professional. It frightened everyone. He immediately wanted the student's name. I was glad I was innocent. How meek was John's voice that morning as he spelled out his name. "I'll see you outside, NOW," shouted the Doctor. "Nurse, setup a new packet of instruments." Dr. Alley made a huge impression on me that morning, one I would not soon forget.

Much later, we rotated again through Surgery. Now the students would scrub-in and become a part (though ever-so-small) of the surgical team by holding a retractor or a suction device or simply standing there sometimes for hours. Surgically opening the chest and the pericardium that surrounds the heart, and then placing the entire patient's circulation on an external by-pass machine was an immense undertaking. This sophisticated gadget kept the blood oxygenated and circulating, thus keeping the patient alive while a heart is stopped. It didn't seem like a time or place to chitchat, but that's exactly what Dr. Alley would do as he diligently worked through his surgical techniques.

Turning to the student opposite, he asked, "Tell me why you chose to pursue the study of Medicine?" Fortunately, he asked the other student first, which gave me time to think about my reply. Now there were two doctors and two students at this operation; the scrub nurse was the second most important person present because knowing and handing the correct instrument to the surgeon, anticipating his every need, was a demanding job. The two students, one on each side held various retractors or at times held a suction catheter, all huddled about the operating table. I stood to the right of the surgeon, somewhat peering over the doctor's shoulder as he worked on the heart.

The scrub nurse stood to my right. She stood on a wooden platform, therefore was taller than I. She leaned over, close to my ear and told me quietly, "Be careful. It's a trick question." Obviously, the Doctor had his little routine for new students. I was grateful for her clue, especially as I heard a "canned" response from the other student: "Sir, to help people, and save lives," the student went on. Upon which the doctor went into a rant and rave, berating the student's contrived response. The doctor added, "There must be a more compelling reason for a young person to commit to eight or more years of study needed to become a physician?" After a time, he turned to me and asked, "Tell me just why you have decided on Medicine for a career?"

Without missing a beat I replied, "Sir, I was born on a farm. We were dirt poor, and I cared not to spend my entire life that way." Yes, it was a bit snide, even exaggerated, but I stated my case with conviction. It seemed that for the next minute everything stopped in that room except my own heart beat. I was sure everyone could hear it pounding during that brief silence that followed.

Dr. Alley turned, peered over his professorial glasses, and simply glared at me. I was damn glad that I had on a mask as he peered at this student. I felt his stare penetrate. "What's your name?" the surgeon demanded. Humbly, I told him. He responded firmly, "I'll speak with you outside, right after this operation, and you wait for me. I'll be a while." I don't believe I said a word after that. I was quiet for the remainder of that long operation. After the surgery, I waited in the anteroom, waited for who knew what? I knew I had been brash, but I waited. Finally Dr. Alley arrived after checking on the patient, now in the recovery room. I remember him addressing me as mister; yes, very definitively I was a mister. "Mr. Burns," he said, "you continue to wait here!" Then he proceeded to dictate his operative notes a few feet from where I sat. I knew, by this time, he was playing mind games with me; but I had little choice but to wait. When he approached, I stood—he extended his hand and we shook with a firm grip. He looked me straight in the eye; then after a long pause he said, "Your response was the most appropriate answer I've heard from students in years."

"Thank you, Sir," I responded, "thank you." Then he departed. Expecting a reprimand, I instead got an offhand compliment.

The next time I would work with Dr. Alley was between my third and fourth years; there was no break between these two years of study, but students could begin choosing electives. Money was real short. Marcia and I had had our first child and had moved into a larger apartment. I had heard that some surgical specialties did not have enough interns and were paying students to come on board (a number of doctors had been drafted for medical services in Vietnam). I enjoyed surgery. There was much excitement and action, and further, I "toyed" with the consideration of choosing surgery as my field of endeavor. Perhaps if I had started college at an earlier time in my life, or if I had come from a different setting ... other than farming ... I might have become a surgeon.

I had gathered much experience from my two summers at the hospital in Little Falls, at least enough to familiarize myself with many techniques. There I scrubbed in on all sorts of procedures; my suturing skills went beyond most students, even beyond a few of the first year Residents at the Medical Center. So I signed onto Surgery as a paid acting-intern. It was a busy surgical service with a large number of inpatients; sometimes this group of surgeons would have forty plus patients in the hospital. I asked the chief surgical resident, if it would be okay with him if I avoided scrubbing into surgical cases and mainly took care of pre- and post-op problems when they arose outside of the actual surgery. As I settled into the caseload, I would arrive about 5:30 a.m. and gather all the clinical data, making sure that I had all the correct lab data on each patient. With that data mostly memorized, I then made early rounds with the Attending Physicians before they started operating. That worked for the first couple of days; however, Dr. Alley insisted that I also attend most operations. There was little rest.

The Senior Resident was a great guy. He was extremely bright, with a vast knowledge of his specialty—plus he was an accomplished concert pianist, educated in the classics. I'm not sure where he was born, but his speech was difficult to comprehend, especially if he spoke rapidly. The patients, on occasion, as well as Dr. Alley found it troublesome to understand all of his speech. Mostly one needed to listen and give his words full attention.

The Resident filled in all the details about Dr. Alley, how he responded to certain matters, especially those that I had not already experienced. First of all, the surgeon did not like short people and this Resident was quite short. He went on to say, "Just be yourself, keep your answers brief and honest." Then he added, "His bark is worse than his bite." I remembered well Dr. Alley's rage earlier over the inadvertent actions of a fellow student.

For the next month, I worked with Dr. Alley, on and off scrubbing in on all of his operations. I found him friendly, yet he continued to castigate the not-so-tall Resident. On one occasion, he raised the operating table to its maximum height, which required the short Resident to stand on two wooden platforms to even see the operation. One time he stated that all students should be screened for a certain height. Those interested in surgery should be at least six feet tall. Dr. Alley would on occasion let me place a few critical sutures, and on one occasion he allowed me to place a couple of sutures into the dacron "skirt" that anchored the replacement aortic valve, stating that from my perspective, from where I stood opposite him, the suture was more accessible from my side of the table. This happened while the Thoracic Resident only watched and held retractors. The surgeon clearly gave me more recognition than I deserved, for what reason I was always unsure. Was it because I was tall? Was it because of the off-hand comment I had made a year earlier, the one about being raised financially poor?

Dr. Alley eventually invited me into his surgical program, an invitation that I gave considerable attention, but in the end I knew I wanted to return to my roots and care for the sick away from medical centers. Besides, I was older and shied away from ten years of further study. Even today, I take pride in Dr. Alley's invitation and the attention he showed me.

One morning the Resident had been awake most of the night, having been on call. The following day, during a lengthy operation, Dr. Alley told the Senior Resident to hold a retractor, which was a put-down for one with six years of post medical school training. While I was simply cutting sutures for him, I saw the Resident doze-off, literally catching a few winks while standing on his feet. Dr. Alley noted his short respite … grabbed a Metzenbaum (a large elongated surgical scissors) and struck the man with its handles on his gloved knuckles, awakening him with a start. "There will be no sleeping here," stated the good Doctor.

Much later, as a Resident physician myself at the Medical Center, if Dr. Alley saw me walking in the hallway, he would always say, "Good-morning, David" or give a short nod or a small wave of acknowledgment; rarely did he ever do this with anyone else.

Once when I stepped into an elevator, the Doctor was already there—I was, by this time, a Medical Resident. He engaged in a discussion, asked if I had ever decided to go into surgery—would I personally let him know? Then added, "We need people like you in our program." I was taken aback, as I again would ponder this offer. He never forgot and neither did I. I always had a fond respect for the man despite his prejudices towards certain others. I wondered, was it because of my honesty, my frankness, that he always recognized this one student, this one doctor, who was in training to be an Internist? Perhaps it was because of my height? Maybe because of my background, my impoverishment, maybe this was the fundamental similarity that welded a bond.

Years later, I heard that Dr. Alley had suffered a severe stroke, which left him without effective speech and the inability to walk. I felt sorry for him, for his personal infirmity and the loss of his hard earned dignity. Life can be like that for some.

Decisions as a Resident

"David, John Carter here."

"Yes, sir."

"There's a newborn being transferred with an acute bleed, blood in the abdomen. Meet him at the ER and bring the infant directly to the OR for exploration. I'll notify Surgery. Oh, and hurry; don't allow the infant to be signed into the ER. Got it?"

"Yes, sir. Where from?" I asked.

"About an hour west of here, can't recall the town; however, I spoke with a Doctor Burke who delivered the baby, likely with high forceps," the surgeon quipped. "Probably bleeding from a lacerated liver or spleen."

There was no doubt that this newborn was from my hometown. I knew and respected this particular hometown physician, with whom I had worked during the summers in between my semesters at the Medical College. He had been our family physician for years. I cringed inwardly as I heard Dr. John Carter castigate this fine, hard working physician. I knew that Dr. Burke was better than someone who would mishandle a delivery. He had delivered thousands of babies, thousands. He was very facile, confident with hard-earned knowledge on how to safely get a baby out through the birth canal.

I felt embarrassed, ashamed that this fine physician, Dr. Burke, could be tarnished by such a glib accusation. My quandary: I also had the highest respect for Dr. John Carter. It was unlike him to castigate a referring physician, especially sight unseen. Perhaps his statement was a simple offhand comment, not intended to be direct. Occasionally a physician at the University would be quick to cast aspersions on a hard working doctor from a local community, and some professors were quick to assume that these local doctors' medical skills were less than those at teaching hospitals. That wasn't always the case. There are good, talented individuals at both ends of the medical spectrum. It's always dangerous to surmise when certain medical facts are unknown, as in this case.

So here was an infant, hours old, bleeding into its abdominal space, clearly a critical situation, no matter where the infant was from or what the reasons for the bleed. I asked to scrub-in with the Chief Surgical Resident and with Dr. Carter. (Normally, with this many individuals, the area of surgery would have been too crowded with such a tiny subject, but I was more than curious.)

It's a huge shock to see that tiny baby, barely six pounds, laying on the large "surgical table," bathed in the cool, intense light of surgery, intubated, a needle in its delicate scalp vein, with blood and platelets infusing into the larger umbilical vein. With anesthesia complete and a scrub with betadine, a minute incision in the abdomen of this tiny subject offered barely enough space for a single doctor to inspect. Dr. Carter worked quickly and diligently. Indeed the patient's interior abdominal space had significant amounts of bright red blood (BRB). Quickly, the organs were inspected and the normally large liver showed numerous pinpoints of hemorrhage, but there were no lacerations of this organ or of the spleen. The multiple, small points of bleeding were packed with an absorbable gel, held in place by the surgeon with additional packing. With this, the many pointed hemorrhages ceased. The surgical staff was relieved, especially myself, knowing there were no signs of any internal trauma. Even though the bleeding had stopped, Dr. Carter ordered me to find the results of the clotting factors (a series of complex proteins that laboratory tests measure).

The surgeons had begun suturing the incision closed when the infant's heart suddenly stopped beating, inexplicably the cardiac function ceased. Immediate resuscitative measures were begun but without any initial improvement. Dr. Carter, with one cut from his scalpel, extended the incision into the infant's chest, across the diaphragm and to the baby's pericardial cavity, to enable direct massage of its tiny but 'still' heart, an organ no larger than one's thumbnail. There continued to be no response in spite of our efforts, everyone was devastated by the little baby dying after only few hours of life. Finally after intra-cardiac injection of adrenaline and prolonged cardiac compression, Dr. Carter hinted at stopping our efforts. However, the Chief Resident continued compressing the tiny heart, but again, without change–yet he continued.

After another minute, Dr. Carter asked, "David, what do you think?" He frequently would ask for my opinion on matters, perhaps to test my decision-making skills or perhaps he respected my opinion. Whatever the reason, this was a tragic situation. I was now more involved than ever, trying to protect the reputation of a doctor back home and swept-up in the emotion of the moment. No one wishes to lose a patient, particularly one that's on the "table," and most especially, a newborn. My answer was aggressive, "Let me?" I asked, as I inserted myself, gently reaching my arm towards the operative field. Again I said, "Let me try," and with one finger I cautiously pressed its tiny heart, the organ now totally exposed by the extended incision. The tiny heart was so pliable so flaccid. I asked for another epinephrine injection directly into the heart muscle, again to no avail. "One more minute," I firmly stated, "sixty-seconds and we will cease." As my index finger pumped, I watched the clock on the wall tick off its seconds: fifty, forty, thirty. "Come on," I softly demanded, as a prayer, as a silent command, as if the patient were a tiny Lazarus. I thought of the parents outside praying, waiting for some good news. Then suddenly, I felt its tiny heart 'snap' to life, spontaneously beating on its own, good solid strong regular contractions. I felt so elated, so thankful, for everyone; it was a rush that was difficult to put into words. To save a life, to go that extra mile, it's like no other feeling. Smiles filled the masked faces; exclamations of success were etched within the visible lines near our eyes.

The elongated incision closed, all vital signs stable, the infant was whisked off to recovery. Because of my schedule the following day, I assumed another position at another teaching hospital at Albany, but I checked on the infant and the little guy was doing well and would be discharged in a few days. There was now an established reason for the abdominal hemorrhage: Hemophilia, the patient's hemorrhage was not because of anything the local physician had or had not done.

Years later, practicing in my home town, I learned that the baby we worked so zealously to save had neurological deficits of Cerebral Palsy. Could this have been a result of resuscitation? Yes, certainly. Could this have been a result of spontaneous cerebral hemorrhage suffered at the time of normal vaginal delivery? Definitely. Should I not have spoken-up at the time of surgery? Who really truly knows? Who knows what life has in store? A tiny newborn deserves all the efforts that any other person does and perhaps even more.

I had asked Doctor Bernard Burke about our efforts that day, that day the child was born, the day Dr. Carter operated. Bernard's response was, "Absolutely. A physician must oblige life at any cost. We cannot know what's in store for people (anyone); that's not our choice." He went on, "Life is always sacred and that alone commands respect."

When our daughter was born, she was labeled as dysmature, a term that meant our daughter spent too long in the womb or perhaps had been under some degree of fetal distress. There was a scant amount of meconium* staining of the amnionic fluid, a telltale sign of some distress before she was born. Our daughter, in her first few days as an infant, took her mother's milk poorly for a couple of days. We were very concerned; however, the obstetrician was reassuring. But in spite of his encouragement we worried.

On my way to the hospital's nursery, I would stop and check my more serious medical patients. On our daughter's second day of life, as I parked by the ER entrance, I noted a disturbance as an ambulance backed to the ER entrance. Its one patient was hysterical, shouting, screaming; she was covered with blood, and naked. The volunteer attendants could not handle this out-of-control woman; they continued their attempts to wrap this naked, disturbed woman with the already bloodied sheet. The third attendant carried a blood soaked plastic bag with the remnants of an infant. The entire scene was a horrendous spectacle; no one seemed to be able to

---

** Meconium: *First contents of the rectum from a newborn, staining implies a degree of fetal distress–an incontinence in-utero.*

control the situation. The continued efforts of the attendants appeared to focus only on wrapping the sheet around the completely naked and crazed woman.

What I witnessed was all nonsense. I shouted to the EMT, "Get the woman in a wheel chair and move her into the ER. To hell with any attempts to wrap that blood-stained sheet around her; this is no place to be concerned with modesty," I demanded.

It was such a macabre scene; the bloody bag contained the remnants of her two-week-old infant. The mother simply had gone berserk at home. No one knew whether the infant had died prematurely or whether the woman literally beat her offspring into a pulp, by herself and against the four walls of her home. Here I was fretting about our own newborn infant, who lay in the neonatal nursery, while the life given by this woman never had a chance. The woman was admitted to a psych ward; our daughter eventually came home to a wonderful life. For some, Fate pulls a short straw.

Medical College Summers

After the first year of professional training, I desperately needed financial help; Marcia was expecting our first child. The Assistant Dean at the College told me that he had never come across a medical student at Albany as financially "strapped" as I was. I had borrowed all the funds and loans available–just to get by. In the two months between the first year and my upcoming sophomore year, I parleyed the local Community Hospital at home to give me a stipend for the two months that I would work there. I worked in the mornings (when surgeons operated and physicians made their patient rounds). I could help in a small way, and they would teach me the finer points of medicine. The experience was inspiring, and the stipend was absolutely a Godsend. Further, I was able to help out on the farm, particularly during the haying season. I found in returning to the fields that the sunshine was an added break from the intense studies of medicine.

At the hospital various physicians took me under their "wing." It was a great experience. Dr. Burke taught me a wide range of clinical skills, which meant so much. He was someone who had made a huge impact upon my life before I had any desire to become a physician. Certainly through the years after, to work beside him had become an honor.

The second summer at home the hospital gave me even a greater stipend than the first year, which again helped towards our added expenses. Experiences of being in the delivery room, in surgery, making rounds with the various physicians at the hospital were a greater head start than I ever had expected. I was able to examine many unusual patients that presented with very rare disorders. For instance, an elderly woman had been admitted with Argyria—someone who had been treated with silver therapy when younger. After years her skin color had turned the shade of slate grey, an appearance that could be initially confused with cyanosis (lack of oxygen). (Much later, while a Resident at a hospital in North Carolina, I had examined another woman who had a slate-gray skin tone. Again, I knew it was someone with this rare disorder.

Dr. Vickers, "Dr. Dan," as he liked to be called, was a well-respected surgeon. His father had also been a surgeon at this hospital. Dr. Dan showed me numerous surgical techniques plus a variety of methods for decision-making on acute patients. He was a busy general surgeon, someone who was well versed in other disciplines of surgery, which included Orthopedics, Thoracic, and even Obstetrics where he would be called for Caesarean sections.

The first laparotomy (an incision into the abdominal space) I attended was at Little Falls Hospital. Dr. Dan invited me to scrub-in, something I had never before known. We scrubbed at adjacent sinks, and I would glance over and mimic his method of scrubbing my hands and forearms to include the elbows. This was a first for me. I thought I had completed the task, when the doctor looked over and said, "Take your wedding ring off, put your mask on, and then start over." Lesson number one, wear no jewelry; lesson number two, place one's surgical mask on before starting to "scrub."

The nurses demonstrated how to enter the OR and how to grab the sterile towels that one is handed, extended with a sterile Kelly clamp, and then to carefully dry, avoid dripping on people or sterile equipment. They also demonstrated how and where to discard the towel that had been used, then how to approach the scrub nurse who would be holding open the sterile gown and then run one's hand into the "held" sterile gloves, how not to contaminate one's self or the operative field. The scrub-nurse then showed how to adjust the overhead lamp so that the patient's belly was awash in bright, focused light. I was beginning to believe I would become a real doctor.

After the skin was prepped with iodine and anesthesia induced, Dr. Vickers' steady hand grabbed the scalpel and without hesitation drew that blade ventrally and midline. A thin trough of flesh opened and exposed a layer of subcutaneous fat that parted. As this incision lengthened, then separated further, pinpoints of bright red blood appeared from the incised tiny vessels causing a small amount of blood to accumulate in this "trough" at midline.

The contrast of parting flesh in that bright light, the brilliance of red blood, and the stark white of the belly with the surrounding white towels emphasized his drastic cut, like a stroke of an artist drawing a steady line. It would be easy to see how someone could become queasy at this sight. Yet I was fascinated and mesmerized by the drama, absorbed by the contrast– the colors, the painlessly divided abdominal wall, the skill of the surgeon. Quickly, the layers of the patient's flesh were parted, muscles pared only with the handle of his scalpel, the "abs" retracted by his unfaltering hand. The uterus huge, appeared as an enormous tumor, but this was life and hopefully there would be no dying here this day. Without hesitation the massive uterus was clamped by his instruments, held by myself while the sharp, special scissors sliced apart the fascia holding tough uterine muscles.

Fortunately I knew what to expect, then stepped back as the surgeon purposely applied pressure to his side of the patient's voluminous belly. The amnionic fluid flowed towards me like a tsunami. I quickly backed away enough to avoid the gush of liquid, as the amnionic fluid poured onto the floor. Without pausing Dr. Dan pulled the infant through the incision and clamped the cord. Very dramatic and my gown and shoes remained dry. Dr. Vickers winked at me, enjoyed seeing my aptitude; the doctor stated simply, "Most students get doused at this stage of their learning." My first C-section, and it was a girl!

On another occasion that summer Dr. Dan had me scrub in for another abdominal operation. By this time he had taught me how to suture an abdomen closed, pointed out all the important layers that would be required to be sewn closed individually. It was just the two of us operating; however, I was mostly holding retractors for him, cutting sutures, blotting dry the few small bleeders. When he completed the operation, he told me to: "close," the abdomen He then snapped off his sterile gloves and walked out from the surgical suite.

Now I had just completed the first year of medical school. There was no way I should be doing a closure of an abdomen.

I believed him, so ordered the usual suture, 3-0 cat gut and began to close the peritoneum, the first layer. It could have taken me a week, but I at least got started, about five minutes into the closure, Dr. Dan reentered and "peeked" in at my work. "Keep going," he ordered. *I thought, "Would he truly expect me to do this?"* Alas, he rescrubbed and returned to finish his work. The doctor was out only for a smoke, oh those old days—filled with cigarette smoke.

Those summers were great—I surmised that I had experienced much more than anyone in my class, especially under Doctors Burke and Vickers's direction. I examined women in labor, checked for cervical effacement, assisted at delivers and delivered babies in some of the easier cases. In the Delivery Room, the most critical direction from the doctor was: "Don't drop that infant!" That was my thought as well with the newborn slippery as an eel. However, with the soft, sterile, warm cotton towel I would wrap the newborn securely. I clamped the newborn cords, set broken bones, applied casts—which were old fashion plaster, much like sculpturing three dimensional work—I loved it.

Bernard J. Burke, M.D., was a favorite for many, but for myself, he was a wonderful mentor, full of encouragement. He gave me guidance, instruction, and conveyed so many great aspects of the profession. He was the most exceptional, dedicated professional man I had ever met. An unusual practitioner, a man married to his patients, all of them; rich or poor, night or day, being born or dying, he would be at their sides. Bernard was the last, the last great one ... no doubt the end-of-the-line for this type of physician. There never could be another doctor like him, at least not in this country.

For years he lived as a solitary individual, perhaps as an Irish cleric, lived in a cluttered small apartment above his medical office. He would either be flooded with patients or alone in his apartment where his evening's entertainment was watching his favorite sports from his old-fashioned rocker that had lions' heads carved into each wooden arm rest. He always sat within the cramped kitchen, everything he needed within arms length: a phone near his side, his portable TV front and center—positioned near the top of the stairs in a narrow hallway—himself sitting in that small room that doubled as a kitchen and the evening's entertainment center. He viewed his sports' broadcast from his oversized rocker, that is, if a patient or a nurse from the hospital didn't call.

The table was crowded with medical charts, numerous textbooks of various disciplines—there were pipe stands, ashtrays with used cigars, leftover food from grateful patients, all in a cluttered eight by ten kitchen.

His charity was legendary. He quietly gave much of his time and money to the poor—he had given air–conditioners to patients with obstructive airway disease. He had given generously to Churches and schools built in impoverished countries all over the world. He used Catholic Charities as an effective organization for getting his money and supplies to people who had need—people far beyond his practice.

Bernard would never let-on about his charity. No, I learned this from the Director of Catholic Charities for the Dioceses of Albany. I met this priest while I was a Resident at Albany. When he became my patient, he confided this information about Dr. Burke. When the good Father had learned of my hometown, he spoke of his exceptional generosity to the poor. After he told of the Doctor's charity, he added: "Oops, I promised the doctor I wouldn't tell a soul, but God knows I'm not likely to leave this hospital alive." Then he added: "Hey, someone should be made aware of the man's wonderful history of charity." That's when I told him I would never tell as long as the doctor was alive. With that promise, the good Father spoke of the Jeeps, the medicines, and the schools, funding that the man was solely responsible for in Central America, in South America, and in Africa.

Bernard always was concerned about the cost of medical care in general. He never sent out a bill to a patient (that I knew of), never had scheduled appointments. Patients simply walked in. If you were ill, then after each examined patient left, he would scan his crowded waiting room and point to the person that looked the worst or needed the most attention. In his office, it was always wall-to-wall people in that waiting room. People sat on the stairs that led up to his office, some waited outside, others waited for hours to be seen. Kids and moms were frequently chosen by Bernard to be examined first.

Bernard would go on house calls—out in weather too cold, in snows too deep—blowing and drifting snows—to see people too poor, too old, and sometimes too sick to be treated outside the hospital, but treatment he would give.

He had delivered thousands of babies. Any cute infant he delivered, he would call ugly, and conversely, he would rave about those homely little ones and called them cute or a gorgeous child, all to their mother's delight. Yet, after forty years of Obstetrics, the State Peer Review Board began a focused of his private practice.. First, they castigated him for not performing enough Caesarean sections, for not keeping proper notes on his patients; both his hospital notes as well as office notes were scrutinized. His patients loved him despite his shortcomings, his abruptness, his sometimes put-on grumpy nature. As he grew older, people brought him food and other gifts, whereas the State and Federal Officials only brought him only grief. They wanted his "hide hung on a fence!"

Drug Enforcement also became involved: their Agents were offended when the doctor couldn't produce records for the supply of ten thousand Codeine tablets he had given out to patients over the past thirty years, handed out in small white envelopes, without record. His personal life, plus years of a charitable medical practice were needlessly scrutinized by these government investigators.

With a full-blown investigation by the State and Federal Offices into Dr. Burke's records, several doctors looked over his written words, his hospital charts—to make sure that enough information was present for the reviewers. His direct care for patients was never in question, and soon the entire town rallied behind him.

After my heart attack, when I could not be there for him, the nurses told me a story, a statement uttered by Bernard. In my absence when he had this difficult case, he simply asked the nurses, "What would David do in this case?" A question that made my ailing heart soar: "What would David do?"

Rarely had he ever asked for anyone's direct help; however, on one occasion he asked me (after I had graduated and was on Staff at his hospital) to evaluate a farmer that had entered with an acute heart attack. The man needed a temporary heart pacemaker. He called me personally: "Bill needs your help, now!" Bill was a neighbor of mine, years ago—when I was working the farm, and Bill was in dire straights. When I was at his bedside, the patient responded: "Jesus Christ, Burnsey, I must be in bad shape to have you here!" With that, Bill's heart fibrillated and required cardio-version with the electric shock. Right after, he awoke he exclaimed, "Jesus, is that anyway to treat a neighbor?" (He was the only patient that ever claimed he could feel that electrical charge while unconscious. He added that he'd been kicked by a horse years earlier and that he did not wish to experience that painful event again; however, he'd rather take the kick from the horse than be cardioverted!) The temporary pacer corrected his unstable heart rhythm, and he was able to, again, go fishing in his senior years.

The Burn Unit: Reconstructive Surgery

As a student it's an interesting perspective attending surgery side-by-side with the surgeon. I was free to make quiet judgments of the work at hand, even though I was still very much an apprentice. I've assisted at many operations at various levels of my professional career as well as dealt with many different personalities. As I had indicated my first year of Medical School, I assisted for the first time at surgery at a local hospital in the mornings and worked the farm fields in the afternoons. It was quite a contrast.

Between my third year and senior year, I worked as an Intern, a student doctor with all the responsibilities of a real doctor, yet I had another year of clinical training to complete. It was a great four weeks, caring for traumatized and burned patients mostly. I loved the roll I played and the professional work that was expected of me.

Caring for burned patients was a daily challenge; and it was tedious labor. The first day "rounding" with the attending physicians, they introduced me as their new Intern. Yet, I was still just a student at Albany Medical College. Later, I returned to re-dress this one patient's wounds, someone who had extensive injuries about his face, neck, trunk and arms—in fact, he needed to be completely wrapped with gauze and a silver based ointment each day. So from behind this mummy-like mask, he asked, "Is your name truly Dr. Burns or is that supposed to be some sort of cruel joke?"

Every day I came to care for him and could begin to understand why he needed to know about everything in his confined space. For as long as I was on that service, he asked so many questions about himself, about myself, and the world outside the walls of that room. I began to appreciate, in small degrees, just how awful it must be to be caught-up in an explosion, to literally lose ones skin, to have your world turned upside-down, to have ones entire persona burned off.

This gentleman would face the rest of his life with a whole new look and not one he had chose.

Every day I made early rounds as the doctors examined each patient and assessed his wounds. I would later return to care for each of the individual patients—some terribly burned or scarred. With our daily shipments of medical pigskin that was harvested from live animals, then sterilized—this material would be applied daily. It was an early, temporary supplement for human skin until the real skin could grow back. Although it would retard infection and limit the ooze of plasma of some patients, it required much labor. I spent hours and hours cleaning and rewrapping this product on the burned areas in special, sterile hospital rooms heated at ninety-plus degrees, gowned in sterile surgical wrap, mask and gloves. I would repeat the pigskin applications everyday after debridement of burned or rejected skin. It was tough work but useful training for my future practice far from a Burn Center.

Working with the Plastic Surgeons at Albany had been very educational; in that position, there were many long, tedious hours caring for individuals terribly burned or injured. It was a great experience helping seriously injured people in the Burn Unit and learning the reconstructive aspects of the work. Many cases involved surgery to revise the predicted scarring from horrendous burns.

On one occasion, working with a senior surgeon, I admitted a 34 year-old patient, a woman the surgeon had previously examined in his office. I was required to complete a full examination for the hospital record. This young woman had a very prominent scar on her neck, conspicuous remnants from a prior thyroid surgery that had been completed at another hospital. In addition, she had developed a partial re-growth of her thyroid gland, and there was a question if this mass was a reoccurrence of her malignancy. She was very concerned about the possible recurrence of the tumor; however, she was equally concerned and ashamed over the amount of keloid formation that had accumulated from her prior operation; it had been particularly troubling to her. Keloid formation can occur from a genetic condition, from poor healing or from poor approximation of the skin edges at the time of "closing" a wound. Sometimes it's no ones fault; the scar thickens and become very prominent on its own.

The patient made me promise that I would make sure that the surgeon revised and removed that obvious scar formation. All went well with the surgery: there was no recurrence of her tumor. As the surgeon began to close the wound, I could see his indifference to the adjacent scar. At first, I was reluctant to remind a staff surgeon about the woman's request, thinking to myself that he certainly would recall her directions at this appropriate time. Then as he further closed the operative wound, I sensed that the surgeon simply forgot or his thoughts were elsewhere. I became worried myself. I was nervous over the commitment I had made to the patient. Should I boldly remind a senior surgeon of his responsibilities and thus keep my promise?

The surgeon's incision was very close to the first, and further augmentation of her ugly scar would surely follow. With about three-quarters closed, I finally mustered the courage and mentioned the promise I made to the woman. Just like that, he stopped, stared first at his work, then at me then back at the mediocre job he was doing. Even at my stage of training, I knew that wound closure could be completed more professionally than what I saw that morning. Surely his thoughts and attention had to have been elsewhere as he closed. Finally after looking again at me, then again at his work, he picked up a scissors and removed all of his sutures. He then surgically trimmed and removed that ugly scar. His final repair was absolutely perfect. It was as if he began to pay attention to his responsibilities, to do the job with perfection. I was greatly relieved.

The surgeon did not thank me or mention it further. However, when I saw the patient a week later in follow-up at the clinic, she thanked me, telling me that for the first time in years her surgery scar was hardly noticeable, and she didn't need to wear those confining scarves any more, the needed apparel that covered her past.

Yes, There is a Santa

It was a terrible blow when I found out there was no real Santa Claus, especially since I remember meeting him a few years earlier. It was a death of sorts; I can still sense my dismay. Someone who had brought me presents every year was now no more. I'll tell you that it was very disappointing.

Now this was a long time ago, in a time that I do not wish to forget. Life in rural America in the 1940's was not fancy. It was the bare essentials, meager, and choices were few. Imagination helped many a kid survive. I thought of the day when I first saw him in person: Santa. It was at a Christmas party at that one room schoolhouse I attended. I was a first grader when on that snowy night the elders, all farmers, all likely standing around outside passing the flask of whiskey, rushed into the building with the news that Santa had arrived! Parents and all of their children, from the eight classes filled that room; everyone could hear the bells ringing from Santa's sled and the heavy foot that he had when he stomped into our schoolroom, clearing the snow from his black leather boots. No doubt his heavy sack weighted his step. I can still remember that scene, snow falling from his red suit so that everyone knew his ride was long and snowy. His persona was exactly the way that books had depicted him—in the amazement of my youth, I saw none other than the real Santa!

Much later, after being told the "news" that in truth there was no true Santa, just the Spirit of Giving, I remember thinking then who in the world brought not the toys I longed for but packages of nuts and oranges into our farmhouse? Who was that man, that impostor who made me believe on that winter night, long ago, in that small rural schoolhouse?

Where exactly is reality and where is that thin line between it and myths? Events of life we knew were real, but looking back, the reality was blurred so many times by the absurd. Much later, far from that scene of the rural school when I was who I am, a doctor, the situations I found myself in were so abstract that I now wonder if those were fact or fiction. On Christmases past there had been too many times of terrible mix for this physician.

When I was a Resident on Call as well as in private practice, I was called on holidays to treat drunks mangled by their cars or attempt resuscitation on a stranger, a stranger who happened to have his heart attack on Christmas Day. I would labor for hours to resuscitate, intubate, standby to medicate, and sometimes all to no avail; and then spend time with a distraught spouse, a family devastated by death. Afterwards, I traveled the short distance home but miles and miles from that medical scenario, to sing seasonal carols, to attempt being festive.

One particular Christmas morning when I was a Resident in training, I had to work on Christmas Day. I begrudged not being with my young family. Life, however, can have its unexpected rewards, for this one Blessed Day it was good I had been there. Moments after my early arrival at the hospital, there was a "code," an urgent call to Surgery. Odd I thought— why were they calling me? A call for assistance in Surgery, was this a prank? Why to the surgical suite? There should be physicians there, particularly if a patient were there for surgery there would have to be numerous doctors nearby.

The quickest way to reach that Unit was to run up four flights to the OR. As I entered without wearing "scrubs," simply in my street clothes, it all seemed so foreign.

There I was on this Holy Holiday, facing a woman on the operating table, about as blue as one can be and still be alive.

It would seem that the doctor there could have handled this predicament. Again, this was a long time ago, but as I rushed into this scene, the surgeon who would perform the surgery simply stood by with arms folded, his hands wrapped in a sterile surgical towel, pondering why the delay? While a nurse anesthetist, was frantically fumbling with this patient's life, or should I say with the patient's death. It was easy to see the exasperations on the anesthetist's face, but she continued "bagging" the patient, trying to squeeze air into the patient, when she had inadvertently, intubated the patient's esophagus, therefore only forcing air into the patient's gut.

The patient was dying, now a deep shade of blue, her heart rate was in the low twenties, dying on this Holy Day. The nurse anesthetist, while totally unsure of what was happening or why the patient was so cyanotic, continued doing that which had not been effective. No one in that room seemed to see the problem except the nursing supervisor that called-in the code. As I rushed in, I quickly assessed the problem. Pushing aside the anesthetist, I removed the errant breathing tube that had been wrongly placed in the patient's esophagus and reinserted the tube into her trachea. Now that she was properly intubated, I hyperventilated her with 100% oxygen. This maneuver allowed lifesaving oxygen into the dying patient's lungs, then to her dying heart, and finally it restored her brain function. This simple act reverted a tragic death, a death that would have occurred while she lay in a hospital on Christmas Day. The entire scene was absolutely surreal; and if the nurse in charge had not called a 'code,' her family would, most likely, have had a sad Christmas season.

Moreover, this woman was someone who had had a spontaneous loss of a pregnancy. Much more important, however, was the fact that her four kids who sat at home almost lost a mother. I admonished the anesthetist as well as the standby gynecologist who waited, oblivious to a rising critical situation; standing by in his sterile gloves and gown, waiting to see his patient nearly die, waiting while a nurse anesthetist compounded her errors.

Finally, after I settled down, I realized that there was indeed a Santa Claus after all. On that particular Christmas Day, Santa wore a white coat and on that particular day, he gave a life, he gave a mom back to her family.

Carolina Nights

Summer nights: there was something very comforting, perhaps accomplished, about these hot, muggy Carolina nights. The scorching sun long set, I would frequently be called into the hospital to evaluate yet another sick indigent patient; someone who had likely waited far too long for his or her care. Driving to the ER at the County Hospital, I would be called to examine the most extreme cases, whether through accident or disease or through pure neglect. Nothing in my training compared to the two months when I was in charge of these clinic patients. I had two great Interns under my direction, both a month away from their books. They worked hard and long, and together we managed all types of medical problems: patients who had finally made it to the ER, people that other doctors in private practice would choose not to care for. These medical dilemmas would eventually be referred to our service, directly under our care. We were on call every day and every second or third night for the months of July and August. Truly, I didn't mind that the Medical Director looked briefly over our shoulders. The "buck" stopped with me. Medical care, surgical referrals, admitting, and discharge were all my ultimate responsibility.

Arriving the last week in June a year before my Medicine Boards, I was assigned on my first day to the University Hospital in North Carolina. I had wished for further training, and thought some time spent in the South might be interesting. I had no idea that some individuals, physicians included, still held lingering Civil War grudges against anyone from the North.

I was assigned to a very busy rotation at the County Hospital, likely because I was a Yankee. I surmised that whoever scheduled the resident's rotations was not happy about having someone from New York in his program. However, I didn't mind the work and didn't mind caring for the poor and the sick.

Before my assignment, I had a single day of orientation. That day included an early morning electrocardiogram (ECG) presentation from a variety of patients. I attempted to sit back and listen while the clinician in cardiology produced several cardiograms, as 'slides' that were projected on a large screen. He then asked for house-staff's interpretations. One was an unusual tracing about which a 'beginner' might jump to conclusions and call an acute ischemic heart attack. Even a beginning student, however, needed to consider that the tracing more likely represented a normal variant. Most of the class thought it represented an acute infarction.

I was sure it was otherwise. The subject was thirty-five years old and his tracing demonstrated what I thought were Delta Waves, inferiorly on a cardiogram from this young man, a patient who had only vague chest symptoms. When I raised my hand, the doctor, who I had not formally met, responded, "Yes, sir. Someone from New York wishes to be recognized."

All I said was, "Sir, one should consider that this tracing may represent a variant of a normal ECG, such as Wolf-Parkinson-White Syndrome, what's referred to as WPW, and certainly not an acute process." I thought to myself, *"Hell, any student doctor at Albany would automatically include this consideration."* Well, I was correct, but I had stolen his thunder, and he held my correct response against me for the duration of the time I was there. From that point on, this doctor addressed me at conferences as "the Yankee" or the "Yankee Doctor," always said with an edge. For some, prejudices die slowly.

Despite this held-over prejudice, I loved the many aspects that the South offered. The wonderful spring exploded green and warm. Flowers of all kinds bloomed in early March. Neighbors were kind and gentle and, of course, the patients were grateful. In general, people we met were wonderful. The summers were scorching hot with high humidity. Escaping into air-conditioned hospitals, the many, many poor sick patients asked only for their health back. Too many of them smoked or drank far too much, and too many had become very ill.

I found unusual solace driving in at the 'wee' hours of the morning, negating the loss of sleep. I was acutely aware of the stillness, the remnant humidity, the heat radiating off the parking lot, cicadas with their night songs. All the certainty of the Carolina nights, along with the patient's medical uncertainty, left an indelible mark on this young doctor. Perhaps, it was the first occasion where I felt I was a full-fledged doctor. Perhaps, it was the needs of those so ill and those who waited. Perhaps I was simply imitating my doctor hero Bernard Burke who was always available, always caring. Those hot summer nights left a distinct mark on me, that narrow margin of time walking from the car into that brick hospital and the atmosphere that I found myself in still sit in my memory. Sick and dying patients were inside, but the walk from the car was an interim between Heaven and Hell, between wellness and disease, pleasure and pain. Perhaps this short walk was a respite, a period of immunity from the world of disease, perhaps even a time for the Holy Spirit to act, to guide.

Standing outside were a disparate group of people: the tired old black men, the custodians on their break, families awaiting an improvement of their loved ones now inside, battling a comeback to health. Most individuals rested against those still-hot bricks, drawing on their lighted cigarettes for strength, sucking in the hot gases, coughing out their waste, praying for a tomorrow; perhaps they wondered about their own slow demise. These narrow passages of time, I remember like yesterday.

I recall the older women with their country ways, the idioms within their speech: "Stop mashing on me," as I palpated their troubled abdomen to find the reasons for their pain. Others stated, "She fell off the roof when she was twelve years old." It would take two or three patients before I caught on that they spoke of their menarche. Everyone it seemed had hypertension and/or heart disease; everyone smoked or used snuff, mashing snuff into their gums with a chewed, softened, frayed twig from their fruit tree at home.

I could have stayed deep in the South forever. Two doctors, both Department Chiefs at the University Hospital had made me offers, and they hoped that I would make the choice to stay in the South. That decision would have been too easy, too comfortable (medically) and, of course, there was not enough snow in their winters. No, I needed more of a challenge … I needed to go home.

Susie

It was the odor I guess: the stench from the burnt flesh combined with the pungent smell of the melted polyester fabric, her singed hair—all had the effect of smelling salts: a quick slap of reality, a sudden start for empathy.

Susie was in rough shape, someone for whom you didn't mind being awakened to help. Until that night I had never thought much about being the lone physician who would be forced to manage a critical situation of this magnitude. I was well trained, confident, and never dwelled upon not having a cadre of specialists at my call. In those first few minutes with Susie, I knew I was a long way from the world of medical centers. That night, I momentarily wondered where life was, for Susie was in shock, in a cloud of confusion from her many injuries, and her vascular system was near collapse. There was also her terrible pain, her dire medical straits, and her severe burns almost beyond description. She also had multiple fractures, respiratory distress, medical acidosis, and who knew what else!

Smoke still rose from what hair remained. Patches of her pale-blue robe had melted, matted into her burnt flesh. Her cough was both weak and painful; blood and soot streaked her sputum. It was all she could do to breathe. She needed a Trauma Center, but the nearest was too, too far away. Mobile support during those years was chancy at best. Simply put, I knew this woman was safer under my care, safer than in most places, safer here than out there, wasting time on some roadway in an ambulance.

After a quick survey, I knew what was needed. Her care would involve two critical periods. First, there was the immediate need to stabilize her labored breathing, her multiple fractured ribs and her collapsed lung. Once on a respirator, she would be able to receive adequate oxygen, receive enough medication for her terrible pain. Then her greater need: to catch-up to her vascular collapse and the need for intravenous fluid replacement.

The second period would involve long-term support to control infection and the need for future grafting. Susie would be moved to a treatment center but first things first.

This was my first night moonlighting at a Carolina community hospital, and I was assured that the work was an easy 12-hour shift. The other resident stated: "Most likely, you'll sleep the night away."

Usually burned patients brought in at the wee hours of the morning are the result of someone smoking in bed, more likely drinking and smoking. That was my first impression as I met Susie that night, the night her luck almost ran out—some would say that it had.

Much of her forearms, neck, face, back, and chest were all badly burned; she also had scattered patches burned on her thighs and legs. An air of smoke was evident with her every labored breath. I worked intensely but with the premise that this woman had fallen asleep with a cigarette. While I worked, I silently grumbled about people who choose to smoke their lives away. Probabilities were that this critically injured woman stood a high chance of dying this night. One might say that this one patient might have been the sole reason I had chosen a surgical rotation at the Burn Unit back at Albany.

First always is the airway. Since she had inhaled too many hot gases with soot, plus she had multiple cracked ribs, Susie needed to be intubated and placed on a breathing machine. This assured good airway, plus helped flush out the soot and debris from within the airways. The respirator allowed a greater percentage of oxygen, moist air and medications to directly treat the chemical bronchitis. We worked diligently. With much to do, I knew I'd be at this all night.

I calculated her burned surface to be about fifty percent. A rule of nines describes each surface area: arms are 9%, trunk 18% per side, a leg 18%. (These are gross estimates necessary to calculate fluid replacement in burned patients.) Necessary fluid replacement is critical because what flows in through the veins of burned patients quickly oozes out with the plasma through the denuded skin. A burned patient is somewhat akin to a sieve; therefore, vigorous fluid and colloid (protein) replacement is critical. The IV was placed at an area that had not been burned. Morphine contained her pain, while a large bore tube was introduced between the ribs and slid into her thoracic space to relieve the tension against the punctured lung and allow the collapsed lung to re-inflate. Fortunately there was another small patch of normal skin to work the tube through. After her fractured arm was splinted, we turned to the more tedious work: the patient's burned skin.

Here we were: a nurse and an aide and myself. They were amazed that I would even treat this patient. Any other doctor, they stated, would have packed this patient in an ambulance, and had the driver go like hell across the State to a real hospital. I explained how patients like Susie needed intense care before that transfer could be safely made. I reminded them it was also the dead of the night. Acute problems needed to be addressed before the patient was ultimately shipped out. This patient's greatest odds of dying were in these couple of hours. Her chance to live would be here with us for as many hours as it would take.

In sterile gowns and gloves we began to remove the burned skin with forceps, patience, and tedious surgical scrubbing. It would take hours. The enormous second and third degree injuries needed debridement and cleansing and then covered liberally with silver-based antibiotic cream before bandaging to retard infection.

I slept little that night as did the patient, and I had no right to moan. As the sun rose, I was leaving for my regular duties. My eyes felt as if they were filled with sand, yet the fresh air seemed like a newfound delight. In the parking lot, I finally met someone who knew the patient; more likely she met me. She had been awaiting my exit, waiting find out about her friend.

She told me that Susie had had lots of hard luck in her life, but she was never short on spunk. Her husband was disabled and in a home. Her son lay silent in Vietnam; her money was always scarce, but somehow Susie had a great resilience and that fortitude had been a medicine for her.

The neighbor went on to describe the first cold night of the autumn. Susie's family had made a fire in their new stove. Later I would find that the mason likely used more whiskey than mortar as he built their chimney. He failed to use a clay thimble to surround the metal stovepipe that traversed the wooden wall. That night as the wind howled, it pulled at the flames sucking hot gas through this hole in the wall. Soon the wall ignited flames that quickly engulfed their home.

Susie had been asleep upstairs as their house filled with smoke. She lost a lot that night: war medals of her dead son, photos of her happier days; all her belongings were consumed. She had searched frantically to locate her Mom, while flames licked at her skin, melted her clothes.

The neighbor claimed to have been awakened by Susie's screams. Susie did get out, the hard way, taking her chances in the dark of that smoke-filled hall, the cold night, and her two-story fall. She flung herself through a window, while her Mother, her house, and part of herself burned that night.

As I walked towards my car, perhaps this woman read my thoughts. She added, "Odd isn't," she said as I then turned back, "Susie never lit a cigarette ... but she may die from the smoke."

My prior thoughts had been admonished, yet I felt elated as I drove to work that morning, drove back to my Residency Program. I was tired but drove wide-eyed awake, with a satisfaction for having done the right thing.

Ode to Bernard J. Burke, M.D.

I never thought I'd see him lying in bed, in an ICU. Never! Although older than I, he always represented strength, wisdom, solutions; he was a problem solver for so many people, the sick and injured included. Here he lie, simply diminished, cut down by the same thing he had always fought against— disease. For more than fifty years, he was the quintessential physician in our small town. He had two things in his life that truly mattered: God and his patients. Everything else was incidental. Oh, his game of golf, that was a life-long struggle for him and his only escape from a steady stream of needy patients.

He was lying so quietly, no verbal exchanges, no testy challenges, no likeness to the curmudgeon he enjoyed being. His only movement was the rise and fall of his chest. Odd that he would be wearing a jaunty stocking cap placed by the neurosurgeon. The cap was even cocked at the usual angle, rolled up like that tan ski cap he wore in the Upstate blizzards. Now he was in a different kind of storm, one of mortal pathology.

His sister sat holding his hand, holding on to hope, claiming that he had squeezed her grip a few times. I tried not to show my doubts about that possibility; after all, he had suffered a severe intra-cerebral bleed. I was reminded of a mentor telling how disease will always beat you in the end, no matter how good one is as a physician. Yet, I never expected to see this once invincible man critically ill in an ICU.

I know his stroke was a blessing in disguise, for Bernard would not lie still for any other affliction. Who could ever imagine this man putting up with the wasting of a malignancy or the blank wonderment of Alzheimer's? Yes, God had taken him totally out of the picture, placed him suddenly into a deep coma, and here he lay quiet— indifferent, hearing no sympathies flow his way. God, who could imagine Bernard putting-up with sympathies? I thought of him other than a typical physician—almost like an Irish Monk or even more as a Celtic Orator. He was totally immersed in patient care and yet lived such a solitary life on his own. Bernard Burke was a complex, stubborn, but dedicated man. In his long and storied professional career, he carried on a one-man campaign to keep medicine affordable and accessible. His office was always open—his small cramped living quarters—eighteen stairs steps above. At all hours, he would allow patients to intrude, examining the sick and down trodden–that's what he did–that's who he was. His depth of knowledge of medicine, his "masked" kindness, his quiet generosity, his charity was astounding. His efforts to contain costs (for the patients' benefit), would cost him dearly. Because as he cared for so many people—the daily stream of patients to his office, others at the ER and always 15 or 20 hospitalized individuals each seen and examined every day—one wondered just how he did it. For years he delivered babies, assisted at surgery, set broken bones, there wasn't much he didn't accomplish each day, except for writing comprehensive notes on each person seen and examined.

Bernard relied on his Catholic faith. His beliefs came from a solid Celtic background. He allowed himself little, if any, deviation from the beliefs he was taught. I always wondered about that wound on the top of his right foot; it was a very odd place for a non-healing sore. He would never address just how or when this first appeared. I recognized it years ago, when as a medical student we were changing into "scrubs" for surgery. It startled me. "What is that?' I asked him. I never got a straight answer about that open sore that never healed. Years later, I witnessed this wound again, again while he was dressing for surgery. I always wondered could it have been his stigmata? We will never know. At his deathbed, I pulled back (and loosened) the sheet that stretched tightly over his large feet hoping to see that foot for the last time, but they had placed socks on his feet. It was odd for someone to have put socks on a comatose patient. I was so tempted to pull one off—but didn't, most likely because his family had gathered about his bedside. Frankly my curiosity at that point had waned— truly what did it matter?

Bernard would live a few more days. I was always disappointed that I did not attend his funeral. As fate would have it, I had been admitted as a patient in a Boston hospital that day—fighting off my own medical demons.

Bernard J. Burke, M.D. had been a great man, a hero of mine—full of encouragement, he gave guidance, as well as instruction. He was the most exceptional, dedicated doctor I had ever met. An unusual practitioner, a man "married" to his patients, all of them, rich or poor, being born or dying, no matter the time of day he would be at their side. The scene in ICU at the University Hospital was a quiet summation for me, seeing this doctor at his end. His thinned Celtic red hair had faded towards gray, his sharp features appeared more pronounced, and his feet seemed larger than normal causing an inappropriate lift to the bed sheets. The stubble on his face aged him further, and the jaunty cap added to the strangeness of this doctor on his deathbed. It appeared that he could be simply asleep, but this was much worse; his great mind was now only a memory.

Oh, the surgeons tried to help, completing a craniotomy to seek out that ruptured artery, but the damage was too massive. The hemorrhage that tore though his gray matter was far too extensive. Yet his sister held out hope, hope that her brother, a learned doctor who had helped so many, many others, would by some means, pull through. As more family arrived, I excused myself and walked to the Radiology Department to look at the post-op brain scan taken that morning. The radiologist reviewed the morbid results with me; he pointed out the bleed that had destroyed Bernard's thoughts.

I returned to his bedside, not mentioning the scan's results. I took one of his large hands into mine, remembering the same hand grasping mine: his congratulations given upon my own admission into his profession. I remembered that hand during deliveries, during surgeries, during so many medical moments, a paretic hand now without feeling.

As I held this hand, a quiet joy came over me, an awareness that this man was dying so quietly, so peacefully. Nobody was invading his last few minutes, no further dramatic attempts were made to pump life anew. Bernard had had a remarkable career, touched so many lives, and now awaited his quiet journey home, just the way he would have preferred.

It would be unlikely that there would ever be another like him.

Not Your Ordinary John

Now in my retirement it's peculiar to be awakened in the dead of night, to hear a voice of urgency. However, during my practice, telephone calls came at any hour, calls from nurses who expected me to be alert and responsive and ready to go. I somehow had trained myself to hear and answer those calls. During the night I would try, and usually succeed, to answer the phone after the first ring. Rarely would it be different. This habit began while on call as a Resident in Training, where three or four residents from different specialties would sleep in the same quarters off the ER. If someone let that phone ring and ring and ring again, then "Hell would pay." In my training there was an element of excitement when called, the realization that when I was called I would not disappoint the nurse who needed help and of course the patient who was in a crisis. Later in private practice, it was simply taking care not to disturb my own family members that were asleep. Generally the ER would not call unless a patient had a serious problem; the same was true with other units in the hospital, particularly at the wee hours of the morning.

On one occasion when I was totally "spent," I had fallen into a deep sleep at home when a patient, who had been in ICU, took a turn for the worse. I received the call about 2 a.m.; maybe I had had thirty or forty minutes of sleep before the phone rang. While holding the phone and listening to the nurse, I fell sound asleep (those wonderful few moments of sleep are heavenly). When the phone suddenly dropped to the floor, I awoke with a start and realized my error. However, I remembered the prior conversation and quickly dressed—then scooted off to the Unit. I then intentionally left the phone off the "hook" so as not to disturb my family (if someone would, no doubt, call back). Meanwhile, the nursing supervisor, who attempted a "call back," heard only a busy signal. She felt she had no other recourse but to send the police to my home.

That night there had been a fresh four-inch snowfall, and as I backed out of the garage and drove away, anyone (particularly a police officer looking to find the doctor), should have observed that a car had just recently backed out of the garage, then had driven off, away from my home. As the police arrived at our home, they failed to notice the obvious: the fresh tire tracks. Instead, the officers began to pound on our front door, red lights flashing, awaking all inside. My dear wife's first thought was that I had been involved in a car accident, while all along I was attending a very ill patient at the hospital. After that fiasco, I never left the phone off the hook again.

On one particular morning, a farmer named John became my patient; even before I examined him—over the phone, I added to his medical regiment on the basis of what the nurse had stated on the phone. John was a middle-aged man with a very serious heart attack. The nurse had said, "He has already arrested* twice: once in the Emergency Department and then as he was wheeled into ICU." Further facts were exchanged and medications initiated, and the battle for his life began. Dying (ischemic) heart muscle, in such a patient, has a potential to become extremely 'irritable' and this irritability will cause extreme autonomy for rapid heart beats, malignant dysrhythmia that will cause further ischemia to the heart from the lack of blood and oxygen. For treatment, time is always of the essence.

With situations like this, I would indeed rush–"fly" out the door, perhaps driving faster than my sleepy mind was prepared for. The drive took less than five minutes for me to reach the hospital. It was a straight shot: a quarter-mile to a four lane road, then one traffic light which I would drive through—if it was red. The trip was a short three miles. I could be at the ER sooner if the roads were clear, and many times I reached my destination in record time.

As I drove towards the hospital, the sun was just breaking dawn for most, but this day a life was waning for this man

** *Arrested: a term that describes when ones heart fibrillates (ventricular chaos)–result–no blood flow.*

named John. Rushing to help was always an odd mix of thoughts, an urgent start, the rush, a half-asleep state of mind. Driving was time given to assess life in general: each patient I would examine in the ER thought their day was likely to be a normal one, a run-of-the-mill day but they sometimes, found themselves at the end of the "road." Truly, how much time remaining has each of us? While driving, my mind would think back to those patients whom I was unable to help.

Rushing to treat a patient, someone I had not seen before, uncertain of what would be needed, confident that if anything could be done to stabilize a patient, we (the nurses and I) could turn around a dying situation. Driving towards a medical crisis is not only an adrenaline rush but also a time of conflict. Families expect a hundred percent; they are filled with hope as well as fear, family members disbelieving, denying that a loved-one could this day die. The nurses also were generally confident that I'd have the correct answers, the right combo of wit and know how.

Already anti-arrhythmic medicines were infusing into this patient called John. I hoped it would help. As I arrived at the hospital, there had been another bout of ventricular fibrillation that had again required defibrillation by way of electrical jolts to his chest. I finally met the man. He was conscious, alert but clearly his disease was trying hard to kill him. After a quick exam of his lungs and heart, I place a catheter into the Radial artery at his wrist that gave us a constant reading of his blood pressure and easy access for blood analysis. His electrocardiogram (ECG) showed evidence of a large ischemic area of dying heart muscle. Often his heart fibrillated as various intravenous (IV) therapies were tried and failed. John's condition continued extremely brittle, his status tenuous.

His lungs became congested, wet with fluid from a failing heart, and continued bouts of malignant arrhythmia threatened any success. Some of these extra beats were erratic, three or four beats that would clear on their own, but other times a single ectopic beat would cause another near-fatal discourse. Other events came in waves that dropped his blood pressures to zero. Most required electrical defibrillation and external compressions of his heart, pumping on his chest to keep the man alive. These were repeated over and over and over, events in which the man's heart ceased to beat normally. He was "buzzed" as many times as it was necessary by applied electrical energy to his chest wall (these jolts would de-energize all electrical circuits of a person's heart).

Everyone hopes that a physician can turn around each critical situation and hope abounds. By this time, John had been intubated and placed on mechanical respirator because repeated CPR had injured so many bones in his sternum and ribs. His ability to breathe on his own was nearly impossible. Further, every occasion when chest compressions were needed, the respirator had to be disconnected, and breathing was induced with an Ambu-bag, a rubber bag that was attached to oxygen and the endotracheal tube in his airway and manually compressed and timed with his resuscitative efforts.

I spent a few minutes to speak with his wife, and I reiterated the grave situation her husband was in. She had a lot to worry about that morning. Besides her dying husband, she was on the phone to her neighbors trying to find someone to milk their fifty-cow dairy. Normally these animals would have been milked and feed by this time.

John's spouse told me, "This is the first time my husband has had a threatening illness." She sad, "He has always worked long and hard." She related that when he started doing his chores at 4:30 a.m., he began to experience shortness of breath with severe indigestion. "He looked ghastly," she said. "I thought he'd keel over right in the barn. I was so scared."

The clock was now turning towards six a.m. and things continued to look grim. Nothing appeared to be calming down his irritable heart, nothing. A standard dose of a beta-blocker has slowed some of his abnormal beats but did not prevent the repeated, near-fatal attacks. Enzymes seeping from his dying heart muscle and his electrocardiogram all pointed to a very large injury. In between all this activity, I was on the phone to Cardiologists at the University Hospitals seeking transport. The entire transfer process required integration of three factions. First, how stable was the patient, then was an airship available (from the National Guard or State Police helicopters). Also a factor was the fickle Upstate New York weather. Furthermore, this early morning, neither University hospitals at Syracuse or Albany had rooms available, and finally the patient's condition, at this point, was far too brittle to consider transport. However, patients this ill, this young needed consideration for early transport to a university setting for urgent cardiac intervention, a process that also consumed lots of time and coordination.

We had been at these resuscitative efforts for over an hour. With every repeated cardiac arrest, there was more electrical injury to the skin on his chest, even with application of thick saline pads between his skin and the paddles—more evidence of electrical burns to his chest— further weakening of his heart muscle with every arrest. Then with the last shock, his normal rhythm pattern did not return. Manual chest compression kept his blood flowing but his heart was now in a terminal phase. The only good news was that whenever a single normal beat was noted, a blip of pressure was measured as acceptable on the monitor. In spite of a plethora of drugs, all seemed for naught.

The nurses and the ER doctor who were helping that early morning, began hinting that, after such a protracted effort, I "call it off." "*When is enough, enough?*" their thoughts read. But it was a thought I refused to ponder. Nurses would occasionally remind doctors of their own opinions during prolonged resuscitations. After all, John's condition was not improving, the skin on his chest burned like 'toast,' clearly second degree injury, elements of his sternum fractured. The other doctor (from the ER) believed all had been tried, and perhaps I was being a bit overaggressive, perhaps, even giving extreme treatment. In other words, I was "beating a dead horse," to use an old country saying. Soon after their opinions expressed, the patient was now in an agonal dying heart pattern (ventricular fibrillation pattern with lessening amplitude noted on the monitor). I still had hope for John, and further, I was in charge. "He was viable an hour ago and so we forged on. I'm not giving up yet," I announced.

All my hopes were based on the results seen when one or two of John's normal heartbeats were noted on the monitor, intermixed among runs of malignant rhythms. Those scattered normal beats registered as a pressure wave on the monitor. I refused to believe that we were killing the patient. This told me that if the malignant rhythms were eliminated, John just might live, but this was a mighty slim shot at success.

Extreme situations require extreme actions and the intravenous medications of: metoprolol, magnesium, lidocaine, pronestyl, and nitroglycerin had done little to help. Perhaps, some had even augmented these malignant runs of chaotic heartbeats, called "Torsades." As a last ditch effort, I decided to inject, into his heart, large doses of another beta-blocker, propranolol.

The nurses drew-up two ampules of IV propranolol, and I gave this "IV push" through a central catheter while CPR continued. Surprisingly, two of John's own heartbeats showed up in between this unfolding disaster. Here again was a glimmer of hope. But after this, his heart went back into that dying pattern. I ordered two more amps of the beta-blocker propranolol. It was indeed a hefty dose. The other doctor was surprised and stated so, the same person who hinted to stop and pronounce the man dead. He said that no one he knew would dare do this at his teaching hospital. (He was a third year medical resident in training, soon to be out into his own practice.) I said nothing in return. With the second dose, a few more random heartbeats were noted, but always the dying rhythm returned. Then more propranolol was injected. Again the other doctor mumbled, "Gees that's a huge dose of a beta blocker ... I don't know?" He went on mumbling under-his-breath, inferring that too much of the drug propranolol had already been given. (Mind you, the patient was essentially dead at this point, except that CPR continued). It was then when I injected yet another ampule, perhaps more slowly than before. Almost miraculously his malignant ECG pattern abated, completely. The nurses and the Resident, all looked aghast. At 6:16 a.m., John had another huge dilemma, complete heart block, no heart rate whatsoever, no electrical activity. His heart flat lined.

Believe it or not, I saw this as a measure of success. After all there was no further malignant dysrhythmic activity. Others saw only an iatrogenic (a doctor induced) disaster. The huge dose of IV beta-blocker ceased the irritability that had been killing him (V. Fib), but another major problem arose, almost as bad: no electrical activity, no heartbeat!

Everyone looked at me, as if to silently shout, *"Oh, Oh, now look at what you've done,"* a subtle inference of what I had caused. While CPR continued I found a large peripheral vein in his left arm (thank God he had a muscular arm). At the bedside I slipped in a temporary cardiac pacemaker catheter. While others continued CPR, I threaded the catheter in through a vein in his arm and the pacing catheter slid into his dead heart with the help from a tiny air-filled balloon at its tip. This is where Divine Intervention really came into play. To everyone's surprise, the balloon tipped catheter slipped into the patient's right ventricle and "captured," in other words electrically "paced" this man's heart in a normal, controlled productive heart rate. John woke up right after restoration of his heart rhythm with no evidence of any change in his mental status and no neurological deficits.

Although attached to a respirator, he couldn't speak but he was very much alive, performing all of my commands. All of us were speechless. The elation felt that morning was indescribable. The joy for this man was indeed palpable. I can only say that something far from the tangible drove me beyond my professional limits that day.

Reflecting back, I was glad that I did not side with the majority's opinion that morning when a few voiced to end the CPR. Rarely do extreme measures make a difference, especially with patients in an agonal heart rhythm. Placing pacemakers into a heart chamber can be fraught with difficulty and having a "wire" inside an already irritable heart can also make matters worse. However, in John's case it saved his life.

As the patient stabilized, I drove home for breakfast, to shower and shave, to prepare for the day ahead. I believe John spent most of a month in our hospital, weeks in ICU, more than a week on a respirator. Although John had gone through a lot, his heart continued to improve, and the pacing wire was removed after his heart functions normalized. He did not need a permanent cardiac pacemaker.

While in the ICU after I removed the respirator, I ask him what he wanted most, believing he would request some home cooking. No, rather he asked for a Manhattan; and for the remaining time in the hospital, John and Louise enjoyed their one evening Manhattan together. He would later have a heart catheterization that would demonstrate a single diseased artery in his heart. John enjoyed almost two additional decades of life with his wife Louise since that day in 1984. He died recently, more than twenty years after his cardiac arrest and several years after his dear wife Louise.

Years later, while filling my car with gasoline, a man from the adjacent pump walked over, recognizing who I was. As I responded, he introduced himself as that Resident physician who had worked at the ER in Little Falls. He went on to explain: "I was there at that protracted resuscitation so many years ago—I assisted with John's care that unforgettable morning." I had failed to recognize the doctor, now older and with a beard. We chatted for a few moments before he added, "I learned a lot with you that morning, during that near hopeless resuscitation. I learned about hope, about perseverance, perhaps more than in all the years of residency." I was astounded that he remembered so many details, as well as humbled by his compliment. Here at a gas station, a serendipitous moment reflecting back to a morning that neither one of us would forget. Two doctors recounting almost every moment of that extreme effort, things that I had waylaid in my mind, indelible events we both carried through the years. We recalled events that we could never let go, moments of a life given a second chance.

Hogs Back and The Stress of Practice

When I was young, I'd walk through the woods on our farm, a vast mix of eastern hemlocks and assorted hardwoods: maples, beech, and cherry. Majestic trees covered the steep slip-banks left from the glacier. This was a place to escape to, a place apart. It was here where I walked to sit and take-in its tranquility. I frequently would pause and wonder in my small way, ponder that which a life could hold or a stress that one could shed. A foot trail ran up the narrow, rounded ridge that our dad called the Hogs Back. I was fascinated by its name as well as its geological formation. Initially I thought that maybe dad made-up the term Hogs Back because of its unique path, its steep slopes sliding downward on both sides a hundred feet to the creek beds at either side below. In these dells, tiny minnows darted in the clear running water of its streams.

In this quiet place, the soft wind moving through high branches was all that one heard. Occasionally a squawking blue jay would break the silence. Other times, partridge arose with a start. In season one would pick the juicy blackberries that laced the wooded perimeter; somehow the choices there seemed endless. This was a place where one could go and dream, imagine all sorts of people that went before: men who had worked the farm, perhaps an Indian hunting for a hare or a hide. It was also the place our cattle would go to seek cool shade in the heat of August.

As a kid, I thought the peace there, the soul searching, could be no greater. For a while, it was that way; for a while, as a youngster, the Hogs Back was almost revered. However, I grew, I studied and met life at another level, experienced another type of place. Then, in this space, I found a much more serious venue. Far from those restful woods, here was an ungodly space; the place was indeed reflective but filled with sadness. Here in the morgue, it was often life and death— lives that had been cut down, whether through accident or by disease. One never knew what day a four year old would fall from the third floor window or what joy ride turned laugher into tears or what summer fun would drown someone.

That youngster lying motionless, lying in a morgue—nothing is as stark. Here is where I would meet my failures, past attempts to rebuild Humpy-Dumpty or the failed efforts to reclaim one from his disease. While others took their lives in stride, I would be at these afterlife exams, at the other end of life far from the living side of normal. In the morgue situations were always strained. Sure there were elements of quiet privilege but outside it might be a sunny spring day with my kids awaiting their game or a snowy Christmas or even the brisk autumn in all its colors. However, inside this room the stillness penetrated and its coolness chilled. Here, bruises and gashes longer red, no longer bleeding, are now aged into maroons and eerie blues; the skin now only an ungodly white, all distorting further a life no more.

This space alone leveled all "playing" fields. It forces one to see life and death as sort of an equal: the Alpha and the Omega. The silence here—broken only by the shrill of a parent or a gasp from a friend, in this unreal world everything is subdued; even bacteria shun the space. Yes, there is little future in a morgue but many "should haves" and "if only." Here life is but a reflection: he was drunk, he was sixteen, and he'll never be any older.

How does one go home, how can one sing songs of gladness or raise a glass of cheer after witnessing such horrible tragedy? I've known doctors who once at home, took long, hot showers, in hopes that the streaming water could wash away the weight of their failures. I've known others that were silent in thought as they drove their car, slowly along backcountry roads until their tears would cease. Dr. Burke told me how after a patient's horrible untimely death, he would retreat to the links ... with a large bucket of balls ... he would drive off his anger, tee off his pain and think of the odds of a hole-in-one that never came—odds that some patients never got.

At home, in the evenings, I would try my damnedest to be up. For there were days when laughter or a simple smile was difficult. Days when you saw your failures, your limits, the mortal side of life, times when the only respite was with the Mercy of God.

At night, the minds of both young and old needed to be freed, so at bedtime I made up stories: fables of heroes on horseback, heroes who always conquered, never failed using images stolen from my younger days spent on the Hogs Back. My wondrous homespun tales made their little minds take flight, and at least in their world and for those few moments, the lives of my children were made right. I took comfort in their peaceful faces as they slept.

Perhaps it is the emotion of the profession that drives us, those powerful feelings from success that propels. However, there are those inevitable failures that can crush most practitioners. I know for me there were times when working on a patient that emotions would grab at my heart and soul. Many times after failed resuscitations, tears would well. Many occasions I would resort to the scrub sink or bathroom in ICU to 'wash up' and simply morn, all because of the enormity of a life lost. Sometimes these emotions would spring-forth for a total stranger, other times for that slim chance of success that failed. Many times I grieved for some poor soul from the 'hills,' for an old man who just lost his wife—it might have been all he had, physically and emotionally.

A word about my profession: I certainly loved my work. It presented so many variations of the human spirit, so many emotions. Speaking of love, I also loved certain individuals that I worked with, unsung individuals that aided in my efforts, efforts that enabled the patient. This feeling was particularly true with the nurses. Some had worked at the bedside of an individual who was critically ill, laboring for eight or even twelve-hour shifts. Working side by side with them made my work light. The list also included my secretaries, technicians, respiratory therapists, laboratory and x-ray personnel, workers who exuded a positive aura, an almost tangible positive force for the care of very ill people.

I can say with certainty: there was a fondness to be around them, to work beside these exceptional individuals who expressed an amazing knowledge of their field and yet, all worked at this small community hospital. There were days filled with tension—critical medical situations that we all had to deal with: Situations that for the most part were far from being positive.

In the late nineteen-seventies, I spent four or five days with a medical college classmate who was a clinical professor at Massachusetts General Hospital. There I was shown the methods of invasive monitoring of patients—newer techniques that had become the state-of-the-art since my Residency and were lacking at our community hospital, technology that was necessary to more effectively manage critically ill patients. Through their Anesthesia Department, I learned how, when and why to use indwelling catheters. These lifelines would be placed into peripheral arteries, as well as positioned deep into a patient's Pulmonary Artery.

I also learned to improvise nitroglycerin use for intravenous therapy. This medicine had not been commercially available; however, at the Boston hospital, the pharmacist there were pulverizing sublingual tablets, dissolving these tablets for parental IV infusion, using a Millipore filter* to assure purity.

Upon returning home, patients in our community hospital, our heart attack victims would now have available in-house, homemade IV nitroglycerin. In the late 1970's, this was a major step forward in treating heart attacks. Further, I was excited about the new abilities to more closely monitor critical patients.

One morning, soon after, a man was brought into the ER. He had passed out while on a sidewalk. Once in the ER, he complained about nothing, and wondered why he was now in the emergency room. As any doctor would, we needed to ask silly questions, like: 'What day is it?' or 'Who is the President?' With these questions, sometimes a patient will feel intimidated, but we need to know if someone is oriented to time and place.

After a fall to the ground, a physician needs to decipher if the patient has an ongoing neurological condition or perhaps

*   Millipore filter: a super fine filter that screens-out all bacteria from a non-sterile fluid entering through *an IV.*

a sudden cardiac arrhythmia or someone with an acute heart attack. However, this gentle man, a grandpa with a large extended family was upset at my questioning, insisted there was not a problem: "Why are you asking these simple questions?" he asked. "I want to go home." However, seconds later, while an ECG was being recorded, he had a sudden cardiac arrest. Sadly, we were not able to restart his heart. After a brief bout of ventricular fibrillation, his heart never would beat again. All of our efforts were in vain. Even with our newer technology deployed, coupled with our older and tried efforts, patients still die.

This man was the first to have invasive monitoring used during his resuscitation. With a catheter in a peripheral artery, the digital transducers demonstrated an acceptable blood pressure during CPR. Here was absolute proof how CPR works. However, in spite of an effective blood flow throughout his body, his heart would never again beat. A death is always humbling.

A Love Story: Harold and Sarah

Harold had been instrumental in helping organize a group of residents who lived in the foothills of the Adirondack Mountains, individuals who started the Volunteer Ambulance Corps that covered a remote area twenty miles from our hospital. It was an odd collection of folks who tried their best to offer emergent transport for the folks out in the North Country. Back in the 1970's, they bought an old, well-used red and white ambulance. There were no trained EMT in those days, but anyone could see these volunteers held their neighbors' best interests at heart. Many evenings were spent instructing those residents in the basics of resuscitation and medical support during transport.

Neither Harold nor his wife Sarah finished high school. Married as teenagers, they raised four children that had all achieved college degrees. The couple was proud of their success, especially since they lived miles, and miles from anywhere in a small settlement where many poor folks subsisted, a collection of maybe twelve or fifteen families whose homes were scattered throughout the rolling hills. These people lived in small trailers or tiny put together houses heated with wood stoves, residents that attended a small, non-denominational church, and lived off the land or did odd jobs to subsist. Some raised a few chickens, hunted deer year round, lived humble lives, independent, not bothersome to anyone in particular. The area was thought, by many to be Appalachia North; however, the residents who lived there, called it God's country.

This day started differently for Harold. He was found unresponsive by his wife Sarah; Harold was taken to the hospital by the same ambulance corps he helped form, but unfortunately, he was deeply comatose. The neurological examine showed an abnormal breathing pattern and a positive Babinski*sign bilaterally; he responded only to painful stimuli.

His poor wife Sarah was beside herself, unable to grasp the how and why of this sudden change, as she tried and tried to awake him. The brain scan was very telling, demonstrating a massive hemorrhage into the thalamic region, a sudden but mortal bleed into his brain; for the most part the damage had been done.

Sarah would not sign a DNR (Do Not Resuscitate) order for her husband. No she wanted him to have all the needed care, at least for a while, until she could see what time and prayers brought her way. Harold was admitted to the Intensive Care Unit where treatment was begun. All too soon Harold could no longer breathe on his own and, therefore, was placed on a ventilator. Each day Harold continued on a downhill course. His medical state required care for numerous metabolic conditions.

After a week in ICU, he no longer responded to pain, indicating further neurological compromise as a result of the edema and the expanding brain injury. Sarah would spend most days at his bedside, silently praying for his improvement, while each day I painted a bleaker picture for his outcome. Yet, she continued to insist that he be maintained on a ventilator. With each new day she became renewed with Hope, stated that she knew he would get better, while the facts indicated just the opposite.

It was now weeks after his admission, and I was convinced that we had given him enough time. Normally, a repeat scan would convince most that this situation was terminal and with that in hand, the ventilator could be discontinued. To further convince her, an MRI exam was setup, a scan that at that time was performed only at Albany Medical Center, the only scan of this type in the entire upstate region, and it was an hour away. Harold required considerable support to carry out this study; therefore, with a nurse and a respiratory therapist, he was sent for this more accurate study. The results were as expected: the Thalamus, that part of the brain necessary for life, was obliterated bilaterally as a result of the massive brain hemorrhage. In addition we noted considerable atrophy of his brain. Upon his return, after I disclosed the scan's results to her, Sarah agreed that the ventilator should be discontinued the following day.

The next morning Sarah again came early and waited outside my office; she stated that her husband would live, despite the discontinuance of the respirator. Surprisingly, when the patient was finally extubated and taken off the supportive respirator, Harold continued to breath on his own. Everyone except his wife believed that there was no way the man could or would ever recover.

Weeks went by and Harold was eventually moved to a regular hospital room, awaiting a nursing home placement. He spent several weeks unresponsive, required total care, continued parenteral nutrition (given through a tube), and Sarah visited at his side every day. In spite of the care, his flesh wasted, and bedsores developed even though an air mattress was employed, even though the patient was frequently turned in bed; his condition predictably and slowly declined.

One day his wife spoke in confidence with me, stating that God had told her that her husband would get better and even walk. I knew that Harold's spouse believed what was stated; however, her heavenly disclosure was almost impossible for anyone to rationally accept, even for a God-fearing physician. I remained firmly a skeptic. Each subsequent day he remained in a deep coma and the extensive nursing care continued, while his poor body wasted from disuse and marginal nutrition.

Weeks later, a nurse called me at 7 a.m. "Doctor," she went on, "you won't believe what just happened. Harold has opened his eyes, and he has even had tried to speak." I couldn't believe it. I had to see this for myself, and as that thought occurred, I recalled the account of the Apostle, the one they called the "Doubting" Thomas.

At his bedside, a couple of hours later, there was Harold, wide-awake, trying to speak my name. Sarah quietly beamed. It was an unbelievable event, and as days went by, Harold began to walk at physical therapy. One or two steps were all he could muster, of course with help, but walk he did. As anyone would realize, he was very wasted, his progress—slow. The most amazing part was that the man seemed to have no loss of memory; he had no hemiparesis. He was oriented, knew my name, and each day his progress inched forward.

About two weeks later, as Harold continued to improve, Sarah waited outside my office, for another early morning meeting; she had some news for me. "What is it Sarah?"

"Harold will die soon," his wife said. "I know the Lord will take him home soon," she went on. "God gave me this additional time with him, and I'm grateful for that." I tried to assure her, noting that he was slowly improving, and there were no new complications. "No," she said. "I can accept his death now; I know he will die soon."

A few days later, her husband died in his sleep. This is a true story, a story with no earthly explanation other than the realization that this was a love story between Harold, Sarah and God.

A Secret No More

Fred was really sick. For a change, this old timer came to my office with a serious illness. Before this day, three or four times a year he would leave his back woods cabin in the Adirondack Mountains and sit fretting in my waiting room believing that death was at his door step. His anxiety belied his good health. This time, however, he presented with marked pallor, weight loss, and fatigue. The raised lesion on his chest combined with his other physical findings were suspect for a blood dyscrasia, probably an acute leukemia.

For as long as I knew Fred, he was always nervous, always uneasy. Although he thought otherwise of himself, he never showed me the calm, cool side of his persona he believed he presented. He had been a widower for twenty years and had no children. He claimed to have graduated from Harvard in 1940 and then "worked for the government," the only given description of his work. He retired to his log cabin that he built and essentially lived as a recluse for the past two decades.

After a number of laboratory test and the bone marrow biopsy I performed, Fred now knew the type of disorder he had: Acute Myeloblastic Leukemia. The disease would soon end his life. Treatments in the nineteen-eighties always fell short at controlling the wild malignant cells. I explained in detail that in spite of his chances, the treatments should begin soon. However, he refused to see a hematologist, refused chemotherapy. Instead he elected to go home and plan his last days. I would see him in the office in two weeks, in case he might need a blood transfusion.

Three weeks later he called, stated he was too exhausted to come in and asked if I could possibly see him at his home. A few days later, on my afternoon "off," I drove the long thirty miles into the foothills of the Adirondack hills, passed the changing season of golden poplars and maples now red from the frost. Beyond the pavement of macadam, coursing over

143

the gravel roadway, I then drove on an even more narrowed roadway. After crossing a small wooden bridge I arrived at Fred's home.

It was like a scene from a calendar illustration: the rustic logs, the porch wrapping the house built on the lower slope of a mountain. As the large majestic hardwoods shed their leaves, smoke climbed from the chimney through scattered pines. This was not a place of a recluse; no, the place where Fred lived was more like a retreat for some mystic.

I thought of this man's life, his worldly travels and then this place for his grounding. I had it all wrong. I had prejudged him as a hermit and a recluse by his nervous gruff manner, his simple dress.

No one greeted me at the door as I knocked. Since the screen was unlatched, I entered the cabin. I was further awed by the interior of polished wood walls, finished natural pine supports, the atrium large and inviting. Row after row of books lined the walls of the main room. A voice from the interior called, "Come through the hallway. I'm back here." I was amazed by the rustic décor and the art on the walls. I had always thought that this nervous man, generally unkempt, quietly unassuming, well, I thought he would have had a more modest house.

I was taken back by his appearance. He was much thinner, with more pallor and weaker. Fred tried to be gracious but couldn't. I pulled up a chair and sat facing the man. After a few personal comments, we both were aware that his status had changed drastically in the past few weeks. I told him that I would draw blood samples for a hemoglobin level before I left, but his raised thin hand fended off any testing. I inquired who was helping him. A neighbor, he said, someone that lived a couple of miles away. Someone who cooked for his meager needs, cleaned up after him.

He thanked me for visiting. "Come, he insisted, help me up and come out to the back." He used a walker and slowly made his way. It was a clear warm day for late October, the grass a deep green highlighted by the scattered, fallen leaves from the hardwoods. There by the lawn's edge was an already dug grave. "That's where I'll soon be," he said, "next to my wife's grave." It was all a bit strange. I was startled by his frankness. "She's buried under those flowers," as he pointed towards her gravesite. Silently I wondered if this was legal? I wondered who would bury him? Then he added, "My neighbor has all my instructions," as if he read my thoughts.

Turning towards the house, he told me, "I have a confession to tell you," then he paused briefly. "I thought you should be the one to know."

"Why me?" I asked.

"Well, I believe my closely held tale will go no further," he added. The pause seemed endless, as I turned to face him. "It's a burden that I need to confess before I die."

"Perhaps you should call a priest or a minister," I suggested.

"No, no, you're the one I trust. I only need to tell one person," he affirmed.

"I'm only a doctor," I told him. "Maybe this should be an item for a higher authority." Again he rebuffed my direction. I had heard secrets from several others; usually individuals who had something to get off their chest, something that they couldn't bear to tell a relative. This was different; I was in his setting, out of my professional enclave. As part of the staff, the hospital always gave me a professional shield of sorts; however, I was not ready for what he told.

Fred paused. "I killed my wife," he bluntly stated, "smothered her!"

God, I thought why is he telling me this, why me? What on Earth am I to do with this information, I thought? "Why" I asked, "Why?"

"I did it in her sleep; she was so depressed, with failing health, failing kidneys, failing eyesight, terrible lungs from smoking too many cigarettes. It was a couple of years after I built this place; I believe she wished it."

"Fred, why tell me this? What am I to do?" I asked.

"Nothing–I hope, nothing. I'll be dead in a few weeks or before—I needed to confess, needed to lift this "off my chest."

"Yes, but I'm not a Confessor."

"With all her ailments twenty years ago, she wouldn't have lived for long."

"Why would you kill her?" I asked, "Why?"

"I loved her, Doc—I loved her."

Driving back, his words echoed over and over in my thoughts: "I loved her." Why would someone kill another for love? It all seemed so incongruous. No one should assume that kind of authority over another, no one! Repeatedly, I heard his words ... and I shook my head in disbelief. Fred died twenty-three days later at his home; his obit noted that his funeral would be private.

Like a Fish Out of Water

The sudden change of pace immediately caught my eye, a quickening in movement, people running, then the posture of that child being carried out, the limp, purposeless swinging of his arms was unmistakable. As I ran to the water's edge, I knew then that this was going to become a tragedy in the making, a drowning so far from a hospital. However, I ran to help.

Treatment of critically injured or dying patients out of a hospital setting is, for any physician, akin to a fish out of water. There is not much one can do. Here are three episodes that I was involved with, happenstances on the road of life.

This was a week after my graduation from Medical College and a week from the start of my internship at the ER at Albany Medical Center, and because of my training, I knew what needed to be done. A five or six year old was found submerged, just a few feet from the beach, in three feet of water. The young lifeguards were at a loss with the complexity of what had just unfolded. Perhaps this explained my own feelings as well, for here was a damn sad situation and we had nothing to work with, other than our hands and mouth. So at lakeside, we began CPR, one hour from the nearest hospital, one damn, long hour.

From the start there was no life, no option but to begin. I took charge, sent one guard to call for an ambulance, another for oxygen, while I compressed and a medical student who had recently completed his third year of studies at Albany also began CPR. I first whacked the comatose child on his sternum with the flat of my fist, without any results. "Easy, easy with the efforts of breathing, don't force so much air." However, already there was reflux from the distended stomach. The student was amazing, as he washed-away the emesis with lake water. The two of us tried our damnedest to bring back life as we knelt, hoping and praying for a miracle. Our emotions were raw while the sands ground away at our knees until someone threw a towel for us to kneel on.

We compressed his chest–worked without stopping, because there was no one else. No one to give his parents a glimmer of hope, only the two of us. The victim's eyes had that God-awful blank stare of death, yet the victim's parents stood over this macabre scene asking, pleading: "Please, please, please, save our child." There never was a hint of life, never any pulse felt, never any pink flush of success, never any real hope.

I could not bring myself to call the young person dead, in as much as I should have. Solely for the sake of his parents, we pumped, pumped to give them time, if nothing else. Time to be near their dead son.

We were glad when the ambulance at last arrived, glad when the paramedics took over, relieved when the flashing lights and the sound of the siren faded over the first hillside. The pall of failure was profound. The two of us looked around the lakeside and saw only three individuals, my wife and my three-year old son, and the student's girl friend. The crowd had abandoned the scene for a happier day somewhere else–the beach vacated. The two lifeguards withdrew to a small building's utility room. This was my first attempt at resuscitation without medical support, away from a hospital. It wouldn't be my last.

***

We had been in Carolina for four months and although we loved the change that the South offered, my professional work schedule had been very hectic. I had been assigned to head the care of indigent patients at the Forsyth County Hospital. The patient load at Forsyth was a never-ending stream, day and night, sick and dying. It had been two months since I had a 'real' day off; the family was looking forward to our planned a week's trip to the Outer Banks and the Ocean, my first vacation in the South. The car was already packed, our two children anxious, my father-in-law recently flown in for the week; we were ready to start our five-hour drive early Saturday morning.

It was a bright sun-filled morning, late September, already a couple hours delay because of the many phone calls from the doctor who would 'cover' my twenty patients. The house we rented was in a quiet neighborhood only four blocks from the Interstate. The traffic would not be a problem.

When we headed out, there would be only one light before the ramp into Rte 24, one stop; then we were truly off to our five-hour drive east. As I waited for that red light to change, I had noticed a Ford Bronco enter the intersection from my left, racing to beat the light. Instead of traveling straight through the intersection, the driver tried to make a sharp left turn onto the ramp. Because of his speed however, he lost control and skidded sideways into the curbing, blowing out a rear tire, skidded further with the Bronco sliding sideway off the road then smashing into a heavy pole, caving in the right side of the vehicle just forward of the passenger door. As our traffic light changed to green, the Bronco was seen to rock from the impact, and all too soon smoke was rising from under the hood that had been bent and forced upward.

Other than this crash there were no other cars to be seen. Our five year old exclaimed, "Dad, did you see that!" I pulled up a safe distance behind the Bronco, and looked about—hoping someone would drive-by but no one did. As I approached the wreck with caution, there was smoke coming from under the vehicle when I noticed the two kids. One about ten years old dressed in a pop-Warner football outfit, helmet on, shoulder pads—he was sitting stunned, no seatbelt, dazed by the impact. The other, a teenage driver, was seen clutching the steering wheel and convulsing, in "status epilepticus," a neurological condition I had only read about. The teenager's eyes fixed in gaze away from the evident depressed skull fracture he had sustained. Real clinical settings, observed for the first time, are always personally amazing—particularly neurological pathology, pathology that had been asked on Board examinations.

The motor compartment continued to smoke and hiss, the antifreeze pouring out. I turned off the key and with my hand, noted a prominent bloody depressed area just over the right ear, and the driver continued to convulse while he gripped the steering wheel. It was a very strange scene, and in the back section of the Bronco was a large German shepherd lying, stunned by the impact. I believe the dog had also lost consciousness but as it noticed me, began to growl and bare its teeth, yet still unable to rise to its feet.

The youngest began to cry. One could see where his helmet had slammed into the glass on the passenger side door, where the window bulged outward. It's likely when the Ford skidded into the pole, with the driver buckled in, the younger lad without a seat belt, careened, rebounded and hit the driver with his helmet.

Here I was, alone, my family awaiting a trip to the shore, still no one else on the road. The driver was critically injured and I was stymied. I did not want to leave the injured boys, but motioned to my wife to drive for help. The younger boys confusion began to clear and now understood what had happened. As I removed him from the car, the dog settled down and remained contained and comfortable in the rear section of the Bronco. The older boy still unresponsive and continued to convulse, continued clutching the steering wheel as if he intentionally held on. Smoke bellowed out from the behind right front fender and fractured hood. Fearful of a possible fire, I elected to pull him out slowly, relieving his grasp easily. There were no other apparent injuries as I went over his extremities and ribs; only the critical skull injury.

The entire scene was so odd. I could look up at the hill adjacent to this Interstate approach and see the hospital where I worked, perhaps three hundred yards from the impact. Yet so out of reach by the steep grade, the escarpment of rock and thick brush. Yet here was this critically injured young man in desperate need of such a Medical Center.

The teenager was placed on his side, lying on an old blanket that had been in the truck—I was concerned that a more generalized seizure might occur. I ran to the car and had my wife drive to a phone or the ER, but before she left the scene—another car did pull up to help. It seemed forever before help arrived, first the police, then an ambulance. With the two-way radio of the emergency vehicle, I spoke with the ER to alert them to the need for urgent neurosurgical intervention for his 'depressed' fractured. At the ER, the teenager was taken immediately to surgery, survived but did required rehabilitation for his brain injury.

***

Years later, we traveled to Hawaii to reunite with our oldest son, who had been teaching school on the Island of Chuuk, in Micronesia. We were meeting him halfway at Maui. We had been told that a day-trip to Molokini, an offshore volcanic remnant that would be a delightful day trip with snorkeling and an experience of a lifetime. The day trip was on a slow moving boat, with about fifty people, most who enjoyed the snorkeling experience. Afterward, there was buffet lunch on the boat's stern.

My son called out from the upper deck. "Dad, Dad," At first, I couldn't see who it was or where he was with the bright sun, directly behind him; again he cried-out, "Dad, you better get up to the bow quickly," he added, "there's a major problem." I left my lunch plate and rushed to the bow; there, the staff had pulled a young adult from the waters, someone in his mid-twenties, now lying on the deck of the boat, while an attendant attempted mouth to mouth resuscitation, breathing all too forcefully and too quickly. Another crewmember stood nearby, I immediately surmised that the swimmer was dead. I could see the ineffectiveness of their efforts, forcing too much air in and no one doing chest compressions. "Oh he's got a good pulse," one young crewmember told me, as he stood nearby. I knew better, simply by looking at the lifeless body, the pupils fixed. "It must be your own pulse that you felt," I retorted. The crew had placed rolled-up towels behind the victim's neck, a position that forced the head forward. Clearly this was not correct.

I repositioned the drown victim, placed layers of towels between the shoulder blades, laid him on his side, compress and expel the massive amount of air from his stomach. "Now, blow that air gently, you're not blowing-up balloons here, simply move some air." *"Here we go again,"* I thought, as I began to manage another out-of-hospital drowning … it was an awful scene, one wrought with failure.

"Tell the Captain to call the Coast Guard," I shouted.

From above and near the wheelhouse, I heard the young captain, "What shall I tell him?" he asked. Heard another crewmember state: "Tell them we have a bit of a problem."

I shook my head in disbelief, the young crew just didn't get it, not sure if it was denial on their part or their lack of knowledge, but their ignorance annoyed the hell out of me.

I shouted, "Tell them we have a goddamn disaster here, I tell them to get a plane out here, quickly."

With continued CPR, there was no response, no sign of life. Too many people had been in the water for hours, snorkeling, some free diving, others with scuba gear: all observing so many wonders in this tropical setting. No one knew just how long the young man was underwater.

The captain calls down, "There's no helicopter available, what shall we do?" Now, I was angry at his ineptness—here we're busting our ass with an acute drowning and he still has no clue.

I'm orchestrating a resuscitation, and now I also have to command the damn boat. "Tell the Coast Guard to get their ass out here, by any means. Commandeer a boat or anything that's fast and floats but get out here."

We were ten long miles off the coast of Maui, on a slow, lumbering, catamaran with about fifty people on board, people ranging from grandmothers to young kids, all supposedly were there to enjoy a day-cruise, snorkeling on a fine sunny day, at Molokini Crater, but now a pall had overtaken everyone. All one could hear was the boat's motors, the lapping of waves on the hull, and repetitive counts of one, two, three–a count of compressions on the dead man's chest.

The victim was twenty-six years old, who allegedly had been an excellent swimmer, someone who flew in from Switzerland the day before. His mother spotted him, floating face down, a hundred feet from the boat. We had been doing CPR for ten or more minutes, and things were not looking good. I had the captain begin to power back towards land at ten knots (full speed), simply to close the distance between the catamaran and the speedboat, hopefully, the fast boat coming to meet us. His parents stood by and pleaded to God and to us to save her son. Repeatedly, I heard their plea: "Please, please, don't let him die." (When in fact he was already dead.) To compound our predicament there was no equipment to aid our efforts. As the crewmembers fatigued, I move my own son into relief, taught him "on the go" about CPR, since he had no prior training.

This was a defining moment, particularly for our son. To see the victim, a young man, physically fit, apparently free-diving, stretching his limits, but then dying. After flying the day before, certainly the twenty-year old should not have been diving, diving deep. It was damn sad situation

I had the Captain move the tourist away from the upper deck's rail, made sure the tourist stop taking videos of our efforts, and I had the Captain give the parents some special attention.

This was another damn sad event, one that I should have simply called a death, but I didn't … didn't have the courage to crush his hopeful parents: his mom and dad, vacationing in a foreign land, I thought the best we could do was attempt a miracle, to go forward with CPR. It would be close to an hour before the victim reached land, another thirty minutes until they reached the hospital. After the Coast Guard personal reached our boat, we transferred the victim on a surfboard, while the seamless CPR continued. There was no room on the fast boat, so I stayed behind on the catamaran, while the EMT and the parents accompanied their son for his final boat ride.

I could have cried, as the rescue boat pulled away, and many passengers did. The hopeless endeavor was over for us; however, not for his parents. As I looked out over the placid Pacific waters, the lumbering catamaran chugging towards shore, the Hawaiian mountains in the distance, and wondered about my short comings, the sadness of the young man's death, and chalked-up another failure.

We had come to Maui, to relax, to reunite with our oldest son, met him at a halfway point, in Maui. He had been teaching school another 5000 miles further westerly, in the Marshall

Islands, on the Island of Chuuk. It was a telling event for everyone on that boat. The chance for success was indeed a longshot, as it is with every drowning victim. For our son, I believe it was his first exposure to a careless death of someone similar to his own age, a young man whose body should have been a picture of health. Instead, it was a body heading to the morgue.

If only we had a defibrillator, injectable medications, an Ambu-bag for assisted breathing, and had these medical necessities immediately available; then a victim like this young man, might have survived. He may have had a chance to relax the next day, on a beach, relax at life, and be alive on Maui. However, we didn't and he wouldn't.

Spiritus Fermenti

Last Time Jack Ran

The last time I saw my brother Jack run, run like any other teenage boy, run like a deer, was a week or so before the accident. Dad had an old REO Speed Wagon, the model name would later be attached to a rock group. However, our family all knew that the name should be reserved for our old truck … it was a 1931 Oldsmobile truck. REO stood for its maker, Ralph E. Olds.

One sunny day in early summer, Dad was in a sloppy drunk state that made this seven-year old cringe. Dad would park his old truck out by the road near our mailbox, on a hill where he could coast the truck and with it in gear, jump-start the machine instead of having to crank it. Dad needed to go to town for more whiskey. Our Mom was adamant that he shouldn't go. Earlier in the year he had a minor traffic accident while driving drunk, and he scraped a farm implement while passing it on the road. Mom wanted no more money spent on whiskey—hard earned cash, money already in too short a supply—money going down the drain for another drink.

Dad wouldn't listen to reason. He needed more alcohol, and by God he would get it. All of my siblings stood by observing this battle of the Titans: Mom holding the line by standing on the narrow, slippery metal running board and dad trying his damnedest to start that old REO. The truck would coast a few feet and Dad in his drunken state shouted, "God damn it, let me go," while mom frantically reached past her husband to turn off the truck's ignition. Mom was more agile and determined to stop him. This was a frightening struggle. Perhaps these things occurred on a daily basis but out of sight—this single episode I remember well, standing helplessly on the lawn observing the scene as this event unfolded. All of us had chosen sides as we began the walk along the side of the road, keeping in line with the moving struggle, hoping our mom would not be injured in the fray. The REO went a few feet as it would begin to start, but Mom would again successfully reach the key and turn the ignition off.

I have that lasting image of Mom balanced precariously on the running board of the old truck, her cotton print dress flowing with the summer breezes while the cold fought battle of the wills unfolded. There were no casual sneakers nor slacks for women, just a modest heeled shoe that offered little grip standing on a short metal step. Mom shouted for us to stay away—so we began to walk along the shoulder of the road. We felt a child's sense of doom especially from my vantage point, while walking in that ditch—now dry from the summer's heat. From our perspective looking up at our parents' struggles, Mom's position on that truck appeared so precarious. What if Mom fell? She was our family's only anchor; our helplessness was palpable.

Dad was never seen as violent even when drunk, but he was damn stubborn and his addiction was strong. In the tug and pulls between our parents, the old truck was slowly advancing towards the town, if only a few feet at a time. Every few yards Mom conquered and overcame Dad's quest. Mom eventually shouted to her oldest son, "Call the State Police." I had believed it was threat, an attempt to give her an edge to finally scare our dad into giving up his intentions. However, Jack ran—ran like the wind towards the house, through the shadows cast by the maples, running to get help for his mom.

When he returned, Jack announced in earnest, "The police are coming!" I distinctly remember that feeling of shame in hearing that phrase. To everyone's surprise Dad simply gave up and jumped out of that old truck and fled across the hayfields. I never understood why he fled. Perhaps he felt the shame as well.

For a long time I would see that perfect image of Jack kicking up his heels, running like hell across our lawn, through the contrasts of the sunshine and shadows cast from those stately trees that bordered our lawn. Later Mom would be furious with our brother; Mom would tell us later that she had only intended to bluff our dad. Mom was emphatic that our problems should never be made public, and by calling the police everyone would know our family's plight. Now as I write this account years and years later, I feel my betrayal over these written words because I'm breaking that trust that Mom always dictated: keep family matters within the family.

Things got worse on the farm. One fine day in June while Dad was away from the farm, Jack decided to work in the day pasture, building a dam down at the creek. He worked in this small stream to create a swimming hole for the summer. When Jack failed to return for lunch, Mom went looking for him.

Aunt Kate's Rampage

Our great aunt lived at the farm until her death in 1948. A retired business woman, Kate had been a milliner, operated her own clothing business in town. She was a very proper woman who expected a lot from herself and those around her. She spent much of her senior years reading, sewing, and entertaining her many friends in our parlor at our farmhouse. Aunt Kate despised her nephew's drinking—she was very intolerant of drunks.

One winter day Aunt Kate became enraged at our dad. He was gone all day, reappearing late one evening and attempted to milk the cows. Physically he was incapacitated, falling and acting foolish when Aunt Kate charged to the barn. This alone was an exception, for our aunt had never before been seen to venture out to the cow barn. As kids, we spent considerable time in the barn, doing minor chores or playing with tricycles or giving whatever limited help a young lad could.

I'll never forget Aunt Kate's surprised entrance. She had on an old winter jacket, a woolen scarf tied about her head, appearing to me as a warrior of old. I never before truly knew of the family's buildup of anger over Dad's drinking, but the events of this one evening, incited Kate's emotions and caused her to burst onto the scene. And Kate had fire in her eyes.

We of course, knew where Dad hid all his bottles of whiskey. They were stashed throughout the barn. Amber bottles were in the haymow, under bags of grain, over the large hand-hewn beams that crisscrossed the stable. Kate sought them all that evening, bottles half-filled, those yet to be opened, even the empties she smashed that day.

As she found them, she threw them at the barn walls—some she even tossed at our Dad. I recalled hoping that none would hit him; he was already in bad shape, in that sloppy drunk state … acting silly, wedged between the cows that temporarily supported his drunken stupor. Dad looked so sad as his whiskey simply washed away that evening.

Aunt Kate broke every bottle she found, and some she pulled the corks before they were tossed. Her rampage that evening is frozen in my memory: the sound of those corks squeaking as they were twisted, the smell of whiskey bottles breaking, the sight of the animals cowering in their stanchions. She frightened everyone but Dad. It was difficult knowing just who we were betraying that night, our allegiances were torn. I knew that Dad would simply go out and buy more whiskey. I disagreed with Aunt Kate's vain attempt to knock some sense into her nephew because her actions were all a waste of anger and money. By this time our father was a drunk beyond reasoning.

The impact of that night would last a lifetime. The tension between family members was unnerving: the shards of brown glass driven into the wooden beams, torn labels pasted with whiskey streaking down the whitewashed walls, the desperation on both our elders' faces. Our aunt's attempt to rid the farm of whiskey was futile, and Dad's day was filled with sadness as he saw his next drink wasted.

Dad's Reckless Behavior–The Ongoing Struggles

Miracles do occur—I know this first hand. For our dad had years and years of alcohol abuse. It was unlikely that he could ever or would ever stop drinking. Although his quest for alcohol affected all of us children, it affected his oldest son, Jack, the most. Our oldest brother was more aware, more observant of just how often our dad was absent. Dad spent entire days off drinking when there was serious and timely work that needed to be completed: crops planted, winter forage harvested, cows milked. At an early age of eleven years, Jack assumed that he was the only one who could be trustworthy to finish the farm work left undone by our father. In completing that undone work, Jack would become a sacrificial lamb of sorts through a terrible life altering accident that would befall him. This tragedy would change our entire family, and change our dad from an everyday drunk into a sober parent. Yes, miracles do occur.

I can still feel that uneasy struggle and the anger felt over Dad's problem with alcohol. These indiscernible chain of events occurred at a time when I was young, perhaps six or seven years of age, dad was drunk most every day.

He almost killed himself with whiskey. He was often reckless, and why was this happening to our family? Why did he need whiskey everyday, and how did things in our close family be allowed to deteriorate? Here is an example of how reckless Dad became when drinking. On too many occasions, Dad showed very poor example with his zealous display of power with the old tractor, working at the tough tasks found on farms, pulling trees or logs or even extracting heavy boulders with the lightweight tractor. Dad would show off, demonstrate how to have the tractor rear-up as if he were riding a horse, like the Lone Ranger on his horse Silver. Dad would push the power, and tether the tractor's front wheels two or three feet

162

in the air. However, this reckless display would come back to hurt him, especially through his oldest son.

Dad became increasingly unreliable, showing up late for milking our dairy, leaving fields unplanted, hay crops left for ruin by the coming rain. The resulting molded hay was not palatable for the cows during the cold winter months, resulting in less milk to market. His drinking lead to further neglect: tractors left running, abandoned in the fields, animals unattended. One day when Jack walked home from our one-room country schoolhouse, he found the tractor idling, attached to a grain drill (a machine that placed the small grains of oats into the ground and in narrow rows.) Jack, at 12 years of age, finished planting the crop that year.

Other times I recall how the cows bellowed, cried out their discomfort as the milk dripped from their overfilled udders as the hired man Frank waited Dad's return. Sometimes our cows would not be milked until hours later, and other times not at all. After all, drunks are only concerned about their own needs and their own schedules.

Smashed

An Emergency Department (ED or ER) in any hospital can be an interesting place, as well as a place of sadness. All types of patients need to be dealt with from those critically ill to people with chronic complaints to others who have nothing but loneliness to deal with. Many poor souls feel they need of a joy ride in the middle of the night, accompanied by flashing red lights and intermittent sounds from the siren. This extreme variety of presenting patients poses a challenge at any hospital, for they all will be seen and treated.

Invariably there are predictable patterns: from ten-o'clock in the evening to midnight small children are likely to be brought in by a concerned parent or grandparent: children with fevers, cough, and upper airway congestion. Less frequently, a child may be carried in after a convulsion caused by a high fever; this is always a frightening experience both for the parent and for the physician. This child needs careful medical scrutiny. From two a.m. onward, most drunks appear because the bars have closed, because of auto accidents or falls or fist fights. Of course, for many everyday drunks, involvement in an accident could be anytime, day or night.

I've had a lifetime of experience in dealing with drunkards, first as a child watching members of my family, then with too many patients in ER experiences. The very worst is when a drunk has killed someone with his car, when a totally innocent person is dead because of a bad habit and frequently a bad attitude.

One evening there was a horrible two-car accident, and it was the drunk who was the first patient to be brought into the ER. He was inebriated, not knowing, and worse not caring, about what had just happened. The man was easy to dislike. Sometimes drunks are comical, sometimes they're entertaining or at least they think they are, but this drunk had just killed someone, someone I knew. He killed both a talented woman with whom I had worked and her five-year-old daughter, as well as injuring her eight-year-old son that had been in the back seat.

The ER got the call as I was leaving the hospital, about 6:30 p.m. on a dark, rainy autumn night. The fatalities had to be extricated from the mangled wreckage. However, the drunk limped away, wandering from the two-car collision, dazed and intoxicated, stumbling around the four lane road in the dark.

He awaited my examination, still very much inebriated and strapped on a gurney; even the head-on collision had failed to sober him. He demanded something for his thirst, "Can't anyone get a drink of water around here?" I examined him with distain, finding only cuts and bruises from the flying glass; he cared little for the profound loss and deep sorrow he had just caused. I decided to suture his wounds without Novocain, perhaps a little pay back, but even without local anesthesia, he felt no pain.

Sure drunks get killed, but this night in the ER a drunk walked away while a good soul, Jackie and her five-year-old daughter were killed. The young mother had worked in our hospital laboratory and was driving home for the family's dinner, her daughter strapped in the front seat, her son in the back. The boy had been smashed so violently within the car that besides his other injuries, one of his eyes now dangled uselessly at his cheek. This would not be the only part of him that would carry life long scars. His mother and sister were both dead.

***

No prom dates, no more birthdays, no grandkids, only grief and a head full of bad memories survived. The drunk, however, was unaware, as he cruised down the road of life in the wrong lane.

Did I hate him? I always pulled back a little short from hate. For far too many years, my Dad was a hopeless drunk. For the first eight years of my life, for some obscure reason Dad needed to drink every day. Sure there were a few sober moments when everyone thought his drinking had ceased, but our mom loved him and never gave up hope.

Mom had a very strong faith, and every night and perhaps all day long, she prayed that our dad would sober-up for good. I recall each night coming into the kitchen, after whatever barn chores a six or seven year-old could accomplish, just shortly before my bedtime. Mom with our two aunts would be kneeling on the linoleum floor, praying the Rosary. I, too, would kneel, pray, and then wonder, wonder shamefully if Mom had it right.

Do drunks ever stop?

Dad's Redemption

My dad stopped drinking soon after his oldest son was almost killed. Sobriety in Dad's case may have arrived through several forces. Jack's accident had to cause our father tremendous guilt. Of course, guilt can give a person a 'reason' to drink No, it had to be something beyond guilt because dad was too far gone to reason with at the time of Jack's near fatal accident. Certainly, all the prayers and rosaries that had been said definitely helped.

The fact that dad stopped drinking was in itself a miracle. The main reason was told to us years later when, in fact, at Dad's last drunken episode he witnessed a messenger—no doubt from God—dressed all in white. This spirit came to him straight out of nowhere. Then it revealed to our dad the path he was on, a path of self-destruction, a path that sure as Hell would bring him to ruin. Was dad exhibiting the DT's or had God shown him special favor by sending a witness– someone who could vividly show our father what Hell was like?

Of course we'll never know. We were young kids at the time, but Mom would tell us long afterward, far too many years later, after our dad died. By Mom's account, she told of Dad's visit with this Angel who had indeed come to demonstrate to him where he was headed. Perhaps, like Dante, this was our father's personal 'Tour of Hell.' Perhaps it was simpler than that. Perhaps all that the Angel needed was to use a mirror, an instrument that caused Dad to see his own miserable existence—because at that point in his life, our dad was a hopeless drunk.

When I first heard this story, I had no doubt of its truth, for I knew my Dad. He was drinking everyday, and every day he came closer to his demise. On a daily basis, all of us were torn by his lack of dependability. Farms have their natural cycles, and even our cows knew he was unreliable. The only cycle he adhered to was his time-out to have another drink.

167

Our mother went on to relate Dad's vision. The look in Mom's eyes and her intent in relating this event years later, told us how real this was. Mom described our father's recounting of that horrible vision of what the Angel pointed out to him. Whatever "that" was–it scared him straight.

For the rest of his life, Dad never drank. He would never again put alcohol to his lips. As a daily reminder, dad kept a pint of hidden on a high shelf in a kitchen cabinet for years and years, and throughout his years of sobriety, he started every day by opening that cabinet to stare briefly at his ticket to Hell. He never told any of us of this daily encounter in our kitchen. Dad never related his heavenly confrontation, but we all knew that our dad was somehow miraculously transformed: the rest of his days were spent responsible, sober, and being our dad again.

***

George and Stephen

George

I have cared for many drunks in my practice, and most would never change, never reach sobriety. All too many would promise, would swear that change was coming; however, most would die a sad, lonely death. Take for example, George, a hard-working farmer who loved to help all his neighbors. He would give the shirt off his back to his friends, but he only stopped drinking the day he died of alcoholic liver failure, end-stage cirrhosis. He was such a character and projected such a happy-go-lucky nature; however, on his inside, he was a tormented soul.

The morning of his last day, he again promised me that he was through with drinking whiskey. He swore that alcohol was behind him. However, that day he smuggled whiskey into his hospital room, lapsed into a coma, and then died later that day after a massive esophageal hemorrhage.

* * *

Stephen

Another farmer--buried in debt, working his 'dogs' off, a man who had a lovely wife and family—lived on a hardscrabble farm, tucked in the hills south of Little Falls. Everyone appreciated just how much whiskey Stephen drank, everyone except Stephen himself. I had been following him as an outpatient over the past few weeks, ever since his dear wife dragged him by the ear into my office.

It was easy to see by the physical signs that he drank all too much: his enlarged and hardened liver, the complexion of his skin with numerous 'spider' hemangioma, his mild icterus (yellow shading in the whites of one's eyes), and then of course the smell of alcohol on his breath.

He had many reasons to drink, or so he thought. He dismissed his excessive drinking through the habits of his deceased father who had lived in war-torn Eastern Europe. "Hey, he drank everyday," so told Stephen, "and was as healthy as a horse until he died." There were other excuses he offered: The work on his mortgaged farm drove him to drink, and so did the worry over his teenage kids. Oh, he had plenty more excuses, but in truth he was an alcoholic.

I continued to see him on an irregular basis, sometimes on days when he wasn't supposed to be seen. I had empathy for the man, and in return, he grew comfortable in our relationship. However, he continued to drink. When sober, he had many redeeming characteristics; he was kind and likable. Anyone could understand the pressures he was under. Farming is like that. His teenage boys were exceptional, excellent in sports, excellent in character--plus they did not drink. Moreover, Stephen was loosing his family, his farm, and his health–and one would not wait for the other. I pleaded with him, asked him often to join the nearest AA, and I thought he would.

For a while he did try to stop, stopped for two days. Then one day, he drank like a wild man, and did not stop until I met him in the ER at 11:30 one night. He was out of his mind, haunted by so many demons, a few real and others made to his liking. He was in liver failure, with alcoholic encephalopathy, a serious metabolic and neurological tailspin: the DT's, the Delirium Tremors.

Stephen was built like an ox, his arms similar to a weightlifter's. Here he was in the ER confused, agitated, and angry as Hell. Fortunately, he was aware that I was his physician, and he still held respect for me. Others working in the ER were complete strangers, and he was very paranoid about them. In spite of his aggressive behavior, I could get through to him, periodically, between his terribly agitated bouts.

Two State police officers happened to be at our ER when Stephen was brought in. The police were there for other reasons, but their presence that night was crucial. As Stephen grew more combative and more confused, he pulled out all his IV's, struggled to wiggle off the gurney, even while he was strapped-down. Sodium Ambutol is a potent relaxant, and Stephen had been given several ampules intravenously. Still he was raving mad. The two State Police officers held the Stephen's arms, one man on each, while I replaced the IV's, but Stephen was able to flex his arms, carrying both Police officers off their feet and with his same movements dislodging the IV's. We had used all the hospital's supply of Sodium Ambutal, plus diazepam IV but acutely, nothing would lessen his hyperactive state. However, eventually the medications caught up to our needs. Stephen was fortunate he survived; he did join Alcoholics Anonymous and has been sober ever since.

Leo

My Uncle Leo was another happy-go-lucky man, happy until he began drinking; then he would turn into a mean bastard. He lived in a house directly across from his family's home. I was never made aware of the dynamics between these two households, but there had to be friction because Uncle Leo spent too many years drinking and smoking. In my mid-teens, I found him after he tumbled trying to reach his home. He was pathetic that night. Maybe our uncle wasn't as lucky as our dad; he certainly could have used some Divine influence. If an Angel had indeed visited him, perhaps, he never told anyone or never took notice. Life can be like that for some.

That night, Leo could only sit on that cold, wet concrete, sit in that narrow walkway that lead to the back door of his house. This cluttered, darkened path lined with garbage cans was a hazard, especially for a drunk. He always chose this approach as his entrance, with the double deck porch in the rear. There was a sense of safety that would allow a wretched drunk a couple of ways into his house. He liked to think this was his home, but over the past few years he was unsure; perhaps it was more like a place for him to crash. Surely, if his wife was awake, there would be heated arguments, and if his neglected kids were awakened, they would again show their disappointed faces.

He didn't want to think about any confrontations just now, not this night. More important was the need to focus on the obvious; how the hell was he going to get up? As he sat there, he could begin to feel the foul water soak through his pants, the cold penetrate his bones. He wondered what remained of that bottle of rye that was under his arm but as he felt through the paper bag, shards of glass sliced at his left hand. "What else?" he thought, as the smell of spilled whiskey filled his numbed senses. A shaky right hand would no longer be quelled by a thought of a ready drink. He wondered whether this late night would be another lost in the DT's. The night was turning colder; he had to crawl to the steps, he had to.

Leo was mild mannered. He loved the out-of-doors and had a great sense of humor. So why did he drink? Drank and smoked and when he was drunk, he was a miserable son-of-a-bitch. No one ever knew what happened inside his brain, but alcohol for him was toxic. His quiet wife never stopped praying for him, praying that someday Leo would stop drinking. Sure she threw him out too many times. It was her only defense. Yet years went by and lives were wrecked. With his sporadic DT's, their lives were made miserable.

Eventually Leo became wasted, the booze shrinking his brain and the cigarettes fouling his lungs while carcinoma grew into that which was left. He had made life miserable for many, but the last four months of his own days were spent in hell. Wild malignant cells grew everywhere, particularly in his bones. Such torment, that one could not help thinking that his pain was his own private Hell, a cleansing before he possibly faced the real Inferno that might surely come.

His children were older the day I saw his daughter at his bedside. She had an odd look as she gazed upon her dying father, a man now only a fraction of himself. I thought I could see on her face a hint of a stoic smile, an expression of favor, as Leo lay suffering in his deathbed. Her look, perhaps, was a silent shout: "Hurt, Dad, Hurt!"

I could see why someone might consider what I thought. Yes, Leo had finally stopped drinking. I thought back to the times when our mom would rescue Leo from himself, times when Leo had no other place to go. At the end of another prolonged drunk, he would be brought to our farm, weak, shaky, probably half starved.

It would take more than a few days of Mom's constant care, her cooking and complete bed rest for his partial recovery. He would stay in the back bedroom at our farmhouse until he could manage the bare essentials such as feeding and washing himself. Even then, it would take additional days before his tremors would subside. He surely was to be pitied. He stayed at the farm until his strength returned. Eventually he would gain enough strength to venture out, walking into our fields, and catching the warm rays from the sun. For a while he would regain his God-given senses. My uncle could laugh again, again tell those humorous stories about hunting as a boy or fishing on the winter's ice. We would hope and pray that this time, after each prolonged recovery, common sense would prevail.

No, slowly as his strength returned, his manners eroded and one could easily see that Leo needed his drink, what AA calls a "dry drunk." Perhaps more simply, he could not put up with his own sober self. Soon Leo's speech included all sorts of expletives; it was Goddamn this and fuck that. Then it became more personal. "Why would anyone work on a fucking farm? You both are nothing more than Goddamn shit-kickers." Or he would add: "I hate this place." On and on he would rant and rave, at myself and at old Frank, our hired man. Then as his level of misery reached new heights, an old drinking buddy would arrive at the farm and Leo was off on another "toot."

Yet Mom recycled her brother over and over, showed him pity when no one else could. For our Mom it was a pure act of love and a work of mercy. Our dad had died at least a year or more before Leo appeared on the scene—needing mom's personal attempts at his rehabilitation. I'm sure that mom thought she could talk some common sense into Leo or continued to pray that God would give Leo a miracle, a miracle like that which had cured our dad. Inasmuch as God reached out to Leo, Leo would have none of it. Our uncle turned his back on many, not just on his family, he turned his back against himself; then walked to the Devil's tune for another drink.

I never had the maturity to confront Leo, especially when he would castigate everyone for his troubles. I would only "turn the other cheek." Thinking back, I should have slapped him hard when he denigrated my work, my Mom, and poor old Frank. When he called us all "Goddamned shit-kickers," I should have slapped him hard. I should have kicked his ass right off the property, right then—immediately. But I didn't.

Lighter Moments

A Garden Party

I was ten years into a very busy practice when my high school basketball coach, Hubie Brown, was named the Coach of the New York Knicks. I was so excited for his success; the perseverance and dedication he had shown to the game of basketball preceded his entrance onto the national scene. It was his ultimate reward for a lifetime of work—and knowing that he began it all with a team at our small parochial school in Little Falls made it that much sweeter. Naturally, there was a flood of press articles high-lighting Coach Brown, along with the team's newest acquisition of the rookie Patrick Ewing.

I had played for Coach Brown, years earlier when he began his stellar career soon after his discharge from the U. S. Army. Hubie had made it to the pinnacle of his game—in some respects both of us had succeeded with our dreams. Meanwhile, I was 'knee-deep' in acute care when *Sports Illustrated* was preparing a focused article about "*Hubie Brown, the Man.*" One of their feature writers called the office at St. Mary's Academy and asked for information about his first position there. A secretary at the school remembered that I had played under Coach Brown, therefore she referred the caller from the magazine to my medical office. As fate would have it, I was caring for a critically ill patient in ICU when the call came in.

I had no idea, at that moment, with that call, national fame was beckoning, when my secretary Michele called the ICU, a nurse relayed the message that *Sports Illustrated* was "on the line." I had no idea that there was a time-line involved. Hence, I had Michele tell them that I'd call them back; however, that day, the demands of medical care forced that return call into the next morning. That was when I discovered my missed opportunity because the issue of *Sports Illustrated* had already gone to "press." *Sports Illustrated*—my one "almost" claim to sports fame, a lost chance for national notoriety for this "second string" bench warmer that had played on Hubert Jude Brown's first team.

Several months later, Marcie, who always tried to expand my world outside of medicine, thought it would be wonderful for me to take the kids to a game at Madison Square Garden. Since the magazine article indicated where Hubie lived in New Jersey, I simply called his home and surprisingly spoke with his wife. I described who I was and my history, plus my desire to visit New York City with my boys to see a game. "Oh, he would love to have you there at the Garden. I'll speak with him and get back to you. I'm sure Hubie will have you sit with the team." *Really?* The thought urged me on. Believe it or not Mrs. Brown called back later with a date, saying that tickets would be sent in the mail. I told her how many would be coming. "Great," she said, "I'll tell him."

Well, the date grew closer and closer but no tickets arrived. My older brother, my two sons, twelve and eight years of age, and our friends' two boys of similar age would join us. The day before the game we still had no tickets. Finally, I placed a frantic call to Mrs. Brown on the day of travel. She apologized for her husband's oversight and said she would check where the tickets might be. In a later call, she informed me that no tickets were ever mailed! Our hearts sank. "No matter, I'll have Hubie leave them at the ticket booth, under your name."

It all sounded very logical. "Six of us will be there," I told her. That afternoon as we boarded the train for the long ride to New York City, the temperature was only 2° above zero. We dressed as if we were from Fargo, North Dakota: mackinaws, down-jackets, mittens, woolen socks, and winter watch caps. The forecast that night told how the temperature could dip to twenty below in Upstate New York.

We appeared quite a sight as the train pulled into Penn Station. Attempts to hail a cab were complicated by the inability for all to ride in a single cab. No one wanted to split-up because I was the only one that knew where we had to go. The kids and my brother, now in the middle of New York City, felt uneasy about using two cabs. Since we had plenty of time, we decided to walk, all twenty blocks!

Brother Tom had a new pair of dress shoes that not only hurt his feet but failed to keep them warm, and on top of that one shoe squeaked, likely from the bitter cold. The wind that night simply ripped the cold through us; we were glad of the extra layers of clothing. As the six of us huddled together to walk, we were quite a sight, even for New York City. There were very few people walking the streets that night, but anyone out would suspect that we had arrived from the "Klondike."

Finally we reached the Garden. Even though we had plenty time, the crowds were already gathering. As we entered the lobby, I immediately foresaw a major problem: line after line filled the lobby, and each of the numerous booths had its own lengthy lineup of anxious, and potentially unruly fans. I would never have the ability or the time to find which booth held our tickets. (All appeared identical, and cutting in line, just to ask an attendant was likely asking for trouble.) This was a major let down for the kids. So the six of us, these overdressed people from God-knows-where, stood trying to figure out our next move.

I directed the others to get in line and buy six general admission tickets. This would at least get us in. Then I thought if I could find the Knicks locker room, perhaps I would find someone to take a scribbled note to Hubie, "Hey, here we are, all the way from the North Country."

My kids have seen some of my past scheming, and already they had become a little nervous. "Dad, it's okay. We'll just sit in general admission."

"No, no, by God a deal is a deal. We've not come all this way to sit and squint at a distant court. No, we were promised court-side seats."

When we found the heavily guarded entrance to the Knicks' lockers, we all walked towards it. I believe my brother as well as the kids took no chance that we'd become separated. A guard, almost twice my size, stopped us and with a firm voice told us that this whole area (the hallway to the lockers) was "off limits." I explained that I needed to get a message to Coach Brown. I could read his thoughts as he looked us up and down, the six of us with our down jackets and scarves, the two younger kids' mittens snapped to their sleeves, our watch-caps in place. I'm sure this New York City Cop thought: *There's no goddamn way you kooks are going to get a message through to Coach Brown.*

I knew I had only a little time before he cleared our group from the hallway leading into the lockers. A flash of schemes flooded my thoughts: *I'll convince the guard that I'm here to meet the team's physician.* (I had read his name from that *Sports Illustrated* article.) Hoping to convince him, I proceeded to tell the cop the entire story. This made the guard appear more suspicious; however, he did listen. "Please call him and he will vouch for me." Perhaps the team's doctor would be a decent guy, sympathetic, and someone who would intervene for our cause; at least that's what I hoped for.

"*Good,*" I thought, as the guard "bought" the story: lock, stock, and barrel. As we stood there and waited, I was somewhat nervous about the meeting with my "old friend," the doctor. Sooner than expected, the team physician appeared at the entrance, no doubt wearing an Armani suit, a thousand dollar necktie and sporting manicured nails. He stood there for a few seconds giving me an indignant look from top to bottom, and with a tirade of verbal disdain the doctor said, "Who the Hell are You?" Then he turned to the guard and said, "Throw these bastards out! I've never met this jerk."

An even larger policeman was called and grabbed me by my coat collar saying, "Okay buddy you're-out-of-here!"

"Wait a damn minute," I yelled. "I have a ticket and so do the others in my group (as the others flapped their ticket stubs at him).

"No matter," the cop firmly stated. "You're out. You heard the doctor." As we were forced from the ramp into the mid-arena seating area, I again demand that he at least, take his hand away from my collar.

After a few steps down the aisle, I re-adjusted my heavy Mackinaw when another well-dressed, very tall young man--likely an ex-player--approached. "What's going on here?" he asked in a kindly manner. The cop acknowledged that he was taking these bums out, and he again grabbed and held the collar of my coat, his grip slightly stronger this time. My kids were wide-eyed with fear that their Dad was getting tossed from Madison Square Garden. My two boys and my brother were aghast; they all pointed to the ticket in their hands, their rights to general admission. My entire troop was lobbying my efforts, as this young representative of Madison Square Garden looked us over.

"Wait, wait a damn minute," I pleaded. "At least let me speak with this gentleman."

"What's the problem officer?" the team Rep asked again, indicating that he was indeed a PR representative for the Knicks' Organization. Great, I thought this is our last shot.

"Is this anyway to treat a fan?" I asked. The PR person told the cop to relax the grip on my collar. Now this was, for sure, the last chance, the whole ball of wax as they say. I told the rep the whole improbable story: the fact that Hubie was my high school coach as well as my conversations with Mrs. Brown the day before. The man accepted my sad tale.

"Wait here," he said telling the cop to keep us there in the aisle while he spoke with the Coach.

"God, he really believed me," I told the kids.

My oldest son chimed in, "Dad, no one could have made-up that story, no one."

The rep was back in a jiffy, "Officer," he commanded, "I'll take over. There's no problem, simply a gross misunderstanding." Then to our group, "Come with me." And he took all six of us to courtside to some seats behind the visiting team's bench. He said, "I'll be back later." Then he added, "Coach Brown will see you in a few minutes, soon after his team takes to the floor. Make yourselves comfortable and don't allow anyone to make you move." (My one son stated under his breath, "As if we could do that.")

"Thank you very much." I appreciated his efforts on our behalf and was ecstatic but the other five were really unsettled, really shaken by the chain of events, especially my boys and my brother by the near ejection from the Garden.

A few minutes later, as the Knicks took to the floor, everyone was engrossed with the team's warm-up. Suddenly, I had a surprised tap on my shoulder. It was Hubie! Kind as ever, he came over to make sure this old admirer was comfortable with the seats.

He apologized about the mix-up and our inability to sit behind the Knicks' bench. "I'll have someone bring over some sodas and chips. And I'll bring Mrs. Brown over at half time; I want her to meet you."

I was elated, but I thought Hubie was just being kind. Why would his wife want to meet me? Sure enough at halftime, again as his team came to the floor for their warm-up, Hubie appeared and said to his wife, "Mrs. Brown, meet Dr. Burns." As I looked over at Hubie, he added with a smile, "This guy is the only damn farmer I've ever known." I guess that said it all. I took it as the ultimate compliment.

Pulling Teeth

"What do you mean, You can't find his teeth?"

"Well, we've looked and searched the entire room but no luck," the nurse on the phone said. "We've checked the waste baskets, looked through the bedding, called the laundry, but his upper denture is missing." The patient was acting normal, as normal as any rascal can, another nurse noted. "One of the nurses' aids thought the patient had been drooling a bit more," she went on. "We suspect that he may have swallowed his upper denture."

"Swallowed his teeth!" Did I hear that correctly? "You believe he swallowed his teeth!"

"He doesn't appear distressed," she went on. "I know this sounds crazy, but we've checked with housekeeping and laundry."

"Have you ever seen a patient swallow their dentures?" I asked.

"No, not really," she said.

I paused—thinking of that possibility, then said, "I'll be right up." Raymond was an irascible old man, moderately demented but "full of the devil." He frequently chased after the female patients, would attempt to get into their beds, and had tried to grope most of the nursing staff. Pulling pranks that made me wonder if, this day, Raymond had played one of his games. Perhaps he threw them out intentionally. We knew he hadn't left the room because he was always tied with a pose.*

I knew the man years ago when I was a kid on our farm. He always had been a character: produced moonshine, gave generous "tasting" to friends, lived in the back hills, lived the simple life. Now in his mid-eighties, he was delightfully

---

** Pose: *a vest-like restraint used to contain patients into a bed or chair*

demented and institutionalized, conveniently, at the top floor of the hospital, the floor referred to as Purgatory.

I found Raymond sitting in bed, in no distress, waiting his breakfast. He smiled as I walked in. In my mind, I was convinced that any person should be gagging and exhibiting much distress if a dental plate were lodged in the back of his throat. Raymond spoke: he denied knowing where his dentures were. I found no evidence of trauma in his throat. Palpating his neck, I could not feel any thing that would hint of something foreign in his throat. With a gloved hand, I palpated deep into his throat and felt nothing. With the majority of my hand in his mouth, this old man did not have a gag reflex. At his bedside, using a pediatric fiber-optic instrument, small enough to slide past any obstructing object such as a set of dentures, I advanced the scope into the esophagus.. Four or five inches beyond the vocal cords, I spotted the denture intact, but I was unable to retrieve it. I then positioned a heavy silk suture beyond the dentures and on one side (of the denture). Then with the small biopsy clamp, I guided by the fiber-optic scope, I grabbed the suture on the opposite side and looped it under and over and then around the denture with several loops. With a surgical clamp, I grabbed the ends of the suture, but was still unable to dislodge the set. They were now close to mid-chest, held by spasm of the muscles of the esophagus. The dentures were bound. I coated Raymond's pharynx with mineral oil and with an oil soaked gauze on a Kelly clamp, and gently coated the oil deep into the upper esophagus (there continued to be minimal gag-reflex.) With steady pressure, I extracted the denture, quite easily, and without much discomfort to Raymond.

"Oh, good, you found them," was Raymond's response. "Now, can I have my breakfast?"

Hardly a Leg to Stand On

"What about the shoe, Doctor?"

"What about it?" he retorted.

"Well, should I remove it?"

"Of course," he stated impatiently, "what would pathology do with a shoe?"

"Gees, I thought, *how the hell do I know? I'm new at this."* What a predicament … here I was with this grouchy old physician, my first day on the job—job of sorts, perhaps it was more like an experiment in learning or a first step of immersion into the world of urgent care. It was during the time between my first and second year of Medical College. I was still unaware of so many things related to medicine. Working in the mornings or occasionally in the evenings at the local hospital, I helped out the doctors in some obtuse fashion, feeling mostly inadequate.

Now what exactly does one do with an amputated limb, let alone one with a shoe attached? After the doctor severed the remaining bits of tissue, he handed off the limb to me. "David, grab hold of this and take it away!" I was impatiently looking for some sort of table to set it on. The limb was wrapped with sterile towels but still a bloodied and a ghostly white--a useless limb. Everyone else was busy caring for this heavy-set, seriously injured seventy-year-old man. Apparently he had driven off the road, and his car rolled over and over, ejecting him. He was brought to the hospital unresponsive. It seemed that just a flap of skin held the compound-fractured, lacerated limb.

The nurses and surgeon were struggling to render medical care, cleaning the wound and tying off the bleeders, oblivious to watching me find a place to set this heavy, useless leg. I can still visualize the image of the black dress shoe, well shined, with blades of grass wedged into the base of its heel. The setting was so strange, then to try to remove that shoe from the

185

amputated limb; it wasn't easy. I pried and pried but the shoe stayed fast on the lifeless foot as its attached leg moved about in all directions with each of my attempts. I was embarrassed to say the least. Everyone else was busy attempting to save a life while I was assigned to simply preserve the shoe.

I wasn't sure if the attending physician just wanted something to distract me from the more important task at hand or if carting the limb about the hospital room was some perverse learning experience intended for me alone. Finally, a nurse handed me a large paper specimen bag … she said, "Just place the entire thing into this. Let someone else worry over the shoe."

I have on occasions like this wondered if my brother's limb, a leg that he lost as a fourteen year old, was treated with similar detachment. It had been amputated at the same hospital, years and years earlier. He had sustained a crushing injury to his knee, and his leg was removed at the femur. Life is unpredictable like that.

Lend Me Your Ear

Soon after beginning my practice, my assigned week of ER duty began on Labor Day weekend, the weekend that brought the end to summer vacations. It was during this time that a unique patient was brought to our ER for treatment of a traumatic injury.

They charged into the emergency department carrying their crying young daughter. The distraught parents together said, "Our dog has bitten her ear off. It's awful; she's lost so much blood." Expressing their fears, the mother held her child, her injured ear smothered by a now bloodied towel. The family had become unglued over their child's injury. As I lifted the blood-soaked dishtowel, it was obvious that they had focused more on comforting the child than on applying pressure to her injury.

It was indeed a deforming injury. The entire outer rim of the ear, and supporting cartilage, was torn free with a loss of half its flesh. Apparently while the Mom and Dad were packing for their long drive back to New York City, their children had been playing with a tennis ball, and as small kids frequently do, the young daughter grabbed the ball with her hand and cocked it back behind her ear in an attempted to throw it. As the dog lunged for the ball, the Labrador grabbed the ball, the ear, and ran. The entire edge of the ear, about a half-inch outer rim, was ripped clear off. A jagged deformity was all that remained.

"Where is the torn piece?" I innocently asked, assuming the father had it with him.

"We threw it away!"

"You did what?" I replied.

"Left it in the waste basket at the cottage. I didn't think it could be used," he stated.

Again I exclaimed, "You threw it away?"

"Yes," he said. I simply shook my head in disbelief. With applied pressure the bleeding had now stopped, and as I gently pulled away the sterile bandage, the remaining external ear looked very odd.

"Let me see, daddy," the child said. When she looked into a mirror held by a nurse, we could see her dejection as she reviewed her deformity. "I can't believe you threw away my ear, Daddy," the girl cried.

I told the parents that there should be a definite attempt to graft that missing piece. "It's a gamble worth taking," I told him "You'll have to drive back and pick up that piece of your daughter's ear." The man looked dumbfounded, "That's almost a two-hour drive one way. It's a haul north into the mountains; besides we have a long trip ahead." I told him, "Call someone, perhaps the person that you rented the cottage from. Have them pick up the piece of flesh, wrap it in a moist clean cloth and drive towards here while you meet them half way. That will shorten the time."

"Hey, that's a great idea," he replied.

I reiterated, "I'm not sure it will be useable, but it's worth a try; your daughter will thank me if our efforts are successful, particularly when she becomes a teenager."

After several phone calls, off he went—with moist, sterile gauze and some crushed ice to wrap the torn flesh, while the mother remained with the child. Over two hours later, the dad was back with the precious commodity, the torn outer remnants of the child's ear. The fragment had not been chewed but offered a jagged line of torn flesh—with small beads of fatty interstitial matter hung from its edges. Under magnification, I cleansed and trimmed its edges and would do the same to the proximal edge of the ear.

I used very fine sutures. My mentors would have been pleased. I placed one suture then trimmed the advancing edge to achieve a fresh supply of fine capillary blood. Over and over, I repeated this tedious process to achieve a viable but bloody edge on her ear before sutures advanced. Innumerable stitches later, the edges were snug and approximated without tension. The post surgical wound bled with pinpoint bleeding—which was good. The wound was secured and protected with lots of fluffed-up gauze dressings. As I completed the graft, except for its pallor, the ear looked very much like a normal ear, perhaps some minimal loss of size.

I told the parents not to wipe the wound nor disturb the dressing in any fashion. If the graft "takes," the ear will be close to normal. The family was very surprised by the ear's appearance before it was bandaged and—to tell the truth—I was surprised as well.

I stressed that their child should not lie on that side and most importantly, the following day after reaching home, they absolutely would need to see a surgeon for day-to-day follow-up. If gangrene set in, the graft would need to be removed. The only question was, would enough blood vessels grow quickly into that cartilaginous outer rim of her ear to nourish the graft? One would know this answer in one or two days.

About a month later, I received a note from the parents thanking me for what I had accomplished. The reconstruction of their daughter's ear had been a success. I'm not sure if that family ever knew I was not a surgeon; however, I was taught well. I had been shown how, with great care and preparation, grafts will succeed. I knew what was best for this child, knew with proper suturing, this graft should "take," and the patient would be better for the time taken by all.

Snow-Fighters

They sat at our large kitchen table. The older man George with his calloused hands, creases outlined with oil and grime, grabbed a piece of Mom's delicious homemade bread, buttered it generously, and mopped up the remaining yolk from his plate of fried eggs. He then carefully folded another slice, using the last sausage and made a sandwich of sorts. Chewing it slowly with delight, he washed it all down with mouthfuls of fresh hot coffee.

Ed, a tall and lanky twenty year old, George's wingman, sat opposite. Ed had already finished his breakfast. Holding his coffee cup with both hands, he pondered, as if in prayer, enjoying the coffee's taste and warmth. Ed ate quickly; it was George that savored each morsel of Mom's cooking.

Years later, I looked back at George, perhaps more likely as an artistic study of the man and my own memories, wondering about all those years that have passed. George, by this time, was now my patient, lying in a hospital bed, his breath labored, nail beds cyanotic, his hands long ago cleansed of that accumulated grime from driving a huge snowplow. Now his one hand was swollen from an infiltrated IV. Generally, he hadn't changed that much in the past forty years.

I explained the need for a central line, an IV catheter placed into the deep vein in his chest, explained also the need of a cardiac pacing wire threaded into his heart. "Perhaps it will only be temporary," I explained.

"Go ahead," he said.

After I dressed in a sterile surgical gown and scrubbed with betadine the area around his collarbone, George's left clavicular area was draped with a "field" of sterile towels. I slid the large bore needle through the skin and cautiously advanced deep towards the subclavian vein. To ease his tension, I spoke about those past winters, telling George how I recalled those wind-swept, snow covered roads that we walked the short mile home from school.

I told George how I recalled three of the Burns' kids walking the road through whiteout conditions and how this one particular day, we could hear the town plow closing in behind us. We climbed above those recent drifts, my older brother pulling me up the six-foot snow embankment, out of that snowy 'canyon' to above the roadway where the air cleared from the blowing and drifting snows.

George was driving the old black and white Walter plow, and as he pulled alongside, the cab door opened, and he told all of us to climb onto the dump box filled with sand. "Hold on," he said. "You're safer there than walking this road." Of course we were thrilled.

"Remember that, George?" No, George couldn't bring back those distant memories, whereas I would never forget that youthful day full of exceptional excitement.

"We're in, George," I said, as the pacer lodged in the right ventricle of his heart. The rhythm then restored to a regular beat. With this hospital stay and medications, George would enjoy many more years of retirement.

***

Odd isn't it that I can recall forty years later how George sat and ate breakfast at our farmhouse kitchen. The gusto of this man's love of our mom's cooking coupled with his hunger from the long work hours drew me back in time. I remembered his short, stout frame, his animated manner of eating, the nasal snorting sounds when he breathed with his mouth full, how his manners held my gaze.

As kids, George was one of our seasonal heroes. He drove that enormous Walter snowplow that kept our winter roads open; that was our lifeline. The plow with its huge V-shape could cut through most drifts. The machine had an attached twelve foot wing on the right side, close to the V-plow that enabled the deep snow to be pushed even further off the roads, pushed far above the ditch and into the fields. Through his efforts, 700 quarts of milk would make it to market each day;

and every nickel helped keep that hard-scrabble farm from disaster.

Our farm was at the end of their district, miles off the state highway. Running northerly, our road "caught" the moving wind-swept snows from both coastal easterlies and the bitter northwesterly storms, winds that were driven by the cold fronts from Canada. Every day the winds played across those flat open fields. Any snow not anchored by a rock or a fence got swept into the roadway.

The road crews amazed many, driving those plows tirelessly day and night through blinding snows. As they kept those big machines working, some men resorted to a flask of whiskey to chase away the cold. The bitter cold was tough on man and machine; frequent breakdowns from cable wear and tear or hydraulic leaks resulted in the two man crew appearing as grease-monkeys whenever they came into our warm kitchen for their break and Mom's cooking.

Mom and Dad made sure to invite them in when the plow arrived at our driveway. Our farm was located at the northern extent of their plowing responsibilities, and our driveway was used to turn around this monster machine and head back. Their work was our lifeline to keep the road open from the continued blowing and drifting snow, and Mom's breakfast added further enticement to the drivers.

When the Little Falls snowplow drivers paused at our driveway, one of us kids would run out and invite them in. Mom always cooked them breakfast, no matter the time of day, a treat to reward their work, and the task was partly a bribe to make sure our road was well plowed. Breakfast was served with farm fresh eggs, homemade sage and spice sausage, and fresh homemade bread with homegrown berry jam on the side.

The men would leave their plow parked in our driveway. Its massive wheels raised its size to even greater heights, and for us kids climbing into the cab was akin to scaling a monument to Old Man winter. The great machine was a cacophony of sounds and smells; with the motor left running, the snowmelt from the engine's heat caused small streams of water to cascade onto its massive frame. Inside the cab a smell of grease, gasoline, and well-used work gloves placed near the heater left a distinct aroma. The windshield defrost warmed the glass, snow-melt trickling down from the thrown snow on top of the hood and cab, wipers still wiping away the trickling melt. The smells of oil and sweat, worn leather seats, a variety of wrenches and tools scattered under foot, a smoldering pipe or used cigar left on the dash all enticed our senses.

As kids we would sit on that seven-foot wide bench seat and absorb the wonders of it all. We peered out, head and shoulders above everything else, sitting in that Walter plow. On occasion the Burns boys climbed in while the men were distracted by fatigue, hunger, and Mom's cooking. We sat in that mammoth cab and pushed levers and pulled knobs until the blade rose, and the extended wing lowered itself, all to our glee. The hiss from the airbrakes brought gales of laughter. Only once did the three of us drive this mammoth down the road, not far … and perhaps not far enough. Those few feet were a combination of exhilaration and out-right fear of being caught. All while the men filled their bellies, we more than filled our imaginations. "Snow-Fighter" was the name emblazoned across the motor's hood. We were in awe, for this moment, this wonder held our thoughts.

The above comprised our normal winter weather, but blizzards represented an altogether different onslaught. These massive storms occurred three to four times a year, and they would clog every road—stop all traffic, sometimes even the largest plow. Occasionally the boss pulled all his men from the roads, while the winds and heavy snow completely obliterated one's ability to see the roadway. Of course today's equipment could, no doubt, keep up with most snowstorms. The newer machines have more power, better hydraulics, and better communications. In the 1940's and 1950's blizzards crippled road travel, and we became isolated along with many other farm families, especially those located in the high country in the Town of Fairfield.

Daily milk production would be dumped or fed to pigs, chickens, or made into butter. Sometimes the butterfat would be skimmed and then shipped to market days later   For the

193

most part; however, farmers' milk during those storms would be, by necessity, dumped—wasted.

Mostly I recall the winds, mounting snowdrifts, and the excitement that nature blew our way while we awaited the snow-fighters with their machine to ram those deep drifts. Backing-up their plows perhaps a hundred yards and then gaining speed, the driver cut into the deep drifts with an explosion of snow. George pushed in the clutch and the machine, as dead weight, lurched forward and wedged into six feet of snow; it was man against the worst of nature. Perhaps a path opened the length of the large truck, and again the whole effort was repeated over and over.

Sometimes the crew would spend an hour just to clear a dip in the road that was filled with snow. At times a powerful snow-blower, mounted on the front of another heavy-duty truck would "chew" into the mountainous snowdrifts and throw the white "stuff" hundreds of feet into the fields. This equipment was used in a limited manner to clear the deeply filled-in roadways because "blowers" were too slow and too time-consuming.

As the winds died and the brilliant sun shone, many roads remained closed by the snow's depth, but the road to our farm would be one of the first to be opened. Neighbors to the North, in the high country, would phone and arrange to have trucks meet them at our farm. Because their roads were buried deep with snow, some portions clogged by ten to twelve feet, these farmers delivered their filled milk cans by horse and sled across the snowy fields, away from the clogged roads.

One could hear the sleigh bells muted by the fluffy snow as those enormous work horses pulled the heavily laden sleds. Team after team, sled after sled, milk cans covered with old heavy woolen blankets, old bear rugs, anything to help prevent the milk from freezing. Trucks would arrive at our farm to pick up the numerous cans of milk brought down from the high country. Some farms in Fairfield Township would have to wait sometimes weeks until roads were cleared of snow.

Viewing the teams coursing through our fields was like a scene out of Currier and Ives: horses lathered by their labor, beautiful matched pairs pulling those bobsleds. The work horses—ones with huge legs, massive hooves sized like hairy bushel baskets—were gentle beasts that were then housed in our cow barn, perhaps four or five teams, harnessed, watered, fed grain and hay for their labors. They rested in the warm cow barn until the milk was driven to town to be processed, cans cleaned and trucked back to our farm.

Hours later, some of the men would go to town on those trucks and return drunk, so drunk that only the horses had the sense to get them back home. I recall seeing those teams head north, the sun setting, the cobalt skies, beautiful crystal white fields and those horses taking their men home. Some men were lying flat on those old bear rugs, sleeping it off, the harness bells ringing, horses snorting to get back home.

Spotsie

"Someone's in the waiting room complaining of back pain," announced my secretary Michele. It was on a Thursday afternoon when no one was scheduled. She added, "He simply walked in, said you'd know him. His name is Spotsie." *Who doesn't know Spotsie?"* I thought. My secretary added, "There's a pharmaceutical representative who walked in ahead of the patient. Do you wish to see him as well?"

"Sure," I said, but before I could finish signing my charts, Michele rushed in: "Spotsie's collapsed onto the Rep's lap. Hurry"

There lay Spotsie, almost dead. The young rep attempted to hold him from injury as Spotsie slid-off his lap onto the floor. As he lay there, I examined him. His blood pressure was extremely low and his pulse thready. The young Rep, "I didn't do a thing to him, (as if defending himself), he simply fell over into my lap."

I sent Michele to the ER for a stretcher, and then the three of us lifted him and moved Spotsie to the ER. He continued to have searing back pain. Although I had never before examined him, I was fairly sure that he was having an acute rupture of an Abdominal Aortic Aneurysm (AAA). He was quickly assessed, and noted to have a large pulsatile mass in his abdomen. This clinically clinched the diagnosis, although there were other numerous finding that pointed to that acute process. Spotsie was whisked off to surgery.

As a post note, I would see Spotsie again but never that pharmaceutical "Rep." Apparently this had been his first day on the job and having Spotsie collapse onto his lap had been a bit too much for his constitution.

Only someone as lucky as Spotsie could manage to survive from that condition. As a diagnosis, AAA had greater than fifty percent patient mortality.

When growing up on the farm, Spotsie had been our neighbor. Along with his sister and a reclusive brother they had operated a hundred acre farm. Their lands were of exceptionally good, dark loam, an excellent farm on which he managed to do as little work as possible. Oh, he drank plenty and always had a fun way about him, a jolly man, even in his later years. He worked just enough to supply himself with beer and liquor.

I was fifteen when I first met him, or perhaps when he formally met me. During those years, our dad had rented their farm. I had been working one of his large fields, discing and tilling the soil the day when Spotsie brought out a cold bottle of Ballentine Ale. He walked out through the fields about 7 a.m.; "You thirsty?" he asked. "Drink-up then," as we clicked bottles. I had been driving the tractor for a couple of hours, preparing the rich soil for the planting of corn that day. It was hot dusty work. It was my first cold ale at that early hour, and it tasted so good; I had an early start at life that day. As a fifteen year old, it was my first buzz—though short, while driving that tractor over that rough sod in an open field.

Spotsie was always a character. He spoke in a manner similar to Peter Lorie, that nasal flat mixed dialect of English and Slovak. Their last name was a homonym assigned to their family at Ellis Island. We nicknamed his sister "Scooter" because of the manner in which she walked through the hay fields, wearing a dress and always with knee-high rubber boots. Fearful for her cats or attempting to find her odd brother John, who hid himself most days from the world; she would walk those fields of thick, tall timothy grass searching for both. Many of the hay fields were a growth of plants taller than Scooter's height, so from yards away and on a tractor, she appeared to be riding a scooter rather than actually walking through the fields. "Scooter" was a different type individual with continued Old-World manners, but kind, very shy, and spoke in a similar monotone, again a mix of Slovak/English, similar to Peter Lorre: almost a singsong way of speech, always with a hand to her mouth that further muffled her words.

Her brother John was a spooky fellow; he never wished to be seen. He'd run into the barn or house or hide in the tall

197

grass. Once my brother Tom and I climbed into the hayloft of their cow barn. It was mostly empty and dark, a large cavernous mow. It was on this floor above the stable where we met John, cowering in a corner. As we froze, he dashed at us, as if he would knock us both down. Instead he scurried past, and like a firefighter, he slid down the makeshift ladder and ran out into the fields. We were shaken by this first meeting; Spotsie insisted that John was harmless, stated that he had had a head injury during the First World War. We would never trust John, and we always made plenty of noise before entering any building, to give him time to run away.

Later in the season we put the hay into bales. These large heavy hay bales would lie in the hay field until the next day and then be placed onto a truck. On a few occasions, these bales would be found the following mornings, piled, shaped like an igloo with a small opening made by Spotsie. It was a love shack, where he and his girl friend would sleep after a night of drinking. He always claimed that it was "cooler" there than in the farmhouse, especially on those hot July nights. However, the truth was Scooter would not allow them into the house.

Spotsie became increasingly a character as he aged, helping my brother Tom with the farm, with light chores, driving tractors, raking hay and then drinking most nights away. He was a tough rugged "bird," survived a ruptured aortic aneurism and the extremes of a surgical vascular graft, then lived for many years afterwards.

Sister Jean Baptist

Perhaps the thing I remember most were the sounds from her movements, the contact of starch on starch. With a quick turn of her head, the wide white bib against her starched collar gave her very distinctive sounds. The movement of her wooden rosary beads strung along the side of her flowing habit, combined to give those muffled sounds to the apparel she wore with distinction.

Sister Jean Baptist was my great aunt, born as Margaret Burns, one of seven siblings, offspring of my Great Grandfather, John Burns. Sister Jean was educated as a teacher, then at the age of forty-one entered the Novitiate to become a Nun in the Order of The Sisters of St. Joseph. She, like her sister aunt Kate, was someone that commanded considerable respect and coming home to what had been her father's farm, she expected things be accomplished: lawns manicured, the weeds clipped, and her nephew's children doing well. It was expected that the five of mom's children be accomplished: whether at piano, diligent in our studies, exhibit discipline and respect.

Her trips back home to where she was born, the farm where her father toiled and died, where the hardships of nineteenth century farm-life trained and shaped her for her resolve in her Faith. These factors no doubt lead her to the demands of her religious order. Her visits were twice a year, summer and winter. It was a long trek for those nuns: commuter rail from Long Island to NYC, then the NY Central to the whistle stop at Little Falls.

Mom would drive us to the station in the old black '39 Chevy to greet the two, as they stepped off that olive green Pullman. In those days a nun could never travel alone; it was an odd scene, a farmer's wife driving two nuns from the train. Perhaps, it was simply an embarrassment of my own, my social discomfort at this scene. I felt, God forbid someone see me, helping the nuns, carrying their baggage from the depot.

I was enrolled in a Catholic school and knew of the hurt I felt when sitting on our school bus and hearing other kids castigate the nuns, mocking their Habits. Well, I never had the courage to publicly stand up for those dedicated women that gave their lives to their students and their commitment to God.

Similarly with my family at the train station, I was uneasy until the nuns arrived at our farm; a place far away from society, a safe place for me to show my due respect to these dedicated women. Perhaps, I had a sense of owning-up to having a great-aunt that had the commitment to be different, someone that could stand apart with pride. Everyone looked forward to their visits, but I wouldn't feel comfortable until the two nuns were packed into our old car and driven to the farm. Even now, I'm ashamed of admitting it.

Sister Jean loved being back home. One could easily notice her more relaxed manner, loving her presence on the land that her father had worked. Our mom would work to make our house special, bake special meals, utilized our best china and the Irish crystal for our table. Of course, my four siblings and I would have to be on our best behavior. Gone were our old clothes. We sat at the dining room table for most of our meals, dressed in our Sunday best, our hands and faces scrubbed. Everything changed when the religious visited our farm. In spite of these minor impositions, these nuns quietly taught us about commitment, and showed us their human side. We heard them laugh, and I'm sure they cried at times as they reminisced, or discussed our dad's alcohol problem. We never had the opportunity to delve into their previous lives, why and how they chose their unusual path through life, all in the name of God.

On one winter visit, our aunt had a nun from Brooklyn accompany her. This nun had never been on a farm, never experienced snow as deep as it would become, piled-high as in our north country. Sister Helen insisted on sledding with us, on the hard- packed snowy road. Her laughter filled that narrow country venue as we navigated the hills, the curves, on the ice and snow. We never imagined seeing a nun from New York City wearing her habit, my sister's snow pants, with makeshift galoshes, earmuffs, mittens, scarf and enjoying this simple winter sport.

Our Dad would block off our hilly country road on certain days and together with our uncle Ed, stop what little traffic there was. Then dad with the old Chevy would pull us on our sleds—sleds in tow and drive to the highest point. He in turn would hold up traffic until we rode those sleds to where Uncle Ed was stationed. Then four or five sleds would race down that hard-packed snow covered road, assured that no traffic could spoil our fun. The nun from Brooklyn became a kid again, someone who let her humanity show. I suppose I was probably ten years old but remembered the joy of riding that sled, on a snowy road, racing a nun to the finish line.

Sister Helen came several times to our farm, and always engaged the country life. In the summer she fed the young calves their bottles of milk, worked side by side in the hay fields, always wore her proper Habit, but with one difference, in that hot dry, dusty hayfield, she left off its starched white collar and bib, as Sister rolled up her sleeves.

Those were great fun filled days, and what past stress the family had had, was cleared from our daily life, and we could be kids again.

In Their Vale of Tears

November

November—it's always been a cloudy, cool, unpredictable month. Many of my uncles and aunts, elders of our family had passed in late Fall. November for me has always carried a hallmark of a dying season, a month when all the efforts of spring and summer oozed into Mother Earth.

I wasn't on call that night. It was my one night off that week, and I was glad because the weather forecast had threats of early winter weather. Reports were unsure if the predicted early snow might turn into rain. As I walked our dog, the air was cold and raw; the first drops of the icy rain pelted my face. Soon it was freezing on my glasses, and then suddenly the road I walked upon was slick.

Back in our warm home, our dog tried in vain to shake off the frozen droplets from his hair. I peered out across the valley, made note of the vast, long line of red brake lights from the stalled vehicles on the Interstate. Later the call came from the ER. The nurse apologized, "Please, Doctor, could you possibly venture in to help? There's been a multiple car accident on the Interstate, a terrible pileup. We will surely need extra help; many people have been reported injured. They're having difficulty getting to the victims because of the icy weather." Our small rural hospital was only a three-mile drive from our house. The nurse knew I'd be there.

As I drove across the black ice, I could easily understand the hazards that the weather posed that night. Other than myself, there were no other cars on that stretch of roadway to the Emergency Room. The icing conditions challenged even the most experienced driver; our four-lane road was all but abandoned. The only stability was to have the two right tires of the vehicle ride off the road surface and onto the grassy shoulder. Since my attempts to gain the hill road over the Gorge View turned out to be impossible, I elected to try the old river road that skirts the hills. This old road had wide, graveled shoulders that allowed for some added traction. As I reached the town, the streets there had been both salted and sanded. One would never suspect the problems that existed out in the countryside.

At the ER, several victims had already been brought in. These were less injured individuals: some fractures or minor lacerations. Personnel from the scene noted that many more were critically injured; however, most remained trapped in their wrecked vehicles.

The first patients I saw were a husband and wife. Both were in shock, both cold and shivering; however, neither demonstrated any external injury. Both were drenched, sobbing, as they sat together on a single gurney with a lost, gaunt look. I tried to speak with them, but they were distant, their emptiness filling the room. As it turned out, no one could reach their deep sorrow.

His spouse was totally unable to speak, shivering from the cold, trembling from their terrible fears. As the nurses worked their cold, wet clothes off and wrapped them both with warmed blankets, the husband was the first to utter their loss. "The kids, no one could find our kids."

In that dark roadway as they climbed out of their wrecked auto, they could not locate their two children. The children had been asleep in the rear of their vehicle. In those few, elongated seconds, an eternity for any parent, their car spun out of control, smashed by other spinning cars, and when it all stopped, their two innocent kids were missing. They had tried to walk about the icy wrecks, the ice covered cars—the road so slippery that at times they needed to crawl—calling out their children's names, but they heard only silence. After all that terrible noise, now there was only silence. "Where are our children?" the husband pleaded in a weak, desperate voice. "We were told they maybe here." That's why they were at the ER. "Where are our kids?" he pleaded.

However, no small, scared kids were brought in that night—only two lifeless, tiny bodies. That night these two people became parents no more. That November night their sadness became exponential. Their lives forever hollowed and emptied. My faint words were unable to reach their deep, deep pain.

I never understood how they could ever live through another November. November—a month that comes every year.

A Mother's Grief

"You killed him! You killed him, you son-of-a-bitch," she shouted as she lunged at me. She repeated over and over, "You killed him," and she grabbed at my lapels. "Where is he?" she threatened. Pulling her person onto me, she kept saying, "You killed him." With tears streaming down her face, her rage was unrelenting. No one had ever attacked me in this manner. I'm sure if she had had a weapon she would have used it. Nurses attempted to hold her off as she pounded on my chest. "You killed him, you son-of-a- bitch!" I couldn't believe this woman was accusing me of such treachery. I didn't know who she was but assumed she was the mother who came seemingly out of the blue into the restricted space of our Emergency Department. Using her clenched fist, she hammered at my chest. As I grabbed her forearms, I could see her slowly lose her strength, as if now totally spent, and in a slow motion she collapsed into the arms of two nurses who had tried to restrain her. Her voice lost its tenor as she sort of slid to the floor. I was taken aback, shaken by her violence, her intent, her grief, and by this sad, tragic day.

It happened in the hot, dog days of August; we had ninety degree humid days all week long. The nights were so sticky, without a breeze and with little rest. The day should have been too hot for anyone to be outside, except, that is, for our youth, teenagers out catching a breeze.

It was in this setting, that humid afternoon, when the nurse called and asked if I could oblige them to "pronounce" a traffic victim. This was not unusual. The Emergency Department, (ER), at that time had no full-time doctor present. In those days there was a private staff physician assigned to the ER to "cover" any emergencies that entered while maintaining his individual "practice." I was not on call, but the nurses knew that I was available, and why disturb a doctor outside of the hospital for a DOA? Many times when someone entered (already dead on arrival), there would be a post-mortem directed by the Coroner. Nurses would need a physician to officially "pronounce" that the patient was dead when the body was received at the ER and then sent onto to the morgue.

"Sure," I said, and sauntered over; no need to rush for the dead. Little did I know what I had in store for myself. The ER was just down the hall from my office. In the back exam room of our ER, lying very still on a gurney, was the victim in a body bag. The charge nurse read the police statement that told of the particulars, described the remnants of his motorcycle, told of the estimated speed he was traveling, the distance to the tree, and then the nurse added, "You don't really need to pull the cover off."

I looked at her puzzled, and then paused, "But I do need to." I could see the reluctance on her face. Gently, I pulled the zipper slowly back, and there lay a young, once handsome teenager, still wearing his black helmet, a helmet now split wide apart over the crown, his blond wavy hair slightly stained with blood. What at first looked like his part down the middle, instead was a gross fracture of his calvarium, his young head split wide into the helmet. After what I had seen in my training, I thought I'd seen it all, but this indeed was a shock. "Get him to the morgue. Let only the pathologist see this lad."

It was all too tragic. I dare not let anyone have this lasting image of a loved one. Seeing such deformity, they would be haunted forever. Quickly zipping the cover closed, I grabbed the end of the gurney, and we headed to the morgue by way of the elevator across the hallway. Out of the corner of my eye, down the hall I noticed this distraught woman barging through the doors, screaming, "Where is he?" just as the elevator opened. The nurse rushed to halt the mother while I pushed the gurney in and pushed down for the Basement and then stepped back into the hallway. That's when she grabbed me. With the untimely death of her son and the intensity of her loss, this mother was unable to contain her overpowering grief, her outright rage. No one would ever forget her headlong accusations toward me on that hot, sizzling day in August years ago. No one could ever forget the intensity of that mother's grief.

Andrew

In a small town, most individuals are recognized for where they live, where they work or how they're perceived. Everyone is known in some fashion or another.

Andrew had not been a patient of mine, although I had known of him for years: knew of his family—a quiet integral family—knew that they were well respected, hard working, and very successful in business. He was easily recognized, tall and handsome. His wife was a very classy woman as well. I remember receiving a call from her during the Christmas season when my office was closed for patient visits. I was making rounds on my in-house patients when she paged me through the hospital operator. She explained that their doctor was away and asked if I would see her husband. From the tone of her concern, this was someone I should definitely examine. Frequently, I made myself available on holidays and weekends for those who could not wait for an appointment. She added her appreciation, stating that he was quite ill and she was worried about him. It was the day before the New Year.

When I met him outside my office, he was pale and looked worried; he thanked me for my consideration. I ushered them both into the office. He explained that they had just returned from afar and were exhausted from travels and the strain from burying his younger brother in another state. His wife spoke up, adding: "This is his second sibling we have buried in as many years." However, she added, "His ninety-five year old father is alive and doing well." She further added the irony, "He smokes and drinks every day and is healthy as a horse."

As I examined the man, he appeared older than I had imagined his age. He had a moderate fever, productive cough, with recent streaks of blood after hard coughing spasms. On auscultation, his lungs were congested, with rhonchi and rales throughout, especially his right lung. He had shoddy nodes at the base of his neck. Generally, he was a worry for any physician. I thought he should be admitted to the hospital; however, he refused, adding that he had a family get-together that evening and needed to be there. After all, it was New Year's Eve. I sent him for an X-ray and told him I would look at it later, after attending my other patients in the hospital. As I handed him a supply of an antibiotic, he asked me to call him later, after I reviewed his chest X-ray. I told him that I would. However, he added, "I want to know the results tonight. No matter what it shows, I need to know ... tonight." I promised I would call him.

After I finished making 'rounds' on my many hospital patients, I reviewed his chest film. I was struck by the extent of the man's pathology. His lungs demonstrated a mass that, no doubt, was suspect for a malignancy and most likely causing an obstructing pneumonia. His words echoed in my mind: "Call me tonight, no matter what." Now here was my dilemma: should I call him on the last day of his last 'healthy' year? Or do I wait to tell him tomorrow, the first day of his new but last year on Earth?

What would you have done?

I picked up the phone. "Andrew, this is Dr. Burns. I need to see you the first thing in the morning."

"Why would I need to see you on New Year's Day?"

"Well, your X-ray shows a definite pneumonia, perhaps an obstructing infection. I will need to follow-up on that."

"Yes sir," then a pause ... with dead silence. "It's serious, isn't it," he added as if he already knew. "Do I need a CT scan?"

"You'll need that plus a bronchoscopy in the coming week. I'll go ahead and make those arrangements if you would like me too."

"Yes, go ahead," he fumbled a bit, but continued: "Thanks ... thanks for calling." Then there was another pause ... as if I knew what he thought ... perhaps stating silently, *"I wish I hadn't asked the doctor to call."* He then added, "Happy New Year."

I wished him good health in the coming New Year, despite the awareness of his dreaded pathology.

211

Trudy

At first I hadn't recognized her, though it had been a number of years since I'd last seen her. Still the woman had lost a lot. Of course, over the past few days she hadn't been feeling well. Complaining of a cough, fever, and weakness, the woman looked pale, older than her sixty-one years, plus she looked worried and worn.

She and her husband had recently moved back into her dad's lakeside cabin, now winterized. They moved from Southern California after he retired from the military. They both longed to spend their senior years nestled in the foothills of the Adirondack Mountains, to relive their youthful memories.

She stated that she hadn't felt well since the move several weeks ago. As the autumn weather set in, Trudy felt it was her response to the cold, damp cottage that made her feel ill. Years ago Trudy had been an acquaintance and a patient. A healthy vibrant woman, full of talent, attractive--my mind tried to imagine how she appeared the last time I had seen her. As I listened to her describe her complaints, my mind scanned for details of how the passing years had mistreated her. I noted the nicotine stained fingers and the palpable nodes felt at the base of her neck. In listening to her lungs, I noted the wet rales, the diminished breath sounds on the right. Few entities came to mind, and all were serious.

As I examined her, she then told me of her inability to accept my parting advice. As I tried recall what that might have been, she added, "I couldn't stop smoking." Almost cruelly I added—pointedly: "No, you wouldn't stop smoking." Then I continued: "Trudy, everyone stops smoking at some point, some have to wait until they die." On this night I had made my third trip back to the hospital to admit yet another sick patient. It was late, almost midnight; I was tired after a sixteen-hour day, with little patience for excuses, but I regretted adding that last point as soon as I had said it.

Walking over to the X-ray Department to view her films, I passed Trudy being wheeled by the technician into the hallway. Jamming the large radiographs into the lighted viewing box always commands the moment, yet what I saw in her lung x-ray would distract most. As Trudy sat in the nearby hall, in a wheelchair, a tube of additional oxygen at her nose, I knew she could see what I was doing through the opened doorway. As I looked over the film of her lungs, under my breath I mumbled: *"I told you, damn it. I told you to stop smoking!"*

I then consciously moved slightly—to block any possibility of her seeing that awful chest X-ray. Silly, but I didn't want her to see her terrible pathology, no not this night. I didn't want her to see the pneumonia filling her right lung, to view the large malignant tumor that distorted that lung, the metastatic nodes that matted the base of her neck.

Trudy surely would now, all too soon, stop smoking.

The Nature of Life

Mom's Later Years

My mother, Louise, survived a decade after that morning when I had inserted a pacemaker into her heart. Mom continued to stay at the farm, a place where she had lived since her marriage in 1932. Mom was reared in a small city—certainly not versed in the hardships of rural life. Married at twenty-three years of age, she came to the farm where our dad's parents and his aunt Kate lived; all were elderly and compromised with various forms of heart disease. All in this generation would die at the farmhouse over the next 15 years. Besides raising five children, Mom cared for her in-laws: she was the nurse for both kids and old folks alike. Our great aunt would be the last of that generation to die in the house; however, Mom gave all these folks terminal care as they became increasingly bedridden in the farmhouse.

Our mother was a great cook and she could stretch a meal to include two or more unplanned dinner guests. Her meals fed our many friends, relatives, and the hired men that worked the fields. Twice, in the late summer and into the fall, handful of neighbors came for a few days to help with harvesting grains as well as clearing fields filled with corn for silage. The only pay they received was Mom's noon-time meal—it was a feast that included generous amounts of roast beef roast beef, mashed potatoes and gravy, home-made breads and multiple berry pies. Neighboring farmers ate like there were no tomorrows; most would praise her for her delicious feasts.

Mom was a diverse woman—she could drive a tractor in hayfields, under the hot dry sun, as dad worked to load the wagon; yet, still cooked our meals, mended our worn clothes, completed the laundry, canned or froze vegetables, made her own bread, her special pork sausage and on occasions made her own butter. Whatever it would take, Mom could give her all.

In her lifetime she had two terrible trying days: the first occasion was when she found her son, Jack, pinned under the weight of that heavy farm tractor. Weeks and months would pass as mom nursed her son Jack back from a crippled right hip, an amputated right leg, back to a functioning teenager, however, both Jack and his mother carried enough psychological trauma to last two or three lifetimes.

The second occasion was when she suddenly found the Love of her life dead—Dad's heart had given out, years after Mom's efforts that striped Dad from his major addiction—alcohol abuse. I'm sure that Mom's persistent prayers converted Dad from a hard-core drunk into a respectable spouse and father. In truth, she experienced enough pain through her years for ten women; however, her daily joys expressed through her five children and her strong faith in her God buoyed her through her long life.

For the most part Mom was a happy person who carried out her duties with proficiency. We had many, many guests stay at the farm: relatives from New Jersey and New York City. Distant cousins of our Dad's would show-up unannounced, whole families would move in for a week or more, sometimes in the dead of the night, in the summers, or even in the winter months.

Occasionally the Emeritus Dean of Fordham University would arrive (always with an established notice). He was my Dad's distant cousin, an elderly Jesuit who loved to stay a couple of nights at our farm and indulge himself in the rural setting, and of course Mom's special meals. On one visit he brought along the Assistant Surgeon General of the United States. Since I was only ten years old at the time, I had expected someone wearing a military uniform.

In her later years, Mom fell and fractured her hip on an evening when our young daughter was staying overnight with her. Mom insisted on making popcorn that night, but the corn kernels were kept high in a kitchen cupboard that required her to stand on a chair to reach them. She did reach her goal, but in turning to step off the chair, she had a mighty fall onto the kitchen linoleum. It's always been a lingering question: Did she break her hip by twisting on that chair, snapping the bone, and then fall or by falling first onto the floor?

My daughter called me stating that Gram had fallen and could not get up. My mom was alert but stated her one hip had considerable pain. Mom kept asking our daughter to give her increasing spoonfuls of brandy, and Marie obliged. "Gram just keeps asking for more brandy," she related on the phone.

I asked my daughter, "On that one painful leg where do Gram's toes point? Where are those toes pointed?"

Marie said, "Her toes are pointed at the doorway; they're pointed outward, away from the other foot." Her descriptions were a definite sign of a fractured hip. I told her to call an ambulance but first to call her Uncle Tom (who lived nearby). I told Marie that I would meet them both at the ER.

Post-operatively, Mom did very well. At eighty years of age, she recovered well from her hip trauma and eventually returned to the farmhouse to live. But a few years year later, when Mom was eighty-five and frail, she lived alone, with help during the day. However, her assistants were not family, and Mom resisted their care. Furthermore, she would not live with her children in their homes. Yes, sometimes for a short week or two but never longer.

One terrible winter day in a full-blown blizzard, she required hospitalization because of a failed pacemaker battery. I made a unilateral decision that she could no longer stay in that fourteen-room farmhouse by herself. Her sister Mary, a couple of years older, required assistance as well. So I conspired to move them together and have twenty-four hour care for both in Aunt Mary's home, the house in which they were both born and raised.

We had the entire first floor cleaned and painted, floors sanded and polished, new linoleum in kitchen--the place looked like a million bucks. One slept in the parlor and the other slept in the living room. There was a roomy kitchen and a large dinning room. I was quite happy with this move, more so than my two sisters who objected bitterly about these living arrangements. Mom's daughters had promised her that she would live at the farm until her death. A wonderful promise; however, living miles from neighbors on roads that winter snows frequently made impassable, Mom became increasingly isolated. She worried about all sorts of problems that only remotely existed, such as strangers breaking into her home. She became paranoid over possible threats, however remote. Her loneliness was compounded by the howling winter winds that made matters worse. And so when she became hospitalized, I forced the issue into a compromise, a resolution: Aunt Mary and my mother would live together, with assistants for their care.

They lived together for three years. We were on Cape Cod, the day when my brother called relating that Mom had been hospitalized. "She's bleeding badly," Tom noted. He said that Mom had already been transfused with eight-units of packed* red blood cells, a significant GI bleed. I drove the five hours, speaking with her physician along the way and arrived about 5 p.m. By now, several more units of blood had been given, but Mom continued to hemorrhage. Her situation was becoming grave; all prior tests had failed to specify the exact site where the bleeding occurred.

When I arrived, Mom was lying on a hard-surfaced nuclear scanning table. She was uncomfortable, extremely frail and worried: an IV in one arm for fluids and blood transfusing into a vein in the other arm. She was pitifully scared—uncertain of so many issues and not understanding what was "going on. Her hands were cold and trembling as I held them. I placed a few more "warmed" blankets over her. I knew she was pleased that I was at her side. "David," she said, "I can't go on like this."

She was correct. "I know," I told her. Mom was in the process of a nuclear scan that would hope to uncover where the pathological bleed was in her abdomen. I didn't feel that the test would be beneficial—it simply delayed the inevitable, the fact that mom was still hemorrhaging and needed a surgeon to tie-off the leaking artery. Certainly, statistics would point that a single diverticulum would account for this significant

---

* <u>Packed cells</u>: *blood for transfusion, consisting of mostly red blood cells*

bleed. Already, I had decided that she needed to be taken to surgery and soon. On a quick exam, her belly was soft with exaggerated bowel sounds, and bright red blood stained her sheets. "I'll speak with the doctor and be right back."

By now 'too many' units had been transfused, with no attempt to intervene, and further, it was clear to me that Mom needed to have an exploratory operation, a laparotomy, to find the bleeding's source and to surgically tie-off that artery.

Unfortunately, laparoscopic surgery was not yet in place at the community hospital, and an abdominal surgery was required to find the wayward diverticulum. Physicians were reluctant to operate, even with my okay. The situation was like the old cliché: making an operative decision on an eighty-eight year old woman with a GI bled was like being between a rock and a hard place. There was no easy answer. However, all things considered, with her blood loss significant, there was little else that could be accomplished by waiting further. I pressed the surgeons to operate that evening. There were no clear options other than transferring her to a Medical Center and approaching the bleeding artery by way of an angiogram to interventional clot-off procedure of that one small artery. This method, however, was also wrought with major complications, especially in an octogenarian.

I was at her side that evening when Mom lay on the stretcher before entering the surgical suite. I held her hand, warmer now but still with a faint tremor. "I don't think I can go through this," she told me. Was she was referring to her survival or were her concerns more profound—the worry about death, her journey beyond? Although the operation clearly posed significant risks, I felt she referred to her last hours, her final demise, passing beyond her long life of ups and downs. Perhaps it was her way of saying that she was indeed afraid of what lay ahead. "I've never had an operation, never been this weak," Mom went on.

I said, "You're eighty-eight and we can't simply let your blood drain away. That artery must be sewn shut, Mom. There's no worry about cancer; it's a diverticulum that's bleeding."

"Glory be," she replied. "David, I don't believe I'll make it." I knew with those last words that we both doubted her survival. We held on to each other; hand in hand, in a tightened grip.

It was sad standing along side her stretcher outside the surgical suite of the community hospital, both silently wondering similar thoughts: Are these Mom's last hours? I held her hands and prayed, surmising that Mom's time had indeed run out. It was true that this frail woman would likely die, something I did not wish to precipitate. However, surgery was a chance that needed to be taken, and soon. In as much as I did not wish to have her die, I knew if God would, this day take her, then that was okay. Sad as her death would be for me, it was okay.

I did not scrub-in with the surgeon; however, I had actually considered it. I saw her in recovery, after the sixty-minute operation, sleepy but alert enough to answer my inquiries appropriately. Mom was comfortable throughout the night, awake at times, but she did have a good rest.

First thing the next morning when I saw her, I knew from looking at her from the nurses' station that she had had a stroke, probably minutes before I arrived. Her breathing pattern became exaggerated—a constant pattern of hyperventilation—alternating with erratic patterns of breathing. I recognized the pathological pattern of Biot's Breathing, abnormal breathing cycles indicative of a mortal brain stem infarct, just as her CT scan would later demonstrate. Mom was unresponsive and in a deep coma. She would never again awaken in this world.

I felt both saddened and relieved. This was mom's "blessed" moment in which to die peacefully, in no pain and with no fears. I believe that this was exactly what Mom had feared, when she said the day before, "David, I can't go through this." However, she did just what all of us will do, one way or another—when we die we all will face the consequences. Our mother died quietly a few hours later, with her first-born, my brother Jack, at her side.

Louise, the matriarch of the family, my mother, a woman of exceptional Faith in God, faith in life, and faith in her children, died after eighty-eight years.

Uncovering a Killer

To uncover occult heart disease requires a doctor's diligence as well as an astute patient or his spouse. The majority of "younger" people that die suddenly have a ruptured plaque within the wall of an artery that is only 40% or 50% impinging on the blood flow, but an acute clot can form to completely occlude that blood vessel. That is when the muscle of that portion of ones heart becomes scar tissue.

Rarely have patients come to a doctor's office to say they have a problem with their heart; rather they may feel anxious, may feel fatigue or they may simply act 'different' to their spouse. Most individuals with serious Coronary Artery Disease have very few complaints and those that feel a 'pain' in their chest or a sensation of aches in their neck or arms can be thankful ... for that red flag will bring them to a doctor. Frequently a physician needs to "read between the lines" or listen closely to the brief words from a patient's spouse. I know because I have missed disease in some stoic individuals, "fooled" by a few middle age patients that "breezed" through their exercise stress test but would go on to have a heart attack. A few have had sudden death.

My strongest suit in medicine was finding heart disease in patients. It was challenging. Some individuals would come to the office because they were worried. My job was to uncover the disease or to make sure they didn't have it. Ischemic heart disease, even in today's standards, continues to be widespread and silent: almost 40% die before a diagnosis is made.

When I finished my Internal Medicine training, few cardiologists were aggressive in their approach to patients with an acute heart attack. Some doctors would even withhold the use of nitroglycerin and only give morphine and oxygen. It wasn't until the mid-seventies when catheterizations were cautiously considered in the acute phase of a heart attack and it was even later, in the early 1980's, before stents were considered as an early interventional tool during the acute heart attack.

The last patient I ever treated conservatively was someone who claimed to have little need for a doctor. His wife 'dragged' him into my office where he described vague shortness of breath only while running long distance. The man was physically fit, and I had to persuade him to take a stress test. Sadly, he dropped dead a few days later before his scheduled test—died while sitting at his desk. From that point on, any suspected heart patient would under-go a stress test within hours, perhaps the same day, if they agreed.

Our office uncovered some startling findings: One man who thought he was well enough to hike through the mountainous highlands and loved to hunt in the autumn; however, his wife was concerned about him trudging about the Adirondack Mountains alone. "There's nothing wrong with me," he firmly stated. But he agreed to prove it by undergo a stress test. In the first few minutes of walking on the treadmill, he collapsed in a fatal arrhythmia: ventricular fibrillation. He was immediately resuscitated and underwent a catheterization that pointed out a critical lesion blocking his left main artery. He was the first of many patients who surprisingly failed at their exercise test, only to live a longer life.

Heart Break

I was never able to lie on my son's bed again, not after that fateful evening. Months, even years after, I couldn't even sit there. The last time lying on that bed I was so sick, shamefully ill, vomiting, with diarrhea, and a weakness so profound that I was unable to raise my head off the pillow. That day I was no longer a doctor, no, I had become, like it or not, a patient. My role had suddenly reversed. I was physically and psychologically thrown to the other end of the stethoscope.

I had cared for very ill patients, people so sick that death could come quickly—at the next moment. I had many individuals flown to University Medical Centers, yet even with the best of care, patients die. However, for some Godforsaken reason I was spared—in spite of a critically low blood pressure, in spite of a failing heart, in spite of serious arrhythmia—I survived.

I came home in pieces, that's for sure, a part here and a part there. To become critically ill is a crushing experience; it tears one down to an elemental level, like being flung into a thousand pieces. Then comes the trick, like any puzzle, patients need to be built back whole; from a person who had been critically ill, they will never again be the same. There is the chance to be better, a chance to be worse, but never the same.

Poetic references to the beating organ in ones chest takes on many different meanings: you can hold someone in your heart or take matters to heart or have someone steal your heart or have heartfelt desires, even lose heart. However, for me, mine was simply heartbreak. For on this day I lost my health, my practice of medicine, and much of my own heart's muscle. I was indeed heart-broken.

Heart disease had been a killer for my father as well as for great Aunts and Uncles. Many died when they were in there forties while a few passed-on when they were in their late thirties. I was always cognizant of that family history although I had never smoked, never had elevated cholesterol, never had hypertension, and was not overweight or prone to diabetes. However, I did have a heart attack; one severe enough that I came very close to dying.

Looking back I could run up three or four flights of stairs at the hospital, hurrying to a resuscitation or just for exercise or simply to save time by not waiting for an elevator—always in a hurry with a full busy schedule. Periodically I would notice the slightest tightness in my chest while running up those stairs. By this time in my life I did have asthma and had chronic bronchitis from an early age. I had used various inhalers with theophylline for several years. Furthermore, I had a cardiologist perform a stress test each year; and with each test, I had great exercise tolerance and could easily advance through stage four or even through stage five of the cardiac stress test without shortness of breath and very little change noted on my cardiogram (ECG).

Several months before my near-fatal event, I had had that year's Stress Test. I thought it showed more than minimal changes although the test demonstrated only "nonspecific ST & T wave changes," a term that doctors use to indicate suggestive changes in an ECG, changes that are not "positive" for anything but changes nevertheless. It's difficult for anyone to firmly label this finding as ischemia, and the cardiologist felt that in lieu of the degree of work measured through my efforts on the treadmill, the changes were irrelevant. I argued the point with him, but he refused to concern himself about the nonspecific changes, and in due respect, he was likely correct.

As for myself, I began to notice an increasing sense of fatigue and evident pallor at the end of my long workday, doing work that I thoroughly enjoyed. These infrequent episodes of chest tightness, though brief, did concern me. Further, I began to develop rare bouts with scotoma, a broken glass visual effect that is most likely associated with migraine headaches. Mine were always associated with overwork and never accompanied by a headache.

With such subtleties engrained in my mind, I wondered if, despite a normal stress test, I, too, could have occult disease. I placed myself on diltiazem (a calcium channel blocking agent), a drug taken as a test to see if this would lessen the visual scotoma and improve my over-all energy. Of course, I spoke with the cardiologist about this therapy. He thought it was premature to start. However, taking this therapy daily, I did notice a change for the better. I had increased abilities and no further scotoma.

Then one day while seeing patients in the office, I experienced waves of nausea, shortly accompanied by vigorous cramps. With a number of people yet to be seen, I had to excuse myself and leave for home. For some reason, I felt a very strange sense that this was going to be more than a simple GI "bug," perhaps a prodrome of an exceptional set of circumstances.

I left for home and I walked-by the ER nursing station, one of the staff on evening shift stopped me to ask what was wrong. "You look ghastly," she noted. I replied almost jokingly, "You might see me later at the ER." I was struck by my choice of words: an off-handed comment, not sure why I even uttered it. It was prophetic indeed. The phrase troubled me as I left for home. It was as if someone else had spoken those words.

***

At home I recalled what an ICU staff nurse, Bridget McKinley, had told me earlier: we were kindred spirits, especially in the care of patients, one of the many terrific nurses that worked our ICU, nurses that cared for the very, very sick. One morning, as I was making patient "rounds," long before my own heart problem, Bridget pulled me aside. She spoke of a profound and disturbing dream that she had just experienced; it was more like a nightmare. She described that I was admitted as her patient to ICU, I was gravely ill … she stated that in her dream, "I was dying." As she described the particulars, I could see her deep concern, notice her tears welling as she brought forth this dream, this oracle. However, I dismissed her concerns as being only nonsense, and then reassured her that I was doing fine. Now at home, her words, her graphic descriptions became foremost in my thoughts.

On that fateful day, the day of my own heart attack, arriving home—so sick that I went into my son's bedroom (he was at College). Within a very short time, I could no longer fathom getting up or out of bed, I was that weak. It was an odd thing, as I attempted to diagnosis the situation I was in. Certainly, one cannot be truly rational as one hopes to resolve the situation at hand, to 'play-down' the reality of the condition. Usually, hope begets hope, then further compromises … then only irrational decisions. For myself, as things became worse, I had my wife call for the ambulance. At first she was surprised that I had "given-in" so soon, but I knew I needed IV fluids, if nothing more.

I knew my status was going downhill. That is when I surrendered and became a patient. The reversal of roles is extremely difficult, and I would come to find that a doctor, when ill, is never truly treated as a patient but rather as a sick doctor. When the Emergency Technicians entered the bedroom, I knew them all by name: Andy placed the IV in my arm and started the infusion of fluids immediately. At that point, I was beyond shame. When placed upon their stretcher, I warned them to lower me down the stairs headfirst, but they, of course, had their protocols, and once the stretcher tilted head up, I became semiconscious very quickly. They rotated their approach, and I was carried headfirst down our stairs to the awaiting ambulance.

The ambulance was so warm, almost comfortable. "Please don't use the siren," I pleaded, but the screaming sound rang forth, adding its signature to their concerns in the rush towards the hospital.

The physician working the ER reassured me that all I needed was intravenous fluids and Compazine as he attempted to plicate everyone's concern. I was indeed a sorry sight as my blood pressure continued to hover in the fifties. I insisted an ECG be taken, but the physician asked. "Have you had any chest pain?"

"No, not really," was my reply.

"We'll do some laboratory studies first, and then we'll see." However, again I insisted because I knew by this time that things were far beyond a simple intestinal virus, for my status continued spiraling down. I was so perplexed, accompanied by the need, at least for myself, to find out what the hell was happening.

When the ECG had been completed, I could tell by the technician's facial expressions that there were major changes. "Let's see," I asked, but all I heard were the stretcher wheels unlock and I was rolled immediately into ICU. One nurse quietly stated that I had "changes anteriorly." I knew that was not good news and began to understand the seriousness they expressed in their worried faces.

So started the race to save my heart, to save this man's life. I was now a patient in the Critical Care Unit, a Special Unit that I was technically in charge of. In some respects, I was pleased that I was there and not somewhere else. I trusted the nurses implicitly; our staff was the best. On the other hand, I placed the staff, the nurses and doctors in an ungainly situation. Things were simply too close, our staff, few in numbers, their burden all too great. Some of the other patients in the ICU were my own patients, and I was as sick as they were.

The rumors flew far and wide: *"Dr. Burns was really sick; Dr. Burns was dying."* The rumors did little for the nurses, as well as my own patients in that ICU. My own patients' anxieties heightened as they likely asked themselves, *"Who will take care of me?"*

My wife was now at my side; however, she had a similar "stunned" look that that I had seen on the nurses. I was sure I could read Marcia's thoughts: *"Am I soon to be a widow? Could my husband die this night?"* It seemed that I was more ashamed than worried, although from the looks of concern fixed on everyone's face, it was very clear that I was in the proverbial quicksand. The more one wriggles with sad thoughts, the more consternation that is sucked into ones psyche.

Within minutes, it seemed that every orifice had been invaded, tubes and needles inserted everywhere: in my arms, in the artery at my wrist, oxygen at the nose, a continued flow of urine output measured into a bag, and yet I was told to try and rest. A bedside ultrasound told of a dying heart, its muscles barely contracting, its output barely twenty percent of normal. Dennis, the ultrasound technician stated the results were "good," but his eyes told a whole different story. I slept off and on throughout that night. My wife's presence played an important part as to which Medical Center I would be transported to in the morning.

The sooner a patient is transferred, particularly those in acute heart failure, the better. Medical Centers can do angioplasty or place an assisted pump into an aorta or perhaps even perform surgery if situations become worse. Marcia caught a few winks on an exam table in my office. It was just down the hallway from ICU.

During the night, arrangements had been made to fly me the next morning to Syracuse. Dr. Michael Jastremski, a mentor and a Critical Care Specialist would accompany me even though it was his day off; when he discovered my predicament, he put on his flight suit. Now it was my turn to fly—to be transported as the critically ill patient into that cold, snowy December day. Dr. Mike was all business as the crew entered the ICU. There was little small talk while our staff supplied all the details, medications, plus their hopes and prayers. They transferred me onto the very narrow stretcher needed for this flight as monitors, IVs, arterial lines, and critical fluids were placed safely on board. There was an obvious rush to leave; Dr. Burke stood nearby looking very concerned, his thoughts full of dismay, while the nurses appeared stern, worried, but gave their best; they all knew the terrible odds between success and failure with anyone who had what I had.

The winter weather mimicked the cold hard facts of acute heart failure. Snow squalls gave a chill of reality to all. There was a short ambulance ride to the awaiting chopper and then another transfer into the airship. Everything seemed cold, blustery, and uncertain as the chopper's blades slowly turned. Air traffic control bantered back and forth with the pilot. Dr. Mike, who tried to be patient, tapped his shoe in anxious cadence. Finally, he said aloud, "What's the hold up?" The two doctors knew the space in this small airship was not conducive to attempt a serious resuscitation. Again he called out, "Let's get going." Yet, ten, fifteen or more minutes ticked off as the chopper blades quietly turned, its jet engine idled, and the pilot gestured helplessly with his hands thrown into the air.

The winds kicked up the cold dusty snow as we all waited, waited for clearance, better skies, and a quick road back. The lake effect squalls continued, as the airship rocked, simply sitting on the pad, buffeted by the strong winds. It would be a rough, worrisome ride through those eighty miles.

A hundred yards from the chopper, I noticed my brother Tom sitting in his Oldsmobile. I was sure he also wondered if his brother would ever make it back. I was further saddened by his vigil, by the circumstances, as my tears trickled down my cheeks. I turned away from Mike so he wouldn't see me cry.

Everyone waited impatiently, expecting yet the sudden thrust when the engine roared to full power—it took me by surprise, the swirling snows, the take-off obliterated any visibility. It was like being surrounded in a frozen fog accompanied by the sense of moving straight up. My brother Tom's watch had ended—ended in a whiteout as we headed west, bucking those lake-effect squalls.

The quick flight seemed to take forever. Strong winds and white out gusts almost forced the chopper to land on a couple of occasions, however, we forged on.

Landing at the University Hospital, nurses and doctors were out in the God-forsaken-Syracuse weather as the winds whipped at their white frocks. I was so glad to see Dr. Bob Eich, a learned cardiologist, someone to whom I had referred many of my more complex patients. Bob had an uncanny medical wisdom about him, a sixth sense of sorts, perhaps a quiet knack for being ahead of the 'game' with certain sick individuals.

I was wheeled directly into their Cardiac Unit. Patty, the nurse assigned to my case was encouraging, quick witted: someone that exuded confidence. She stated with kindness: "I know you're a doctor and are close to Dr. Eich, but I'm in charge here, and I'll relate to you what's happening with your heart. Don't worry, you're going to get better." As sick as I was, I found her words important. I would spend more than two weeks in the CCU at Upstate Medical. There were entire blocks of time and even complete days disappeared from my memory, times when I had absolutely no recall.

Medically, I suffered from a "Stunned Myocardium," another term for injured heart muscles that functioned minimally, if at all. In laymen terms—I had acute heart failure. Repeated heart scans and the ECHO, showed very poor cardiac output, the heart's muscle barely contracting. Dr. Eich continued with his encouragement—even though my situation day after day showed little improvement. My dear wife was so strong and supportive. The children all arrived on scene the second day, our oldest, returned from college—home for Christmas.

Most likely the doctors told me of their plans, but one morning, a couple of days after I was transferred there, I was taken into the Catheterization Lab for the doctors' first look at my Coronary Arteries. They were eager to evaluate the anatomy my heart and check the damage that already had occurred; they also worried that my heart had such little reserve at this point, that another ischemic event would certainly be fatal. The Staff would then know if further problems loomed, if other arterial obstructions threatened my survival or how extensive was the disease? Would heart surgery be a forced option? This aggressive and early catheterization was somewhat controversial but something I favored. Due to a recent infarct, pros and cons aside, Dr. Eich wanted to visualize the other arteries of my heart. Even though I can't remember all the details of what happened that morning, I do know that I almost died during the procedure. When the dye was injected, there developed severe spasms of those arteries. My heart rate flipped into a rapid pattern and the weaken heart developed more and more ischemic pain, that much I do recall. I was aware of the "excitement" that occurred as I became semiconscious.

Drugs were injected intravenously to 'break' the spasm, to convert the malignant arrhythmia back into a normal pattern. I do recall the doctors' excitement, the shouting of orders: "Give him more, more." Then as my condition stabilized, the doctors were reluctant to 'fuss' beyond what had been attempted. They halted further studies that day, and I was wheeled directly back to CCU. I was drenched in sweat, as were the physicians who had been in that catheterization room.

The study was aborted without much new information. I believe the procedure caused more problems than it solved. The next few days were a total blank, little or no recall. My wife knew how seriously ill I continued to be because she witnessed my bouts of inappropriate behavior, a giddiness at times, and then tears from the worry. The physicians had a difficult time deciding if my swings of emotions were from emboli (blood clots to the brain) or from being over medicated or simply from the stress. I'm sure it was likely a combination of many factors and the underlying fears that my next heartbeat could be my last.

I've thought often about having been so ill that a person, as my Dad used to say, "Doesn't give a damn whether school keeps or not." I had seen so many people die, those sick or traumatized, die slowly and some all too quickly. It's not that I wanted to pass on, but rather that I was so weakened and psychologically devastated by the extremes of an illness, illness that brought a person close to the edge of dying. I believe many have had thoughts to ask themselves: Why not? Never did I consider post-traumatic stress disorder (PTSD) as a regular component of patients critically ill until I suffered from it myself. This is now recognized all too commonly and treated early.

Eventually, of course, things slowly improved and a week after my first study, another catheterization was performed without any complications. The second study noted only one artery that had serious blockage. My left anterior descending artery of the heart, the artery so named "the artery of Sudden Death," so called because it supplies blood (oxygen) to that part of the heart where many important functions are concentrated: the electrical conduction bundles, the muscle of the anterior wall of the heart, a large portion of the left ventricle.

Fortunately, I survived and was sent home. I would see Dr. Eich weekly for a month. To tell the truth, psychologically

I was a 'basket case.' I had wide swings of emotions. I became much like a recluse. I suffered from shame, the shame of loosing my practice, shame of being a doctor and not preventing this horrendous sequence of events.

Finally at home for weeks I could not meet with anyone without becoming emotional. My response could bring tears, or I might have been giddy for surviving, happy to be home. When I told some friends that I could have died, I silently pondered if I would have the strength, both physically and emotionally, to go through this process, somewhere down the road of life. Besides truly wanting to improve and to return to my former self, return as a doctor to my practice of medicine, I did not want to dwell upon the possibility that my practice, the work I thrived on, work that defined me, had been killing me softly.

Sick patients were the grist that challenged my existence. If I could not practice medicine, I felt I would be lost. Dr. Eich instructed me to take three months off—to walk, read, and have some fun. He would study another stress test before further plans were to be considered. Since his advice seemed reasonable, I started on a strict diet. Even though my cholesterol had been very good, I was switched to margarine and a high fiber diet; in truth I was miserable.

***

Sure Enough Things Got Worse

As the third month rolled around, it became the Ides of March, and as I walked three or four miles each day, I began to notice something new. I began to develop chest pressure. If I stopped walking the symptom abated completely, and if I walked faster it returned. I was so perplexed, disbelieving that my arteries would become narrower so soon. For a couple of days I told no one. As long as I had no symptoms at rest, I would attempt to work through the new symptoms. However, I couldn't do it. I needed to slow down my gait and walk less distance just to be safe. I began denying that which was so obvious. Again, here is the main reason that people die at home, by discounting even the slightest symptoms.

An unusual event occurred one night and to this day I've never put this occurrence into words: About three o'clock in the morning, I awoke with severe chest pain, severe. Awoke with a start and swung out of bed; I sat on the edge of the mattress, wondering what the hell was happening. All the while the pain grew more intense. Suddenly, the entire hallway in our 1790 colonial home began to fill with a peculiar bright light. A light of such odd properties that it appeared to take-up space, like very bright cotton that would fill a jar. Although the door to our bedroom was open, the brightness did not stream into the room; it never entered. Further surprise: there was absolutely no fear on my part over this strange occurrence.

I turned to awaken my wife (she was sound asleep)—my shouts did not awaken her. "Marcie wake up!" still, no response. I reached over to shake her, but as I tried to push on her, she didn't move, and did not hear my words. It was then that I saw myself lying there in bed under the covers, asleep. It was all so freaky. I was viewing my own body, and I for some Godforsaken reason was experiencing a horrible chest pain, on the edge of the bed, yet still in the bed. Even now as I put this very strange awakening in writing, I have a chilling

235

sense about me as I recount that simple remembrance of a night I cannot forget. It remains so very visual in my memory. Going back to that March night, as I gazed at the bed— I saw that both myself and my wife were fast asleep—I slowly turned back, for I could not forget that odd, but intense light. And as I turned towards the hall, the peculiar light source was receding; the brightness was being pulled back in a very odd, three-dimensional manner.

For years after this, I could not sleep if there was the smallest, tiniest shaft of light in a room. Even to this day, any light source will immediately wake me from sleep. In my heart, I know that this episode was all too real to be simply a dream. Certainly, it could have been a nightmare, but I'm convinced that it wasn't. I truly believe this was something supernatural. Perhaps my angina was so terrible that my heart had malfunctioned or stopped. Who really knows? I do know what I believe and continue to believe: when that peculiar light returns, if ever, my soul will be on its way "home."

In the next moment (of that night) I was no longer sitting, but I awoke from under the covers with severe pain, and as I swung out from under the sheets, I was sweaty, with severe indigestion. However, I was quite unsettled by my awareness that I had been sitting up and I had witnessed that light. I can't explain it further. I went to the bathroom and after I swallowed a few gulps of antacid, placed several nitroglycerin tablets under my tongue. The pain subsided completely. It was now about four o'clock in the morning. I stayed awake until daylight returned and then called Dr. Eich at home. He scolded me for not going to the hospital but added that since I now felt improved, he wanted me in Syracuse as soon as possible. He added, "I will set up a catheterization this afternoon at two o'clock. Oh, and don't eat anything, just liquids."

This was my third catheterization in three months, and I was devastated. As I lay there in the catheterization laboratory, while cardiac catheters slid silently through my arteries, I prayed that I would have the strength to face whatever came my way, whatever they found. With the first test dose of dye, I could see that narrowed lesion blocking my artery, as viewed on a nearby monitor: a very tight, dangerous obstruction of the same artery that caused the earlier heart attack. I turned away for fear there would be more (obstructions), and there were. A significant number of additional arteries had become involved. After all the diet restrictions, after all my daily exercise, rest and less stress, my disease became more threatening in just three months.

This wasn't a bit fair, but then disease is never equitable. Clearly, I would need surgery to restore blood flow to my heart and get back my life. Angioplasty was out of the question because of the technology, because of the number of arteries involved and the extent of obstructions. It was a rude awakening. The cold hard facts of disease were staring me in the face.

The surgeon that I preferred was, Dr. Fritz Parker, whom I had worked with in Albany, when he was a surgical resident, and the surgeon I had referred most of my own patients for By-Pass surgery; however, he was away on vacation. I told Dr. Eich, I would await his return. A few days later I was scheduled, but Dr. Eich would not let me go home. He insisted that I remain in a special unit until surgery could be completed.

Saint Patrick's Day, March 17 was the day for surgery. My dear wife pinned a knitted shamrock on my hospital gown; however, it didn't help with the schedule, for increasingly emergent patients required the earlier slots. I kept being "bumped," rescheduled to 11 a.m., then again to 3 p.m., and then it became 6 p.m. Finally, the surgery was completed by 10:30 p.m.

I had cared for Coronary Bypass patients while in training, and learned that this surgery is a horrendous insult to the integrity of the human body; and yet it is an important operation, a lifesaver. It has been modified through the years, and this approach to redirect blood around those clogged arteries continues to improve the lives of many. To open one's sternum, place the blood circulation onto a heart-lung machine, and redirect the circulation to several small arteries is nothing short of a huge accomplishment as well as a credit to the expertise and training of the surgical team and to our own human endurance.

The painless awakening after the long hours of surgery was an odd mix of sensations: the first image was a bright light from something I could not decipher (a different sort of light than the "heavenly" light of days ago at home); it was the over-head surgical lamp. My fragmented senses also knew that people were lifting my helpless body. With my groggy, post-operative mind, I equated this as if I had been lying on a road somewhere from some accident: I could not move and people were attempting to carry me away. "Can you move your toes? Try the other foot, good," stated the surgical resident checking my neurological status. He then added: "Good, you've not had a stroke." His statement was my first recall that I was in a hospital.

As I was rolled into the Recovery Room, I regained my orientation. I was ecstatic that I had survived; perhaps now my life could resume a normalcy. Later that night, Dr. Fritz told how I was involved in a surgical accident: A towel clip, an instrument that clamps the sterile towels to the skin at the edge of the surgical wound, and holds the cloth boundaries in place. One of the instruments used that evening had a handle longer than normal, and that handle came into direct contact with the cautery ground under my back. A "Bovie," a cautery machine used to 'zap' an electrical charge to small bleeders, had, in my case, 'cooked' the skin repeatedly, around and deep into my rib cage. It would be days before this injury would define itself. It would take several more months for the third degree burn to heal. This is only one of many scars that I have had to carry through this life of mine.

Ultimately, I was unable to return to my profession. In follow up, Dr. Eich insisted that I had only one patient now to care for and that was myself. My heart function continued to be marginal, continued with anginal symptoms, continued with bouts of depression while I mourned the loss of my profession, the loss of my identity. This became a shameful occurrence. I was literally ashamed of being a doctor and not "catching" my condition before all this had happened.

Within a year, one of my sequential vein grafts closed off leaving only the internal mammary artery and one vein graft open. Fatigue, dysthymia (low grade depression), and atrial arrhythmia haunted my daily routine. Dr. Eich sent me to Boston, to Mass. General Hospital for a second opinion. However, after extensive testing there, Dr. Charles Boucher found no ready solution. I would remain compromised from having a normal life, restricted from the endearing practice of medicine, from the care of patients—people who lived in the economically forgotten north country of Upstate New York. I became like the old, used jacket hanging in a closet: no longer worn by anyone, no longer having a use.

Marcia soon recognized the need for substitutes for my lost profession. She assigned watercolor art classes at the local community college for me. She knew I had a talent to draw, a process I used in my practice, drawing in medical charts a chest x-ray or where a catheter tip was positioned in a patient's chest or the drawn description of what trauma had done to the patient's face and bones. It was so much easier to describe a medical state with a drawing rather than with words, and it saved time.

Art became my new quest; and through this medium I found a new pursuit, found new friends. More importantly, I found new accomplishments for this goal-oriented individual. Life does go on, enduring efforts through my brush—and now as I paint my life's experiences through the words of this manuscript.

The experience of being critically ill, personally, set in motion a belief that an ill physician is never totally a patient—a doctor is not a true patient, simply a sick doctor because the doctor-patient bond is never completely established. In some respects I became aware of this deep into my own illness. Perhaps it's not completely understood or even recognized.

After a period of recuperation I wrote articles about this and was asked to speak at physicians' conferences. I have spoken at the American Psychiatric Association in San Francisco, at the American Academy of Family Physicians in Los Angeles, and at American College of Physicians in Washington, D.C. It was at these conferences that a number of doctors approached me and agreed that this was indeed the case for them, during their own serious medical setbacks. One in particular was a psychiatrist who had had an amazing life experience, a man that awoke from a dream in which he was dying; it was so graphic that when he awoke, he knew from the message in that dream he was indeed going to die. So he woke his wife, and after a period of convincing her, she drove him to a noted hospital in Washington, D.C. There, the doctors could not or would not believe him, castigated him and told him to go home and go back to sleep. However, his wife was his faithful supporter, and she insisted that he be kept and monitored. "All right," stated the ER physician, "We will attached a heart monitor, and keep him in the ER until sun-up." At 6 a.m. the man arrested and required a prolonged resuscitation. He went on to say that he was never accepted as a patient, simply as a sick doctor. I know this may be a concept that is difficult to understand, but I believe that a sick doctor throws off the "comfort" level of the attending physician that treats another (doctor).

Other physicians told believable stories of their treatment and their indifferent patient-doctor relationship. For me, it wasn't that I was neglected; far from that--the main problem was that the attending physicians included me in all decisions, frequently stating, "You know, you're a physician. You know what needs to be done." However, at those moments I wasn't (a doctor); I was a patient, albeit, a sick one.

After returning home—after realizing Dr Eich's directive that I not practice medicine—I would occasionally return to our small hospital and walk through the ICU, the ER, occasionally through the medical/surgical floors, and through the laboratory. Everyone seemed to fawn over this "used-to-be-doctor." At first my visits were heart warming, nurses were friendly, compassionate. However, it soon became clear to me that after each visit, I would become exasperated, more lonely, certainly more sad and grieving from my losses: lost needs, a lost profession. I needed to get on with a life, a life without patients. On my last visit to the ICU to the Unit I had been in charge of, as I spoke with the nurses at their workstation, I noticed that one of my "old" patients was in bed three. Roy was dying of heart failure. As I walked over to his bedside and held his hand, I saw the evidence of his past hard work had eroded—his once prominent working hands were now wasted, and his cyanotic fingernails showed the effects of his illness. Roy looked up sadly, his eyes filling as he spoke his faint words: "Doc, if you were here caring for me, I'd still be able to work. Look at me. I'm on my last leg." *'Enough,'* I thought; there would be no further visits to my past, no further efforts to mine my past for a little offhanded praise. Roy died that night, as did my attempt at gathering past glories.

Syncope

As I reached for a warm dinner roll from the table's center, suddenly my hand had no strength--then the entire right arm weakened. Just like that, my world began to crumble. Within the next milliseconds, I tried to deduce what was going wrong. Then there was more, much more: a terrible general weakness overshadowed all; even my vision became darker. *"What the Hell?"* I silently thought. My wife was dumbfounded as I quipped, "I'm going to pass out," and then slid off the chair and into a squat position. Perhaps one or two more seconds ticked by. My mind told me, *"Lie down, lie down, Lie Down Now!"* My thoughts told me, but I didn't—and who would, in a crowded restaurant? Who wants to appear more foolish than he already has? Strangely time seemed to have slowed. I was now my own patient. *"Yes, I must lie down,"* I again thought. As the seconds ticked by, I read the fearful expression on my wife's face. I knew things didn't look good. However, the squatting posture had briefly stabilized the situation. All the patrons in the restaurant took notice; most wondered whether I was simply another kook that had come into their lives. A young man rose from the nearest table, grabbed my arm, and asked to help me out. "No, no," I pleaded. "I can't stand up; for sure I'll faint."

"Come on, he stressed, I'll help you."

I don't know just how many minutes had lapsed as I lay there unresponsive. I'm sure that my dear wife and the patrons bet that I had died. My first recognition was the EMT standing over me as I lay on the floor while they rolled the stretcher to my side.

There is no greater embarrassing moment than leaving a restaurant without paying the bill. Yet out they rolled me into a waiting ambulance. I had been in one before, and the second ride is quite similar to the first: flashing lights, swerving motion, intermittent sirens, and much shame. I made mention that this was all an overkill, defending my integrity by stating that I had simply fainted. They wouldn't buy it. There were IV's and heart monitors, yet I continued to down play the need.

As I was efficiently transferred into an exam booth at the ER, one attendant said to the nurse, "He has a history of heart problems." So far no one knew that I was a doctor, assuming my wife had not told. I prefer not to be known as a physician while being carried into a hospital: there are too many suppositions about doctors treating doctors.

On this occasion there was much attention given: an ECG taken, then an attending physician entered and after a brief exam, concluded that I most likely fainted (there I thought, someone who thinks like I do, finally someone in my corner). Minutes later, he came back to tell me that my ECG was much improved from the last exam. As I pondered that point, the doctor promptly left to find the results of my blood analysis, saying that he'd be right back.

My wife was now at my side, again we waited. Much later, the doctor returned to state that things looked good, and I would soon be sent home. With my mind numbed by the day's events, I thought that was a good idea; however, Marcia had a different take, "My husband is a cardiac patient." And then she insisted that I be monitored throughout the night. "He's never passed-out like this before. I'm not asking a lot," she said.

The attending physician replied, "Mrs. Burns, your husband's cardiogram is much improved [there's that statement again], but if you insist and since his history is

Important to recognize, we will keep him until the morning."

The next day at 7:45 a.m. a doctor was at my bedside. "How are we today?" he greeted. (I'm always annoyed by this expression, 'How are we?') "I'm substituting for your doctor, and things look good. I've checked your chart and lab data. Reports are favorable. So you'll be discharged soon."

"How is my cardiogram from this morning?" I asked.

"It's improved," he added, (there's that phrase again).

"If you don't mind, I'd like you to show me the change for the better, compared to my previous."

"Surely," he said.

My cardiogram had been normal, even though I had a major insult to my heart. The doctor returned with the two tracings, one from seven years ago and the most recent. The name on the reference tracing was the same as mine; however, the other tracing demonstrated a Left Bundle Branch Block (LBBB). That's a conduction defect of the heart's electrical circuitry, an abnormality that I've never ever exhibited on the tracing. As I reviewed the tracing, I noticed the name, but the listed age of that patient was eighty-five years. Now, I was very disappointed, with my mind more clear than before—I realized I had never before had a cardiogram at that hospital. How could two doctors on the staff overlook such a simple obvious fact: the discrepancy in the age of a patient? How can competent physicians not see the obvious? "Doctor," I asked, "How many times have you ever seen a Left Bundle Branch Block revert to normal?"

The Cardiologist thought for a moment, "I believe your tracing is the only one."

"Doctor," I asked, "have you noticed the patient's age at the top of the ECG?" His face flushed red with embarrassment. "Doctor, I'm a physician, also, and I expect more than this from fellow professionals. Two doctors in this hospital have made the same simple but grave error in interpreting two electrocardiograms."

I've always been tough on incompetence, even my own. As my wife drove me home, she more than I, questioned the actual episode that I had been through. "I called our son," she said. "He'll call you soon."

No sooner had her words been spoken, as my wife's cell phone rang. It was our son calling from California where he was a Resident in Internal Medicine, "Dad, how are you doing?"

"Fine," I stated. (Denial is a wonderful deceiver.)

"Listen to me, Dad, what would you do if one of your own patients with a heart problem had had a major syncopal episode? What would you do?" I knew where he was going with his query. "Dad, please give Dr. Charles Boucher a call today." It was more a directive than a request. That afternoon, when I called the doctor in Boston, my long time physician, friend and associate, I told him how these events unfolded.

He also was direct. "I want you here by six in the morning tomorrow or sooner. Then I'll decide what course we'll take. Oh, don't eat anything after midnight, but drink lots of water."

It was then when I began to realize that this likely was not a simple bout of fainting. My denial was replaced with some cold hard facts of life (again). Denial: the killer of so many people with heart disease. This is why nearly forty percent of heart attacks kill before the patient becomes aware of their diagnosis. Of course, I knew this. I had met too many in the ER that were already dead.

The next day at 6:20 a.m., I met the Senior Fellow in the Division of Cardiology. After examining me, he explained Dr. Boucher's decision to complete a heart catheterization that morning. After I signed all the permissions, the doctor began the early phases of my heart study. First, an arterial line was inserted into a small artery at my wrist, and a larger introducer was inserted into my right femoral artery, in my groin. This is an entry, a conduit that act as a doorway, allowing larger bore catheters to be moved in and out of my arteries and of course in and out of my heart. There are two main arteries that feed the heart, the Right and Left Coronary; each requires a different stylized catheter to enter.

This was my fourth heart procedure, dye injected with high-speed imaging to uncover any hidden narrowed arteries. With the first dose of the dye, anyone could see on the video screen the damn blockage. The Right Coronary Artery was severely obstructed by an elongated plaque, more than two inches in length. Here was the reason I had fainted.

There I lay on a twelve inch wide cardiac table, both arms and legs strapped on swing-out extensions, IV's in both, an arterial line at my wrist, all while facing a deadly situation. In truth, I felt like I was on a crucifix, at another crossroads of life. It was the worst feeling, a combination of great Hope that something could be done, and outright fear—a sinking despair that my life will be substantially shortened. It was a moment of living on the edge, so very close to the point of dying. Here I was again, facing life's unknown—it was as the Polish poet Mikiwiecz wrote, the author who raised the basic tenet: "What are we truly, when everything has been taken away, when we are laid bare and vulnerable, when we desperately plead our case to our God? What are we when we selfishly ask our Creator for more? *Nothing ... simply dust— perhaps."* And yet, we continue to ask for more, more time, more health: the greed of existence.

Doctor Boucher came near, "You saw the lesion?" he inquired.

"I did." In a serious mode he continued, "I'll review the high-speed video and return shortly to discuss just where we go from here and what is needed." Dr. Charles has always been a great source for medical direction, has always been there for me. I particularly liked his response: Where *WE* go from here? Because he and I were in this predicament together: I felt that way with my own patients—it's a packaged deal: he makes the call, and if he right—I reap the benefit.

After a long twenty minutes he came back. "Initially it looks like you will need to undergo another by-pass operation." These were his first words, words that ground painfully in my thoughts, words that left a speechless pause. I thought, *'No way, there must be some other alternative.'* I knew how difficult this type of surgery would be, and I said nothing in return. He continued, "It's a very elongated lesion. I believe it's too long for angioplasty." He paused at my silence, and then added, "I will speak with Dr. Igor Palacios. He's been experimenting with an intravascular device, a high-speed knife that shaves off the obstructions from within. I can review this with him if you like."

"Sure," I grabbed at the chance. While others juggled with my fate, I thought about that name: Igor; perhaps it refers one who is some sort of monster scientist, then the word Palacios. I concentrated on the sound of that name; perhaps it referred to peaceful. That was more in keeping where my thoughts should concentrate, as I lay on that special procedure table. I was definitely eager to meet the man, and hopeful that he would have a solution. Increasingly time passed, as everyone waited. Then the word finally came that Dr. Palacios would come to review the imaging, and most likely decide what would be the best course.

Further time elapsed, while nurses and technicians began to prepare for my next phase: opening a seriously plugged artery. Dr. Boucher returned. He had spoken with my wife and said, "This is a great device, if it works. Of course, greater risks are involved but greater returns if everything goes well. There's a chance that the high-speed knife might rupture the wall of the coronary artery. That of course, will force emergency surgery, so it will take some more time to set things up." (Meaning a standby cardiac surgeon and a standby surgical suite to be able to acutely intervene.) "You understand, of course," stated the doctor.

I had little sense of time. At that point, I was unsure just how many hours had lapsed as everyone waited—for the required backup. While the staff cleared the equipment used in the prior procedure, I told them just how cold I felt, as I shivered from the uncertainty.

They re-draped my naked body with a heated blanket, then with new sterile sheets while a Cardiology Fellow inserted even a larger introducer into my femoral artery. "This will cause a bit of discomfort." He went on to say, "There will be a need for a second 'port' to accommodate an aortic pump that will be used only if things go 'badly.'" (In other words, if the artery ruptured, my blood pressure could go to zero.) With his statement, the seriousness of where *"we"* were headed finally set in.

We waited and waited for Dr. Palacios. I dozed off and on as another hour lapsed. I awoke in a start and needed to pee, feeling that my bladder would soon explode. I told the nurse I had to stand up. Of course, that was out of the question; I was strapped down, with numerous intravenous connections, under loads of clean, sterile drapes that could not be disturbed. I was sedated silly; happy about everything except that full bladder. A nurse stated she would place a urinal, from under the sterile drapes, between my legs, an offer I could not fully appreciate at that time. "Go ahead and pee, go ahead," reaffirming it was okay.

"It's not aligned correctly," I insisted, aware that the placement of the urinal did not seem correct.

"Don't worry," she said, "it's okay, believe me." I could no longer hold the huge volume, a volume of urine, fluid and the dye that had been injected earlier. Shamefully, I could hear my urine flowing down the mechanical table, dripping onto the floor, it sounded like gallons flowing, cascading all over. I could have cried, and maybe I did; I was so ashamed and vulnerable, lying there peeing like a two year old or some old man in a nursing home. Doctor Palacios took my mind off my pity as he quickly appeared. "Hi, Dr. Burns." he said in a heavily accented voice. His heavy eyebrows and dark eyes were features that fit his name; the surgical cap and mask reveled no more. As assistants mopped the urine from the floor and the sterile drapes were reset, the doctor stated, "Sorry about your troubles, but don't worry about the urine." He reassuringly explained, "You'll see; the lesion you have is perfect for our machine. It will mechanically shave off the plaque and you'll be better for it. It works like a small dental drill. You'll hear the whirring sounds and there will be pain. Most of your pain will be from my need to close off the artery for the knife to work. We will close off the Coronary artery to your heart, in order to work on it. This prevents particles from going down stream into the muscle of your heart. You let us know about the pain, please. We'll give you morphine whenever you ask for it."

As Dr. Igor Palacios began, everyone about me was scrubbed and gowned and busy, watching monitors, placing catheters that inserted discretely into my diseased artery. My only awareness occurred when that Coronary artery was totally closed off. It was then that the ischemic pain was excruciating, horrible. Despite IV morphine, there were tough long moments of hot, searing, penetrating pain, from my heart muscle crying out for oxygen. The repeated episodes of pain went on and off for what seemed to be hours as that artery was intentionally closed and then opened, over and over.

Dr. Igor, when finished, brought an impressive intravascular photo for me to view. The lumen of the five-millimeter artery appeared in the photo as large as a mailing tube. Oddly, I wondered just how that photo was taken. I could tell he was very pleased with his efforts. He then discussed, mostly to himself, whether to include an extra long stent into the same vessel. He asked, "What do you think?" while at my side and then answered the question himself. "Yes, we will place the stent!"

It was afternoon before I was wheeled into recovery, drenched in sweat, exhausted, as I entered a large recovery room that overlooked the Charles River—a room with a magnificent view. In spite of what I had been through, I felt elated. Through the huge windows, sailboats played on the Charles, coursing in the sun and shadow. People were enjoying life, people totally unaware of the high drama that had occurred on shore, nine stories up, high above the flowing River. All the while the recovery room stereo played Ray Charles singing "A Wonderful World." The words to the song are now not easy to forget: "I see trees of green, red roses too."

It felt so good to be alive. I was euphoric from the apparent success and the morphine: all had helped —I was both thankful and exhausted. I had gone though an ordeal that could have been a disaster, but here I was high-- and above the world outside. I dozed off to sleep, thinking to myself, *"What a wonderful life."* I'll never forget that six hour morning along with those three called Charles: *the doctor, the river, and the singer.*

Of course, there was no going home that day. I was closely watched and critically unstable; my wife worried and the physicians continued their concerns. Because too many situations could arise, I would stay the night in a Special Unit, monitored and closely observed. The nurses in that Unit were great. They reminded me of those back home in Little Falls. It is amazing how attached we become, extend our complete trust with one or two individuals that work for our medical needs. I have wondered this myself, caring for total strangers, and within minutes, professionals and strangers bond, whether with a doctor or a nurse or both. In an instant people place their lives totally in their hands. I've always been amazed by this rapid transition as I bonded that night.

Eight hours later, with things now more stable, it was time to remove the "introducers" that were earlier placed in my groin, those standby "ports." It was time to extract these devices before something clotted off, like the main artery to a leg. But these large tubes inside my arteries would not budge. The more the doctors pulled to extract them, the more spasm (and pain) occurred in the artery in which they had been placed. The pain was most unusual; it felt like my entire aorta, along with the entire length of my Femoral Artery was being extracted! I had excruciating pain with greater amounts of morphine injected, yet the arterial spasm held on as if it were some cruel Tug-of-war.

The doctor began to carefully hold continued pressure, to pull, and to slightly twist at the introducer; the process caused continual severe pain. The intensity was worse than the earlier heart procedure. Probably because of the pain, there occurred a precipitous drop in my blood pressure. Again I was fading into unconsciousness as attendants lowered the head of my bed (Trendelenburg position). The doctors worked feverishly, pushing fluids, giving nitroglycerin. My dear wife was beside herself as she yet again envisioned her love dying. After all the earlier work and extreme efforts to reverse an obstructed artery, there I was having serious chest pain, marked hypotension, and coming very close to loosing consciousness. Desperately, as her concerns mounted, Marcia called out: "Can't someone please call 911?" We were in one of the highest ranking hospitals in the country, with the best-trained physicians, and yet my dear Marcia pleaded for EMTs to come and help. I must have smiled through my tears at her deeply honest but oddly humorous plea.

Needless to say, the introducer slowly moved and eventually was extracted. I was discharged the following morning and have remained stable since.

Aunt Mary

Mimi's Passing:

She was old, now the last of her generation—her four brothers and two sisters had all passed. This day, here she lay on our son's bed. The springtime sun was streaming in; it highlighted her frail body, her weakened state, her obtunded sleep. It was fortunate that we had her in our home.

Believe it or not, I contemplated ignoring my aunt's medical condition. I was tempted not to treat her fever, her dehydration, the mounting sepsis. She appeared so peaceful; and if it were not for her fever, one would assume that she was asleep. I wondered if perhaps I should simply let her be, with her sepsis. An unusual thought from a doctor, a devious thought for sure. Could I live with my intentional neglect? Could I allow her die this day or the next, to die from renal shutdown and a kidney infection?

I spoke to my wife about these thoughts; she flashed back a look to the contrary. I didn't stop there but called my long time friend Bernard, a physician also, and asked him. "Aunt Mary is septic, dehydrated, obtunded, yet she appears so peaceful. Should I ignore her state or treat her? I'm trying to decide, what do you think?" It was an odd question to pose to such a moral man.

"Oh, you're thinking about playing God," he quipped. He went on, "So her body is old, but her mind has been bright. Why do you ask for such an onerous thing, of your own aunt mind you? Do what's right!"

I knew what he would say before I had asked. The question was a major deviation from all my prior medical decisions; it was unlike me to become pragmatic, especially with my own aunt.

***

If I hadn't treated Mary, I would not have had the pleasure of seeing her on that summer's day at the beach, at water's edge. I would not have heard her tell how the warm sun felt on her face, how she loved the smell of the salt air. For another year, I would not have heard those old but forgotten stories when, as a kid herself, her dad brought home small incidental things after his menial job, trinkets for her alone. I would not have seen her simple joy every morning with her daily soft-boiled eggs and buttered toast.

She certainly would not have seen that chickadee eat from my hand, almost every morning. Certainly we both would not have had the experience at the rest stop on the Mass Pike, as we waited in line for the women's room. "No, I'm not going to let you go in alone," as I defined the limits. When we neared our turn, a teenage 'angel' from Iowa discovered our dilemma and guided my aunt, hand in hand to the toilets. My relief was palpable, although I have wondered since what my alternative would have been and the commotion it may have caused? Would I have chosen to bring her into the men's room, or take David with Mary—into the women's room?

If I had not called the ambulance that day and had not begun intravenous treatment, I would have missed those tender moments. When the need arose, her frail aged body naked, I lifted Aunt Mary into her warm sudsy soaks or onto a seat under the streaming warm shower, a similar task that I had fulfilled years earlier with our hired man Frank. Either way we both knew what was best. It was then when Mary told me, "David, we've come full circle" She had frequently given me a bath when I was a baby, and now the need was being returned. Two people, my first patient and my last, both with aged bodies in need and without shame. It was, again, the circle of life, the dependence for care, the giving and the taking, favors returned; my first and my last.

Aunt Mary was the only one of seven to live to ninety-one. As expected, when her days dwindled down, she was eventually confined to the nursing home that was part of the Little Falls Hospital. There the nurses and staff were excellent; they treated her like royalty because she was someone easy to like.

On two-earlier occasions Mary almost died; perhaps she had passed and then returned? The first had occurred earlier in her own home on St. Patty's Day. A friend, Father Frankhauser, made a special four-hour trip to see her. That night, the weather was miserable with freezing rain, dreadful winter conditions. I drove to Utica to meet him at the train, despite the treacherous roads. The ice built on the windshield so quickly that the defroster could not keep the windshield clear. Several times I had to stop to clear the burden from the ice.

He stayed for only an hour, and as he was leaving he gave Mary a special Irish Blessing. Saying goodbye to the priest, I stood behind her when suddenly without uttering a word—Mary collapsed and fell back into my arms. I carried her to the nearby sofa, and lying there Mary had no pulse and no respirations. My first thought was this was a lovely way to die, at eighty-nine years of life and on St. Patrick's Day, right after her special blessing. This was her first near-death experience, her total collapse. I timed her apnea and her pulseless state into a long three minutes and decided that I would not perform CPR. Then like Lazarus, she awoke as if nothing had happened. I was truly amazed.

It would be months before her next episode; Mary was in the nursing home when this event occurred. She had been weak for days and had received the Last Rites of the Church. On Sunday, after Mass we stopped to see her, she had become obtunded, difficult to arouse. We called the extended family, believing this day would be her last. Her respirations became increasingly shallow, and as we gathered around her hospital bed. However, although in a weakened state, she awakened and asked if those present would pray the Rosary with her. After a few prayers, Mary became totally unresponsive, even deeper than before. As we continued to pray, she stopped breathing, again for all too many minutes. I listened to her chest: there was neither pulse nor breath. As we called the nurse, I thought this had to be her final minutes. In spite of the dire findings, after a very long timed, four minutes, Mary awoke and without a pause, prayed along with us—never missing a verse of the Hail Mary.

The following morning, the nurses felt that Mary was the only patient ever to 'attend' her own wake. She told the nurses how she had such a wonderful time with her family gathering at her bedside … the day before.

She lived for three more weeks and continued to improve. We flew to the West Coast for Easter to be with our son, Michael. The evening before we intended to return home, Aunt Mary died in her sleep.

We arrived back home just before the funeral Mass, unsure of the arrangements. While shaving the morning before her funeral Mass, I heard the sounds of spring in Upstate New York: geese flying north. I remembered how Mary always loved those vernal sounds. In my mind I knew what I would say when asked to speak at her Mass of Christian Burial:

Today I heard the Canada Geese 'honking' north, and thought of Mimi:

This season of change—seasons ahead without our aunt.

A woman born, lived, and died in this little town,

High school, then Normal School, finally the teacher.

A single woman, Irish and parochial,

Applied for a job, but they didn't hire Catholics there.

So she came home and stayed in this small town.

Oddly, she told me—in her later years—her wish to have become a nurse,

And for sure, I told her, she already was one:

She had cared for her mother, Gramma, in her dying days,

Cared for her brother Leo, as he died in so many ways,

For her sister Helen … attended her long suffering months,

Dying with ostomies, metastasis, as Mary quietly sobbed,

From pressures too great for any sister, any nurse.

On evening visits, Mary buried her head on my chest,

Quietly sobbed her exasperations … over the

Urostomy that soiled Helen's cachectic abdomen

So many fears, yet so few tears, as she toiled

Cared for my mom, kept her company in her last years,

Mary shared her family home, where both were born.

A generous and caring Aunt … now a memory

God Bless … Mimi.

My Mother's Bed

I slept in my mother's bed a few months ago. For the first time in over sixty-five years I slept in the room where Mom and Dad had slept their entire married life. It was the same room where they loved, laughed, and cried; it had been a place for their tears from difficult times and a place for their dreams of better days. I rested in this very place where they experienced many joys: joy in each other's warmth, joy in their children, and joy in so much love.

For me this night became introspective into generations past, people like my parents who are no longer here but are still a part of us through their spirit and through what they had given us. Our folks worked hard and worried like all of us. They had stress, ever returning stress over events large and small somewhat like Prometheus chained to his rock, suffering repeatedly. Even now similar commotion fills our own days, nonsensical things that frustrate us daily. Yet in a few years these worries simply vanish, as with all of our flesh. It seems that emotions are recycled, for like a bottle in the ocean each returns—to burden.

I awoke in between dreams. This cold October night, a bright moon was shining on the porch roof, its light enhanced by the coat of frost. The moonbeams danced into this home of five generations. Simple beauty—a scene repeated for every generation that takes notice.

This stay was a time for me to savor, to delight in thoughts of my great-grandfather arriving at this farm. Probably he also slept in this room while raising his children: loving, crying, rushing to complete all the demands that the nineteenth century threw at him.

I reflected on all the human emotions of generation after generation, all the lost time, distractions by things unimportant. Why the rush I thought? Why fall back into a slumber of sleep? The room, the house, the surrounding countryside was steeped in complete silence, the penetrating stillness of night, the moon-glow, and the crispness of the outside autumn air. In that quiet country setting, with the immediate world so very still, I took comfort in that time spent. It was exceptional.

I knew there—others were sound asleep in the house. As the silence continued, I began to appreciate the loneliness that our mom slept with each night after she was widowed: three decades were made empty by the death of her Love. That void was then made worse by each of her five children leaving the nest, one by one. I wondered: if I lived alone in that farmhouse—would that found silence be so poetic, would the stillness echo so kindly?

My own life is now a retrospective, a transition that has come all too quickly from then to now. My time perhaps—winding down, the degree of slope unknown. I recall lying in my parent's bed as a child, feverish, while the measles affected my lungs, wondering then what it was all about. While others played outside, I lay prone, each repeated cough a burning pain. It was weeks before I was well again.

After all these years, I still wonder, not of the time lost, not of the Way, but still I wonder?

Conclusion

We all have pre-formed impressions of what a doctor is or who they should be or how he or she should present. I too have also had preconceived notions of what a patient would expect from myself, especially on the first encounter. I remember, when as a child with measles and a pneumonia, I needed an injection every day, and when the doctor came to our farm house–my mom would brush her hair–remove her apron, then tidy-up the room where I lay–before the doctor walked in. As a child, I realized that respect mom had given to the visiting doctor. For myself, I thought appropriate attire was an important part of patient care. On evenings or weekends on call, I would never respond with summer shorts or jeans; casual was okay but I believed people should be shown respect through attire, and the respect of my profession.

In this story, in the Preface, I spoke of a Dr. Kantor, a Pediatric Intensivist at Syracuse, who through past phone conversations—always gave needed advice for the care of critical patients in our ER, if that was required. Over the years, I had generated a mental image of the man, however, upon meeting him that morning (after he flew-in with the chopper), at this critical situation (in our ER): here was this slim man wearing jeans, a very elongated and graying ponytail—now all business at saving a couple of young lives. I had never been disappointed by the man's talents, his knowledge, but I had his image all wrong, and after that morning I became much less concerned with any doctor's attire.

Doctors, young or old, tall or short, or whatever attribute one has, doctors are, for the most part, diligent individuals who have given-up much to achieve more than the majority of people in our society, and in my case, it was a response to the sick and perhaps, to those dying people.

My life has been a great ride, certainly not the usual path for a professional to take; however, I wouldn't change a thing.

I recall a young pharmaceutical representative telling me, after he heard where I was reared, "I can't believe that you were ever a farmer?" With that I replied, "Hey, I can't believe I'm a doctor." With a perplexed look, he said after a short delay, "Oh yes–I … I can understand … what you mean."

Becoming the Professional

The process of acquiring a medical education was indeed a busy four years, packed full of learning, plus a wide-range of experiences—mostly good and a few less than that. Students are buffeted by all sorts of interactions—similar to the metal ball in old fashion pinball machine—all sorts of bumps, pushes until one succeeds or is "down the drain." It's an odd process.

At first, I marveled at those graduated house-staff members that were so knowledgeable, accomplished at the "job" at hand. Students, on the contrary, were generally uncertain, unsteady to the task—but slowly we learned, surely we all became polished to a professional sheen. Somewhere in that transition, somewhat unbeknownst—we all evolved into the doctor status. And like any race, some finished in better shape than others. The day I graduated, I was both humbled and exalted upon the conferred Degree: a Doctor of Medicine.

Perhaps at a point, somewhere between my fourth-year and my internship, I would take note that a few patients began to confide more in myself—than with the Senior Attending physician. The first occasion was with a woman who was about to have a breast biopsy, but had a degree of distrust with her surgeon:

"I know he (the surgeon) said that he would tell me the honest results of that biopsy, but I don't believe he will if it's cancer."

"What would you like me to do?" I asked her.

"Please be honest with me; please let me know as soon as possible—what I must face."

I told her I would.

After her operation, as she was returned to her hospital room, after obtaining permission from her surgeon, after I reviewed the pathology of the specimen, and then spoke with her—I also met her daughter in that room as well:

"Your mom wishes to know the full report of today's operation, is that your opinion as well?" I asked in front of her mom so not to conjure any distrust. She agreed with her mom's request.

I told her: "I have both good news and not-so-good news—first, the not-so-good: The lump was malignant."

"I wish I hadn't asked you to be truthful," was her immediate first words.

I went on: "The malignant lump is non-invasive—it is what's called an intra-ductal cancer—that means the bad cells are all confined to that intra-ductal tissue from the lump that was removed. Of course, the total block of tissue needs further processing; however, after a full review, you will find yourself, surgically cured." I could see the strain on her face—erased.

I've been energized through these writings—it has been a wonderful trip back through the pages of my life. I have attempted to honestly recount those distant events—memories of both the good and gritty times. I had never thought of myself as a writer, looking back when Sister Eunice taught eight-grade, I was always lost for words for her writing assignments; Sister would be pleased to know how I've come to find eighty thousand. And still, there are so many more medical accounts waiting to be told.

Writing is similar to painting a work of art: we all start with the same letters—it's all about application—much like using the similar pigments that Van Gogh or perhaps Andrew Wyeth had used—again, it's all about application. Life itself is how one applies oneself.

Now with this task complete—I will pick up my brush and paint.

D. B.

Breinigsville, PA USA
27 July 2010
242489BV00001B/4/P